C000145483

Alexander
the Great

Keyne Cheshire

CAMBRIDGE
UNIVERSITY PRESS

CAMBRIDGE UNIVERSITY PRESS
Cambridge, New York, Melbourne, Madrid, Cape Town, Singapore, São Paulo, Delhi

Cambridge University Press
The Edinburgh Building, Cambridge CB2 8RU, UK

www.cambridge.org
Information on this title: www.cambridge.org/9780521707091

First published 2009

Printed in the United Kingdom at the University Press, Cambridge

A catalogue record for this publication is available from the British Library

ISBN 978-0-521-70709-1 paperback

ACKNOWLEDGEMENTS
We are grateful to the following for permission to reproduce copyright photographs:

akg-images: p.10 right; akg-images/Peter Connolly: p.34; akg-images/Erich Lessing: pp.52, 53, 84, 85, 114 bottom; The Art Archive: pp.139 left & right, 141; The Art Archive/Archaeological Museum Salonica/Alfredo Dagli Orti: p.10 left; The Art Archive/Archaeological Museum Sousse Tunisia/Gianni Dagli Orti: p.153; The Art Archive/Alfredo Dagli Orti: p.90; The Art Archive/Gianni Dagli Orti: p.114 top; The Art Archive/Museo Archeologico Nazionale di Napoli/Alfredo Dagli Orti: p.158; The Trustees of the British Museum: p.69; Keyne Cheshire: pp.63 & 67; CSPS, photographersdirect.com: p.154; The J. Paul Getty Museum, Los Angeles, Artist unknown, Alexander the Great in the Air, from *Weltchronik*, circa 1400–1410 with addition in 1487, tempera colours, gold, silver paint and ink on parchment bound between wood boards covered with brown leather, Leaf 33.5 × 23.5 cm: p.176; Livius.org: pp.47, 122; Maya Vision International: p.96; © 1990, Photo Scala, Florence – courtesy of the Ministero Beni e Att. Culturali: p.15; Spectrum Colour Library/Imagestate: p.91; Werner Forman Archive: p.88

Cover picture
Alexander reading Homer by Ciro Ferri (1634–89)/Galleria degli Uffizi, Florence, Italy/
©1990 Photo Scala, Florence – courtesy of the Ministero Beni e Att. Culturali.
Alexander reclines engrossed in Homer's *Iliad*. The banner floating above his head reads, in Latin, *unus non sufficit orbis* ('one world is not enough'). Alexander appears to hold one world in his hand, but his passion (the winged Cupid overhead) leads us to imagine other worlds for him to conquer.

Picture Research by Sandie Huskinson-Rolfe of PHOTOSEEKERS.

Contents

Maps and plans

Preface

Alexander III was just under 20 years old when he became king of Macedonia, but he soon embarked on the greatest conquest the world had ever known. Within ten years of crossing from Europe into Asia, he was sole ruler of lands now part of Greece, Albania, former Yugoslavia (FYROM), Bulgaria, Turkey, Syria, Lebanon, Israel, Egypt, Jordan, Iraq, Kuwait, Iran, Turkmenistan, Afghanistan, Uzbekistan, Tajikistan and Pakistan. Cyprus, Armenia and parts of modern Libya were nominally under his sway as well. With staggering rapidity Alexander's conquest spread Greek culture far and wide, and altered for ever the Greeks' understanding of the world and their place in it. The effect was so profound as to give birth to a new epoch, the Hellenistic Age, that would endure for over 300 years until the death of the famous queen Cleopatra of Egypt, herself descended from one of Alexander's own generals.

But who was this Alexander? Pragmatic, philosophical; virtuous, murderous; stubborn, visionary; pious, patricidal; megalomaniacal, generous; diplomatic, vengeful; courageous, lucky. These are some of the ways ancients and moderns have represented him, and the varied and contradictory list testifies to the impossibility of our pinning down the character of a legendary figure onto whom people have projected such varying personas. Still, there are some things we can say for certain. He lost his father at 19. Despite his youth and relative inexperience, he could inspire battle-worn soldiers to win victories against formidable numerical odds and to conquer the toughest terrain. He pondered the possibility of his own divinity, and many while he lived thought him a god on earth. He faced the threat of assassination, and he murdered the man who saved his life. He married daughters of former enemies and forced his generals to do the same. He struggled to balance the interests of his native Macedonians against the pressures of holding together a huge and unwieldy empire. Finally, even as he prepared for further conquest, a sudden illness – suspicious to many – took his life at only 32 years of age.

This book presents this complex and intriguing character and his deeds primarily through extracts drawn from ancient sources, especially Arrian and Plutarch. Inevitably, their interests largely influence the focus of this book; some aspects of Alexander's life (e.g. battle narratives and miraculous events) are often related in great detail, while our sources say almost nothing about other dimensions (e.g. the social history of the non-elite and the administrative details of running an empire). Accompanying notes flesh out the historical and cultural context of Alexander's life, and explain unfamiliar terms. Other useful aids include a timeline, maps, battle plans, a list of the ancient sources for Alexander and glossaries of important terms, people, gods and heroes. The questions that follow each extract encourage the reader to look closely at what the passage can tell us

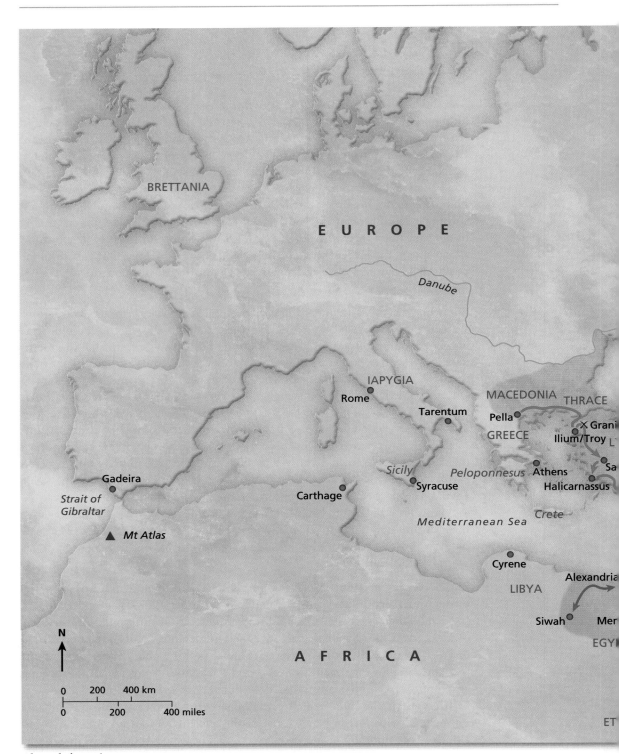

Alexander's empire

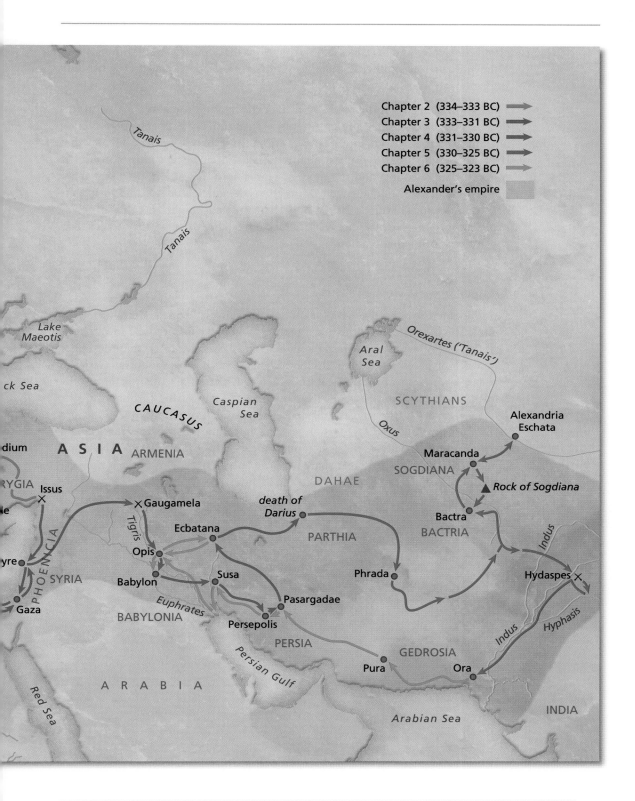

Chapter 2 (334–333 BC)
Chapter 3 (333–331 BC)
Chapter 4 (331–330 BC)
Chapter 5 (330–325 BC)
Chapter 6 (325–323 BC)

Alexander's empire

Tanais

Tanais

Tanais

Orexartes ('Tanais')

Lake
Maeotis

Aral
Sea

ck Sea

CAUCASUS

Caspian
Sea

SCYTHIANS

Oxus

Alexandria
Eschata

dium

ASIA

ARMENIA

Maracanda

SOGDIANA

Rock of Sogdiana

RYGIA

Issus

DAHAE

ne

X

death of
Darius

Bactra

BACTRIA

X Gaugamela

Tigris

Ecbatana

PARTHIA

Indus

Opis

tyre

PHOENICIA

Babylon

Susa

Phrada

Hydaspes X

Gaza

SYRIA

Euphrates

Pasargadae

Persepolis

BABYLONIA

PERSIA

Indus

Hyphasis

Red Sea

ARABIA

Persian Gulf

Pura

GEDROSIA

Ora

INDIA

Arabian Sea

about Alexander and his times. These questions tend to increase in difficulty and often build on one another so that they (I hope) may lead students to begin asking informed questions of their own.

Finally, I must caution the reader that the extracts (and the battle plans) in this book do not necessarily represent events as they actually happened. Conflicting ancient accounts accompany nearly every episode of Alexander's life, so that the student who seeks the fullest picture possible of any event must consult the other ancient accounts and the modern scholarship that attempts to sort them out. This is the sort of detective work that has delighted students and historians of Alexander for centuries. In the hope that this text might encourage further exploration, I frequently cite variant accounts and offer at the book's end suggestions for further reading.

Acknowledgements

I am indebted to several others for my relationship with Alexander and for the completion of this text. Of the many teachers who have inspired me towards the Classics, it is W. J. McCoy who sparked in me the passionate interest in Alexander that will not be extinguished. Students in seminars I have taught at Carleton College, Minnesota, and Davidson College, North Carolina, have only fanned the flames. The editors of this series have been most encouraging throughout. Eric Dugdale's many astute suggestions and corrections to my notes, questions and translations have spared this text an array of infelicities. Any errors that remain are mine alone. Finally, I am most grateful for the support of my wife Alyssa and daughter Earle, who inevitably share in all my adventures. This one has been no exception.

Introduction

Macedonia and Greeks

After the break-up of Yugoslavia in 1991, tourist shops across Greece teemed with t-shirts bearing slogans such as 'Macedonia is Greece' and ' ▤▤ [Greek flag] ♥ Macedonia'. A new country on Greece's northern border had just proposed to call itself 'The Republic of Macedonia', and the t-shirts were part of a concerted campaign against the name. Because of Greece's opposition, the new state joined the United Nations in 1993 under the *provisional reference* (i.e. not a formal name) 'the former Yugoslav Republic of Macedonia' (FYROM).

This recent controversy testifies to the power that the name 'Macedonia' still holds today. It is true that Greece has expressed concerns that FYROM's proposed name will pave the way for territorial expansion into Greece's northern province of Macedonia. In reality, however, Greek opposition probably has as much to do with national identity and cultural heritage. A new Macedonia might suggest that 'Macedonian' is somehow not 'Greek', and could consequently seem to threaten the Greeks' claim on Alexander the Great, the king of Macedonia (336–323 BC) who famously conquered the Persian Empire.

The Greek view of Macedonia in the fourth century BC was quite different. Greece was not a nation at all, but rather consisted of independent city-states who shared a common Greek culture and spoke regional dialects of the Greek language. These Greeks, or 'Hellenes', inhabited parts of modern Greece, modern Turkey and colonies around the Mediterranean. To an Athenian at the time, 'Macedonia' was the back of beyond, a remote and rather unsophisticated region whose Greekness was questionable at best. Macedonians did not participate in the Panhellenic ('all-Greek' and 'Greek-only') Olympic Games. They drank wine straight, without diluting it with water, a habit of 'barbarians' such as the Thracians, not of Greeks. Macedonia was neither a democracy nor an oligarchy like most Greek city-states, but a monarchy whose power derived from the support of the army. Finally, though evidence suggests that the Macedonian language was linguistically related to Greek, the Greeks themselves seem to have thought it a non-Greek, 'barbaric', tongue.

For its part, however, Macedonian royalty and prominent nobility had, since the Persian invasion of 480 BC, sought to cultivate a Greek identity. The royal court used the Greek language, distinct from the native Macedonian tongue, and invited prominent Greek poets such as Agathon, Timotheus and maybe even Euripides to the capital at Pella. Macedonian nobility were educated in Greek culture, including philosophy, literature and music. Macedonians asserted that their royal ('Temenid') house sprang from men of the Greek city of Argos, descendants of Temenus, who himself was a descendant of Zeus' son Heracles. Not surprisingly, Greeks began to question Macedonia's professed Greekness most vocally during the reign of Philip II (Alexander the Great's father), whose growing power and influence had begun to affect the Greeks themselves. The Athenian orator Demosthenes, for example, warning against the growing threat from Macedonia, disparaged Philip as 'not only no Greek, but wholly unrelated to Greeks; not even a barbarian from a land that one might call worthy, he is a pestilence from Macedonia, a region yet to produce even a decent slave for purchase' (*Third Philippic* 31).

Macedonia under Philip II

Macedonia rose to power thanks largely to Philip's innovations in his army. He introduced the sarissa, a pike so long that an enemy was forced to face three rows of them before reaching the serried ranks who held the weapons. Philip also masterfully combined infantry and cavalry manoeuvres, so that the two contingents worked in concert like never before. A new corps of experienced and lighter-armed soldiers called Hypaspists ('Shield Bearers') facilitated this cooperation. They could protect the infantry flank when the cavalry charged ahead and, if necessary, they could charge forward to support the advancing cavalry. This cavalry, too, was a formidable force, specially trained to attack in a wedge formation that could punch through enemy lines and thereby render an entire army vulnerable. Finally, improvements in siege technology made taking rugged hilltops or city walls only a matter of time for Philip.

Through early military victories Philip gained control of the mountainous region of Upper Macedonia. He did not subjugate its people, but rather united their nobility with that of his native coastal plains of Lower Macedonia. He incorporated Upper Macedonians into his court and into an army of regionally defined infantry battalions and cavalry squadrons. These regional units took pride in their unique cultural identities and naturally rivalled one another in skill and courage. At the same time, they reaped the benefits that the whole Macedonian army won, and so quickly came to identify with Philip and his goals.

Military success brought Philip access to financial resources. Victories in Thrace won him silver and gold mines, which enabled him to enhance his army and hire Greek mercenary soldiers in great numbers. As he acquired more territory, Philip parcelled it out to chosen Macedonian nobles, at once increasing Macedonian interests in the new lands and rewarding those nobles who supported him. He also required eminent Macedonian families to send their sons to him to serve as Royal Pages. This was an opportunity for the noble youths to establish personal relationships with the king and to learn from him first-hand. But it was also a means of controlling the powerful nobles. Families whose sons resided with Philip were more likely to remain loyal.

Marriage won Philip alliances, too, both within and beyond Macedonia. He married Olympias (Alexander's mother) from Epirus to the west, Phila from Elimiotis to the south, Audata from Illyria to the north-west, Philinna and Nicesipolis from Thessaly to the south, Meda of the Thracian Getae north-east of Macedonia, and

Cleopatra, a member of a powerful native Macedonian family. Although polygamy did sometimes lead to strife within the palace, Philip was clearly willing to risk such tensions for the diplomatic advantages his several marriages offered.

Philip II and the Greeks

Philip always had his eye on the Greeks farther south, working hard to cast himself and Macedonia as Greek. He was the first Macedonian king to enter the Olympic Games, where his horse won a victory. The Athenian philosopher Aristotle famously tutored his son Alexander. And Philip also welcomed other influential Greeks to his court, where he lavished them with 'gifts'. Through these contacts, he acquired a nuanced understanding of the Greek city-states, their unique interests and the conflicts between them. As he exerted increasing influence in the Greek world, he worked to ensure that most Greeks either did not recognize Macedonia's growing power or were too preoccupied with affairs closer to home to do anything about it. This included bribing Greek officials and supporting variously the interests of different city-states at different times.

When the Greeks did unite to resist Philip, they suffered a decisive defeat at Chaeronea in 338 BC, and Philip swiftly installed Macedonian garrisons in key cities. Philip did not absorb the Greeks into a Macedonian empire. Instead, he formed a confederation of Greek city-states called the League of Corinth. The League's treaty bound members not to attack one another and obliged them to declare war on any who did. The designated leader of this new League and its 'Common Peace' was none other than Philip himself.

Philip recognized that a common war could keep this new confederation intact, and Persia made an ideal target. King Xerxes of Persia had led a destructive invasion of Greek lands in 480 BC, and a Greek war of revenge against Persia was just the common cause that Philip needed. The current weakness of the Persian Empire made the idea even more attractive. It was plagued by revolts; just before the battle at Chaeronea, in fact, the Persian Grand Vizier Bagoas had poisoned King Artaxerxes III Ochus, killed any competent successors, and was ruling the empire through Ochus' youngest son. The Greeks were well aware of Persia's plight and knew that an empire in disarray was more vulnerable to attack.

The proposed invasion won the League's enthusiastic support. The League declared war on Persia in 337 BC and named Philip commander-in-chief for the invasion. By 336, Persia seemed even worse off. There had been revolts in Egypt and Babylon. Bagoas had poisoned his puppet ruler. The successor, Darius III, eluded Bagoas' attempt on his life, but was now ruling an empire governed by unreliable satraps whose loyalties were highly questionable. This was the Persian Empire against which Philip sent his generals Parmenion and Attalus with 10,000 men to prepare the way for the larger invasion to come. And so it was that under Philip II, Macedonia, a kingdom of the Greek hinterlands and of dubious Greekness, rose to become the Greek world's champion of Panhellenism.

Alexander III as king

When Philip was assassinated in 336 BC, Alexander III was not yet 20 years of age. He swiftly acceded to the Macedonian throne, but also assumed leadership of the Corinthian League and its Panhellenic interests. As king of the leading state in the Greek cause against Persia, Alexander proved himself a master of public relations. He would regularly cast his conquest in Greek terms, taking advantage of historical and mythological parallels in the works of Homer, Herodotus and Xenophon. He would retain Greek Companions and surround himself with Greek philosophers. At intervals during the campaign, he would sponsor at great expense Greek athletic and dramatic festivals that included performances by the most famous Greek talents of the day.

Alexander also proved a good student of his father's diplomacy. He had learned the value of spending resources lavishly. He had seen Philip honour non-Macedonians and even bestow on them traditionally Macedonian offices and titles. He had watched (and even intervened) as his father used carefully negotiated marriages to forge a network of alliances. The reader who observes Alexander's use of diplomacy throughout his campaign may well wonder whether Alexander approached the peoples of the Persian Empire and beyond in a manner very like Philip's management of his Macedonian neighbours, including his 'fellow' Greeks to the south.

Plutarch and Arrian

All eyewitness accounts of Alexander's campaign are lost. Those works we do have were written centuries after Alexander's death, but we know that they used a wealth of earlier accounts, many of them first-hand. The variety of the extant sources, the contradictions within and between them, and the different 'Alexanders' they offer can dizzy a reader, but a full reading of them all affords a magnificent – if kaleidoscopic and vertiginous – view on his life and deeds. A listing of the major extant works and those sources now lost to us appears under 'Ancient sources' on pp. 177–9.

The present text includes translated selections excerpted primarily from Plutarch's *Life of Alexander* and from the *Anabasis of Alexander* by Arrian. These works complement one another well, primarily because their approaches to Alexander are so very different – one biographical, the other historical. Furthermore, because both offer statements of their authorial purposes and even something of their methodologies (Plutarch at p. 8; Arrian at pp. 28 and 31–2), one can readily track how these authors' aims and perspectives shape their accounts.

Plutarch (Mestrius Plutarchus, AD *c.* 46–120) was a Greek from Chaeronea, a town on the Greek mainland east of the Delphic oracle. Though he spent much of his life there, he travelled widely, visiting Athens, Egypt and Rome, where he taught and lectured. In a series of works known collectively as the *Moralia*, one finds reflected a wide array of interests, including religion, politics, literature and morality. One jewel in this collection, *On the Virtue or Fortune of Alexander the Great*, explores the question of whether Alexander's achievements were the result of his courage or of divine luck. Plutarch is probably best known, however, for his 'parallel lives', a series of 50 biographies of famous Greek and Roman men. Forty-six of them are paired with another life (hence 'parallel'), each pair treating a famous Greek and Roman who share something with each other in career and accomplishment, in virtues and failings. Plutarch paired his *Life of Alexander*, the source for many excerpts in the present text, with a biography of Julius Caesar.

Arrian (Flavius Arrianus Xenophon, AD *c.* 86–post 146) was a Greek native of Nicomedia in the Roman province of Bithynia, on the south coast of the Black Sea (see map on pp. vi–vii). He was a student of Stoic philosophy who led an active administrative and military career. Under the Roman emperor Hadrian he served as senator, then consul and then governor of Cappadocia from AD 131 to 137. This last appointment included his successful leadership of Roman legions against an invasion by the Alans from across the Caucasus to the north-east. We last hear of him serving as archon at Athens (an honorary post of great distinction) in AD 145/6. Arrian published verbatim lectures by his teacher, the famous Stoic philosopher Epictetus, which he had copied in shorthand as a youth. He composed treatises on hunting and military tactics, several biographies, and a description of the entire Black Sea coast. He wrote a history of his homeland Bithynia, an account of the emperor Trajan's campaigns in Parthia, and a description of his own military tactics used to drive the Alans from Armenia. His ten-book *Affairs after Alexander* is lost, but we still have his *Indica*, a work full of Indian memorabilia that features the exotic voyage of Alexander's admiral Nearchus from the Indus River to the Persian Gulf. In his seven-book *Anabasis of Alexander*, a central resource for the present text, Arrian openly glorifies the king and mitigates his faults for posterity.

Plutarch and Arrian offer remarkably different perspectives on Alexander, but the authors also have much in common. Both were Greek intellectuals living under the Roman Empire and both sought to present their Greek heritage to their contemporary audiences. The studied prose of Arrian imitates and combines the styles of the historians Xenophon, Herodotus and Thucydides, a testament to his profound respect for those famous Greek writers of five centuries earlier. Plutarch for his part looked back wistfully to an age of greater piety. In presenting a Roman figure on the heels of an earlier Greek, his parallel lives inevitably led his readers to consider the celebrities of Roman history in terms of Greek accomplishments.

When FYROM in 2007 renamed its capital's airport 'Alexander the Great', Greece saw an aggressive attempt to appropriate part of its cultural heritage. Indeed, Alexander's Greekness is as old as our earliest literature about the king. Although the works of both Plutarch and Arrian do acknowledge a distinction between Macedonian and Greek, as their sources certainly did, the Greekness of Alexander the Great is for them never in question. Plutarch's *Life of Alexander* is the *Greek* life of the pair, so that Alexander was for Plutarch as fundamentally Greek as Caesar was Roman. When Arrian likewise searches for his parallel to Alexander, he looks to the literary heart of Greek culture, the works of Homer, and he returns with Achilles, the *Iliad*'s most formidable and transcendent Greek hero.

When reading the excerpts in this text, therefore, one must beware. These are treatments by men who felt a very real connection to Alexander, a figure who did not seem so distant to them as he does to most of us today. Plutarch, remember, as a native of Chaeronea, was born just a stone's throw away from the battlefield where Philip and his son defeated the Greeks in 338 BC. Alexander never even saw Arrian's native Bithynia, but Arrian insists that his own fatherland, his people and his whole life's career are inseparable from the story of Alexander the Great. This kind of passion is contagious. I know from personal experience that it is all but impossible to resist the visceral reactions that Alexander inspires. And so I encourage my readers to make Alexander their own even as they critique the accounts of his life and the phenomenon that he became.

Important dates in the life of Alexander

Date BC

480	Xerxes invades Greece
359	Philip II becomes king of Macedonia
356	Alexander III is born (around 20 July)
344	Alexander tames Bucephalas
343	Aristotle tutors Alexander
340–339	Philip II besieges Byzantium Alexander founds Alexandropolis
338	Battle of Chaeronea Formation of the Corinthian League, which declares war on Persia Philip II elected commander-in-chief of the proposed war King Artaxerxes III Ochus of Persia assassinated by Bagoas
336	Darius III becomes king of Persia Philip II assassinated Alexander III becomes king of Macedonia
335	Campaigns against Thrace (spring) Campaigns against the Illyrians (summer) Sack of Thebes (October)
334	Crossing to Asia (spring) Battle of the Granicus (May)

334–333	Taking of Gordium (winter)
333	Battle of Issus (November)
332	Siege of Tyre (January–August)
	Alexander becomes Pharaoh of Egypt (14 November)
331	Foundation of Alexandria
	Siwah and the Oracle of Ammon (winter)
	Battle of Gaugamela (1 October)
330	Burning of the palace at Persepolis (May)
	Dismissal of Greek allies at Ecbatana (June)
	Darius III dies (July)
	Alexander assumes the Persian title and dress of the Great King (July)
	Execution of Philotas and Parmenion (September)
329	Capture and execution of Bessus (summer)
328	Taking of the Rock of Sogdiana (summer)
	Alexander kills Cleitus (November)
327	Marriage to Roxane (spring)
	Proskynesis affair (spring)
	Pages' conspiracy (spring)
326	Taking of the Rock of Aornus and crossing the Indus River (winter)
	Battle of the Hydaspes (May)
	Mutiny at the Hyphasis (June)
	River journey begins (November)
325	Campaign against the Malli
	Mouth of the Indus (July)
	March through Gedrosia (September–December)
	Alexander reaches Carmania
324	Purge of satraps and generals
	Alexander in Pasargadae; Cyrus' tomb restored
	Mass wedding at Susa; payment of soldiers' debts (April)
	Mutiny at Opis (June)
	Death of Hephaestion at Ecbatana (October)
	Campaign against the Cossaeans (winter)
323	Return to Babylon (spring)
	Alexander dies (10 June)

1 From birth to kingship

Plutarch's purpose

Plutarch (see Introduction, pp. 4–5) composed a series of biographies commonly known as his 'parallel lives'. They are so called because Plutarch often published these biographies in pairs, in which the life of a famous Greek was followed by that of a Roman whose career or accomplishments were comparable to the Greek figure's. As Plutarch states here, his 'life' of Alexander was published together with that of Gaius Julius Caesar. The philosophical intent of these works was to illustrate virtues and vices in the well-known figures of history.

As you read the excerpts by Plutarch in this book, consider how he abides by his aims as presented here and to what extent his focus must necessarily affect how we interpret the contents of his work. A useful approach may be to note which aspects of his account are the 'face' and the 'eyes' of Alexander and which are the 'body'.

Plutarch 1   I compose in this book the lives of Alexander the king and of the Caesar who overthrew Pompey. Because of the multitude of their recorded deeds, I ask my readers not to criticize my mainly summary approach, if I fail to report all their famous acts or to relate any one of them fully. I am writing not histories, after all, but lives, and an illustration of virtue or vice does not always reside in the most conspicuous deeds. A little thing – a remark or joke – often reflects character better than battles with countless dead, better than the greatest armies readied for war, better than the sieges of cities. A painter captures his subject's likeness through the face and the expression of the eyes that reveals the character of the person; he pays very little attention to the rest of the body. In the same way, I must be allowed to focus more on the signs of the soul and use those to depict the life of each of my subjects. I leave their grand exploits to others.

> •   Think of a renowned individual of the present day. What famous acts would you suggest best reveal his or her soul or character?

Alexander's birth

Plutarch 2   There is complete agreement about Alexander's lineage, that he was by his father a descendant of **Heracles** through Caranus and by his mother a descendant of **Aeacus** through Neoptolemus. And it is said that **Philip**, upon initiation with **Olympias** into the mysteries of **Samothrace**, fell in love with her – he still a youth and she an orphaned child – and so engaged to marry her after prevailing upon her brother Arymbas. Then, before the night of the marriage's consummation, the bride dreamed that amid peals of thunder a lightning bolt struck her belly. A great deal of fire was kindled from the bolt, then scattered, bursting into flames and spreading everywhere. Later, after the marriage, Philip dreamed that he was placing a seal upon his wife's belly, and that the relief on the seal contained the image of a lion. While the other seers were apprehensive at the vision and said that Philip's marriage demanded more scrupulous attention, **Aristander** of Telmessus said that the woman was pregnant, for nothing empty is sealed, and that she was pregnant with a child quick-tempered and lion-like in nature. A serpent, too, was once seen stretched out beside the body of the sleeping Olympias, and it was this most of all, they say, that dampened Philip's desire and affection for her, so that he ceased his frequent visits to her, either because he feared some magic or drug from his wife, or because he was keeping himself safe from intercourse with a woman who appeared to be enjoying a union with some greater power.

Heracles Greek hero more familiar today by his Roman name Hercules. Heracles was the son of Zeus and Alcmene. The royal house of Macedonia traditionally traced its lineage back to Heracles, and therefore ultimately to Zeus himself.

Aeacus another son of Zeus, and grandfather of Achilles. Both Achilles and his son Neoptolemus participated in the Greek conquest of Troy.

Philip king of Macedonia and Alexander's father, properly Philip II.

Olympias Alexander's mother. She came from the region of Epirus to the south-west of Macedonia. She was married off to Philip to reinforce a strategic alliance between the Molossian dynasty of Epirus and the kingdom of Macedonia.

Samothrace an important centre for the worship of the chthonic (underworld) deities called Cabiri. We know almost nothing of their 'mysteries', or initiation rites.

Aristander prophet who hailed from Lycian Telmessus (in modern Turkey), a city famous in antiquity for its seers. He makes his first appearance here before Alexander's birth, and proves later to be Alexander's most important seer during his campaign, until he disappears from all records after 327 BC.

Roman medallions of Olympias and Philip, c. third century AD, a testament to the desire to identify in some way with this Macedonian royal family even six centuries after Alexander lived.

And there is another story pertaining to this situation. All the local women had been participants in the **Orphic** rites and the ritual orgies of **Dionysus** from very ancient times. They were called Klodones and Mimallones, and were often thought to behave like the Edonian and Thracian women around Mount Haemus, apparently the source for the word *thrēskeuein*, meaning to engage in intemperate and superstitious acts of worship. Olympias herself was supposed to have achieved such ecstatic bouts of divine possession more zealously and barbarically than the rest. She would also provide the revellers with giant tamed serpents, and these would often slither out of the ivy or the mystic **baskets** and coil around the women's wands and garlands, to the horror of the men.

Orphic term referring to rites held in honour of Orpheus, son of a Muse and Apollo. According to tradition, he was one of the few figures to have travelled to the Underworld and to have returned, and though he was ultimately dismembered by a band of Thracian women, his head continued to sing posthumously. For these reasons, he is associated with rebirth, and mystery cults of Dionysus frequently celebrated him.

Dionysus Greek god of wine. He was the son of Zeus and Semele, who was incinerated when Zeus revealed himself to her in the form of a lightning bolt.

thrēskeuein Plutarch derives this verb (meaning 'to worship') from the word 'Thrace'. The words bear an even greater resemblance to each other in Greek.

baskets *liknoi* in Greek, typically carried on the head during rituals in honour of Dionysus.

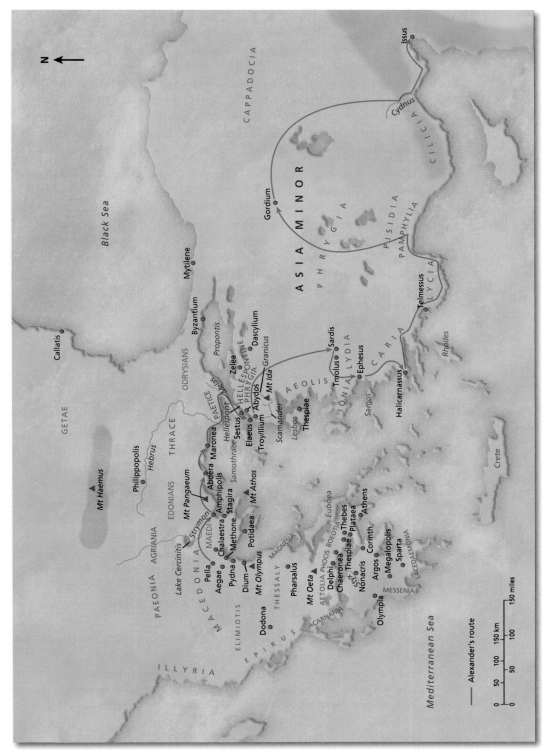

Alexander's route from Pella to Issus

3   At any rate, after Philip's vision, he sent Chaeron of Megalopolis to **Delphi**, and they say he returned with an oracle from Apollo ordering Philip to sacrifice to **Ammon** and to revere that god above all others. The oracle declared, too, that Philip would lose the eye with which he had peeked through the gap in the door when he caught sight of the god in the shape of a serpent sleeping with his wife. And according to **Eratosthenes**, when Olympias sent Alexander off on campaign she divulged to him alone the secret of his conception and exhorted him to aim for things worthy of his birth. But others say that she denied this, saying, 'Will Alexander not stop pitting me against **Hera**?'

And so Alexander was born near the beginning of the month **Hecatombaeon**, which the Macedonians call **Loüs**, on the sixth day – the very day on which the temple to Artemis at Ephesus caught fire. At this, Hegesius the Magnesian made a pronouncement tasteless enough to put out that blaze, for he said that the temple of **Artemis** had naturally burned down because the goddess had been serving as midwife to Alexander. All the **Mages**, however, who happened to be at Ephesus considered the destruction of the temple a sign of future loss, and so they were running about, striking their faces and wailing aloud that ruination and great misfortune had been born for Asia on that day. But Philip, who had only just captured **Potidaea**, received three messages at the same time: first, that the Illyrians had been defeated by Parmenion in a great battle; second, that Philip's

---

Delphi   home to the famous oracle of Apollo. An arrow did strike Philip in the eye at Methone in 354 BC.

Ammon   Egyptian god whom the Greeks identified with Zeus.

Eratosthenes   scholar and head of the library at Alexandria in the third century BC. He wrote on a great range of subjects, including geography, mathematics, astronomy, comedy and history.

Hera   Zeus' notoriously jealous wife, who persecuted many of his mortal lovers. The suggestion that Alexander was the son of Zeus could have caught the attention of Hera and endangered Olympias.

Hecatombaeon, Loüs   the mid-summer month. This would put the date of Alexander's birth at about 20 July 356 BC.

Artemis   virgin goddess frequently associated with hunting, who presided also over midwifery.

Mages   members of a priestly class of Medians, a people conquered by the Persians. Under the Persians they continued to play a fundamental role in religious matters, including sacrifice and the interpretation of omens. It is not clear why they would have been in Ephesus.

Potidaea   city captured by Philip in 356 BC, probably in August.

racehorse had won a victory in the **Olympic games**; and third, that Alexander had been born. Philip was already pleased by these developments, as one would expect, but his seers encouraged him to even greater delight by proclaiming that the child born in conjunction with three victories would be indomitable.

> 1   What might have been the perceived significance of the lightning bolt and the scattering flames?
>
> 2   What do the particular omens here related tell us about Olympias and her newborn son?
>
> 3   What do you make of Plutarch's account of these omens – did they occur or were they invented after the fact?

Alexander's appearance

> Physiognomy, the notion that a person's character is tied to his physical attributes, was widespread in the ancient world, and therefore important to Plutarch's treatment of Alexander's character.

Plutarch 4   The statues that portray Alexander's physical appearance best are those by **Lysippus**, the only sculptor Alexander thought worthy of depicting him. Lysippus captured perfectly, in fact, those traits that many of Alexander's successors and friends later tried to copy, such as his neck's gentle lean to the left and the moistness of his eyes. **Apelles**, in painting him as wielder of the thunderbolt, did

---

Olympic games   Panhellenic games in honour of Zeus at Olympia. The chariot race and horserace were generally thought the more prestigious competitions. Victories in these events were credited not to the riders, but to the wealthy sponsors, who footed the cost of the equipment, animals and training. The games of 356 BC probably ended on 28 August.

Lysippus   one of the many outstanding Greek artists, writers, engineers and philosophers invited to the Macedonian royal court. King Archelaus (ruled 413–393 BC) had already begun this tradition, later renewed by Alexander's father Philip II (ruled 360–336 BC). It would have lent a Greek flavour to the kingdom of a people who were generally seen as primitive by the civilized Greek. Lysippus, famous for introducing a great degree of realism to his works, had already sculpted Alexander as a boy when Alexander appointed him court sculptor upon his succession to the throne.

Apelles   contemporary of Lysippus and Alexander. He was commissioned for 20 talents to compose this painting for Artemis' temple at Ephesus, probably the very temple built by Alexander in place of the one that was supposed to have burned on the day of his birth. The talent, strictly a weight of gold or silver, is difficult to convert into modern currency for several reasons, but a *very* approximate amount of £300,000 (about $600,000) per talent may serve. Apelles' commission would then come to around £6 million ($12 million). The prices put on top Rembrandts and Van Goghs today are comparable in value.

---

not get his complexion right, but made it too dark and swarthy, for they say that Alexander's skin was fair and would turn red, particularly on his chest, but also on his face. I have read, too, in the memoirs of **Aristoxenus** that his skin exuded the sweetest scent and that a fragrance hung about his mouth and all his body, even permeating his clothes.

> 1 According to Plutarch elsewhere, Lysippus sculpted Alexander with a lance and criticized Apelles for depicting him with divine attributes. To what divinity does Apelles liken Alexander in the painting described here?
>
> 2 Besides adding to the Greekness of his reign, what other advantage could the writers and artists in Alexander's retinue offer him?

The taming of Bucephalas

> The following episode describes how Alexander broke the untameable horse Bucephalas. Alexander prized this horse, and kept it with him on campaign until its death in India, where he founded a city in its name.

Plutarch 6   Philonicus the Thessalian once brought **Bucephalas** to sell to Philip for 13 talents. They went down to the plain to test the horse, but he seemed far too wild to handle. He would endure no rider nor any command from Philip's attendants, but kept rearing back from everyone. This displeased Philip, and he ordered the horse away as utterly wild and unbroken. At that, Alexander spoke up from nearby, 'What a horse they are losing, because they are too ignorant and cowardly to handle him!' Philip said nothing at first, but when Alexander repeatedly spoke out and appeared highly distressed, he said, 'Do you criticize your elders? Do you think you know more or can handle a horse better?' 'This one, at least,' Alexander answered, 'I could handle better than the rest have.' 'And if you cannot, then what price will you pay for your brashness?' 'I shall pay for the horse myself.' There was

---

Aristoxenus contemporary of Alexander and a member of Aristotle's philosophical school. His description suggests Alexander's divinity, for a unique fragrance often accompanies divine manifestations in Greek literature.

Bucephalas meaning 'ox-head'. Arrian (5.19) records that the horse was named for a white marking on his forehead in the shape of an ox. Bucephalas, however, was also a Thessalian breed of horses, and that is probably the origin of the name. Many apocryphal details quickly attached themselves to the compelling relationship between Bucephalas and Alexander. In the *Alexander Romance* (1.17), a highly fantastic chronicle composed by the third century AD and attributed incorrectly to Alexander's court historian Callisthenes, Bucephalas is a man-eating horse that only Alexander can manage. Here the price of 13 talents, over three times more than the cost of any other horse on record, may be exaggeration as well.

laughter. Then the price was set. Right away Alexander ran to the horse, **grabbed the rein**, and headed him towards the sun. Apparently, he had noticed that the horse was spooked by his own shadow darting here and there on the ground in front of him. Alexander soothed him a little by doing this, and then stroked him. When he saw the horse was now full of pluck and spirit, he tossed his cloak lightly aside and deftly mounted him. Then, pulling the bit a little with the reins, he checked him without striking him or cutting his mouth. Once he could see that the horse had stopped his menacing behaviour and longed to be put to the gallop, Alexander relaxed the reins and now urged him on with a bolder voice and a kick of the foot. Anxiety gripped Philip's attendants, so that they were silent at first. But when Alexander turned the horse around, proud and overjoyed, a cheer rose from everyone. His father, they say, actually wept for joy and kissed Alexander's head when he dismounted. 'My son,' he said, 'find a kingdom to match yourself. Macedonia cannot contain you.'

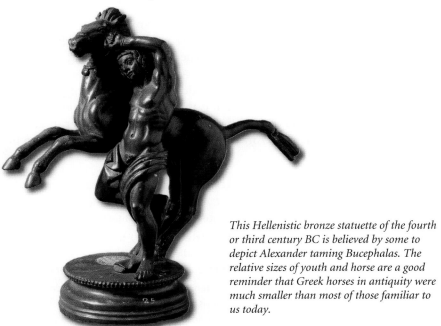

This Hellenistic bronze statuette of the fourth or third century BC is believed by some to depict Alexander taming Bucephalas. The relative sizes of youth and horse are a good reminder that Greek horses in antiquity were much smaller than most of those familiar to us today.

---

1   What elements of legend or folktale might Plutarch's account of this incident contain?

2   How would you describe Alexander's relationship with his father, based on this account alone?

3   Would you agree that Plutarch is trying to draw a parallel between Alexander's temperament and that of Bucephalas? If so, what is it?

---

grabbed the rein   control over horses is often used as a philosophical metaphor for control generally, especially over oneself.

Aristotle

In continuing to describe Alexander's youth, Plutarch highlights the future king's keen interest in philosophy and literature.

Plutarch 7 Philip observed that, while Alexander's nature was stubborn and he resisted any coercion, reason could lead him easily towards what was necessary, and so he himself would try to persuade rather than to command his son. Philip deemed overseeing and training Alexander an important business, and, to quote **Sophocles**, 'a job for bits and rudders aplenty'. He therefore did not entrust this work entirely to the teachers of **music** and the usual studies, but sent for **Aristotle**, the most noted and erudite of philosophers, and paid him an appropriately handsome fee. He resettled Aristotle's native city of Stagira, which he had desolated, and reinstated its former citizens, who had been either exiled or enslaved …

8 It was Aristotle, I think, more than anyone else, who instilled in Alexander his interest in medicine; Alexander not only found delight in the theory, but also would aid his friends when they fell ill, prescribing treatments and regimens, as one can see from his **letters**. And he had further an innate passion for learning and reading. In fact, he considered the *Iliad* a supply of military valour for the road – and he would call it that. He took the edition by Aristotle, the so-called 'Casket *Iliad*', and always kept it next to the dagger under his pillow, according to **Onesicritus**. Any other books that were not available to him while inland he

---

Sophocles   fifth-century BC Athenian tragedian. The quotation serves as a reminder that the Macedonian court was steeped in Greek literary traditions.

music   *mousikē* in Greek referred not only to musical instruction, but also to reading and mathematics. The 'usual studies' would probably have included grammar, rhetoric, dialectic, geometry, arithmetic, astronomy and music theory.

Aristotle   (384–322 BC) student of Plato. He later founded the so-called 'Peripatetic' school of philosophy at Athens in 336. He was in fact not yet so renowned a philosopher when he was invited to Macedonia in *c.* 343 to tutor Alexander. As Aristotle's influence in Greece grew during Alexander's campaign, however, his opposition to some of Alexander's policies threatened to undermine Greek support of Alexander's rule. Philip had sacked Stagira in 350.

letters   letters are frequently cited by our sources for information about Alexander, but those attributed to him tend to address personal details rather than political or military matters. Many letters from antiquity are known to be spurious. Ancient education seems often to have included the composition of letters that famous people might have written in various situations.

Onesicritus   chief helmsman of the fleet and famous in antiquity for a highly embellished account of Alexander's (and his own) life. He claimed falsely, for example, to have served not as helmsman, but as chief admiral!

would order from **Harpalus**, who in fact sent him the books of **Philistus**, many tragedies by **Euripides, Sophocles and Aeschylus**, and **dithyrambs** by **Telestus and Philoxenus**. Alexander admired Aristotle in the beginning, and loved him no less than his own father, since, as he himself used to say, it was because of the latter that he lived, but because of the former that he lived nobly. Later, Alexander came to regard Aristotle with a fair amount of suspicion, not to the point of causing him harm, but his greetings, which did not possess their former ardour and affection, were proof of estrangement. Still, that zealous longing for philosophy that was born in him and grew with him from the start did not recede from his soul; his respect for **Anaxarchus**, the 50 talents he sent to **Xenocrates** and his high regard for **Dandamis** and **Calanus** testify to that.

1	What did Philip mean by the quotation from Sophocles in this context?
2	Why might Plutarch have followed the Bucephalas account with this discussion of Alexander's education?
3	Based on your own knowledge of the *Iliad*, what elements of its content might Alexander have found useful to his campaign?

A proud father

Philip appears to be grooming Alexander as his successor by providing him with important experience in both administrative and military affairs.

Plutarch 9   When Philip was marching against Byzantium Alexander was only 16. Yet even so, Philip left him in charge in Macedonia, both of general affairs and of the **royal seal**.

Harpalus   boyhood friend of Alexander's. He served as treasurer during most of the campaign.

Philistus   of Syracuse; he wrote a history of Sicily.

Euripides, Sophocles and Aeschylus   the most famous of the Athenian tragic playwrights.

dithyrambs   songs set to dance in celebration of Dionysus.

Telestus and Philoxenus   two of the genre's most famous composers.

Anaxarchus, Dandamis, Calanus, Xenocrates   the first three accompanied Alexander on his campaign; we shall see more of them later. Xenocrates refused the invitation to join him, but instead wrote a theoretical four-volume work, *On Kingship*, and sent it to Alexander.

royal seal   this indicates that Alexander was effectively regent in Macedonia, at an astonishing 16 years of age.

During this time Alexander subdued those **Maedi** who revolted; he captured their city, drove the barbarians from it, and then introduced a mixed population and dubbed the city Alexandropolis. At **Chaeronea** he took part in the battle against the Greeks, and was famously the first to break through the ranks of the Thebans' Sacred Band. Even up to the present day people point to the ancient oak beside the Cephisus River and call it 'Alexander's Oak', for he had pitched his tent near it then. (The mass grave of the Macedonians is not far away.) Because of these deeds Philip loved his son excessively, as one would expect, and was even delighted to hear the Macedonians call Alexander king and Philip general.

1 What skills does this brief account suggest Alexander possessed?
2 Why might Philip have permitted Alexander to wield such power at so young an age?

This inscription from the Acropolis defining Athens' relationship with the League of Corinth is the source of the extant text presented on the opposite page.

Maedi members of a powerful Thracian tribe on the upper Strymon River. They were frequent enemies of Macedonia. Alexandropolis would technically have been a military colony, not a true city.

Chaeronea site of an important battle in which Philip established a thinly veiled sovereignty over the Greek city-states. That battle was fought in August of 338 BC, a little after Alexander's eighteenth birthday. Here Philip placed Alexander in charge of the left wing of the Macedonian army; Alexander would have had the experience of several generals at his disposal. Diodorus (16.86) records that it was Alexander's wing (not necessarily Alexander himself) that first broke the line of this Theban Sacred Band, a highly respected military contingent composed traditionally of pairs of male lovers.

The League of Corinth

This fragment of an inscription was found on the Acropolis at Athens. It is probably a section from the treaty that established the League of Corinth between Philip II and the Council of Greek city-states (except Lacedaemonia) after the battle of Chaeronea in 338 BC. The governing council of the League comprised representatives from the participating city-states, but at the same time gave Philip of Macedonia the upper hand in matters of League policy. The League could pass a decision only with approval by the Leader, who was also commander-in-chief, and a majority vote of the Council. Philip was appointed Leader from the beginning, and a declaration of war on Persia was one of the League's first acts. All members of the League were required to contribute money or forces to the effort. After Philip's death, Alexander immediately inherited the title of Leader (but not of commander-in-chief) through his accession to the Macedonian throne.

[Oath. I swear by Zeus, Earth, Sun, Pose]idon, A[thena,]
[Ares, all the gods, and all the goddess]es. I shall abide [by the]
[Peace and shall not break the tr]eaties
[with Philip of Macedonia, no]r shall I wage war
[with hostile intent against any of those] abiding by
[these oaths, neither by land] nor by sea.
[Neither city nor cita]del shall I seize,
[nor any harbour by wa]r belonging to any of those
[sharing in the Peace –] not by any means
[or contrivance. Nor shall] the kingship of Ph
[ilip and his descendants] be overturned by me, nor the
[constitutions in place] among those states when
[the oaths concerning] the Peace were sworn by them.
[And I myself shall do nothing to op]pose these
[treaties nor] shall I allow another to do so, insofar as
[I am able. But if anyone at all] breaks faith concerning
[this treaty, I shall bring aid] whenever summoned
[by those wronged,] and I shall make war on the violators
[of the Common Peace] whenever
[the Common Council deems it meet] and the Leader
[demands, and I shall not a]bandon the …

Inscriptiones Graecae II² 236a

1   The lettering in square brackets represents reconstructed text, i.e. text that does not appear on the recovered stone. What do you suppose permits a modern epigrapher to reconstruct this inscription with such confidence?

2   Who is represented by the first person 'I' in this inscription?

3   In what ways does this treaty appear to limit the freedom of the Greek city-states?

4   What freedoms do they appear to retain?

A son and mother threatened

> Philip had apparently not yet officially named a successor, and Olympias and Alexander seem to have viewed their situation as precarious, as the following two episodes make clear. Their fear for the future was perhaps not unfounded; new kings would often begin their reigns with the elimination of other pretenders to the throne.

Plutarch 9

But there were troubles within the household, specifically **Philip's marriages** and his loves, and the disease of the women's quarters compromised the character of the kingdom, leading to many reproaches and great quarrels. Ill-tempered Olympias, a terribly jealous and indignant wife, exacerbated these problems by goading Alexander on. **Attalus** started the most public quarrel at the wedding of **Cleopatra** to Philip, who had fallen in love with the girl despite his age. Attalus was Cleopatra's uncle, and now thoroughly drunk he called on the Macedonians to pray to the gods that Philip and Cleopatra might produce a legitimate child as successor to the kingdom. Angered by these words, Alexander answered, 'And me, you dirty scoundrel? You're calling me a bastard?' and he hurled his cup at Attalus. Philip leapt up then, sword in hand, to confront Alexander, but luckily for both of them Philip's wrath and the wine made him stumble and fall. At that, Alexander insultingly mocked his father: 'Look here, men! This fellow has been preparing to cross from Europe to Asia, but has fallen flat in crossing from couch to couch!' After this drunken act, Alexander settled Olympias in **Epirus**, while

---

Philip's marriages these were indeed numerous, but all of them effected important alliances with the royal house (see pp. 2–3). While the marriages appear to have been primarily political, there were certainly rivalries between the wives, each of whom would naturally hope that her son would become heir to the throne. At the same time, having multiple wives was rare among Greeks, so that Philip's relationships would have led to moral judgement as well. The rivalry combined with the questionable morality leads Plutarch to refer to the situation as a 'disease of the women's quarters'.

Attalus a politically powerful and noble-born Macedonian. He, Philip and Alexander are all drunk in this episode. While most of the Greek world customarily drank their wine mixed with water, the Macedonians were notorious as heavy drinkers who drank their wine unmixed.

Cleopatra a native Macedonian, not to be confused with the famous Cleopatra VII, queen of Egypt (see p. v). Her Macedonian blood might naturally have presented a threat to Olympias and her status within the palace. A 'pure' Macedonian son by Cleopatra could conceivably become a legitimate heir and displace Alexander as Philip's successor.

Epirus Olympias' homeland. By leaving for Epirus and Illyria (to the west) respectively, Olympias and Alexander effectively entered a voluntary exile. Though Alexander returned at Philip's invitation, Olympias remained in Epirus until after Philip's death.

he himself resided among the Illyrians. Meanwhile Demaratus the Corinthian visited Philip. As an old friend of the royal house he could speak with candour, and so, after the initial greeting and niceties, when Philip asked how well the Greek city-states were getting along with each other, Demaratus replied, 'Oh, how utterly fitting that you, Philip, express concern about Greece when you have filled your own house with so much ugly discord!' This gave Philip pause; he sent for Alexander and with Demaratus' help persuaded him to return home.

> 1 Plutarch writes of two spheres here: the private domestic sphere and the kingdom's political sphere. What details of this story would suggest that they are not so easily separated?
>
> 2 What insight into Philip's (and Macedonia's) relationship with the Greek city-states does his exchange with Demaratus offer?
>
> 3 What factors might have led to Philip's recall of Alexander?

Carian wedding plans

Plutarch 10   **Pixodarus**, Persian satrap [governor] of **Caria**, wished to marry his eldest daughter to Philip's son **Arrhidaeus**. By uniting their families in this way, he hoped to insinuate himself into an alliance with Philip. When Pixodarus sent Aristocritus to Macedonia for these purposes, Alexander's friends and mother once again began bringing him tales and alleging falsely that Philip was busy settling Arrhidaeus on the throne through the ties of a grand and celebrated marriage. Alexander was distraught at this and so he sent the tragic actor **Thessalus** to Caria to persuade Pixodarus to forget about Arrhidaeus, who was a bastard and of unsound mind, and instead to seek a marriage to Alexander. Pixodarus far preferred this option to his earlier plans, but when Philip caught wind of it, he entered Alexander's room with Parmenion's son **Philotas**, one of Alexander's friends, as witness. He upbraided his son harshly, bitterly reviling him as low-born and undeserving of his noble status, since he was content to become the son-in-law of a Carian man who was slave to the barbarian king of Persia. Philip then wrote to the Corinthians, demanding that they send Thessalus back to him in shackles, and he

---

Pixodarus   after the death of King Ochus of Persia in 338 BC, Pixodarus sought to split from Persia and initiate an alliance with Philip, whose plan to invade the Persian Empire was by that point common knowledge.

Caria   a Persian satrapy (province) in south-west Asia Minor (see map on p. 11).

Arrhidaeus   younger half-brother of Alexander, known to be weak-minded.

Thessalus   like Aristocritus, a Greek actor. Actors were not uncommonly employed for political negotiation at this time.

Philotas   his father was Parmenion, son-in-law of Attalus.

banished from Macedonia Alexander's companions **Harpalus** and **Nearchus**, as well as **Erigyius** and **Ptolemy**. Later, Alexander recalled these men and promoted them to the highest rank.

---

1 Why do you think tragic actors would have made good go-betweens on diplomatic missions?

2 Why might Philip have chosen Philotas as witness in this instance?

3 What conclusions may we draw about the tensions between Alexander and his father throughout the episode?

4 Why might Philip not have exiled Alexander on this occasion?

Philip's murder

In 336 BC Philip was stabbed to death by Pausanias, one of his personal Bodyguards, at the wedding of Cleopatra, Philip's daughter by Olympias, to Alexander, king of Epirus. Theories of conspiracy abounded.

Plutarch 10   **Pausanias**, who had been maliciously abused by Attalus and **Cleopatra**, killed Philip after failing to obtain justice from him. Most of the blame then fell on Olympias, for allegedly encouraging the youth in his anger and even goading him on. But some of the reproach surrounded Alexander, too. They say that when Pausanias, after being wronged, ran into Alexander and complained bitterly,

---

Harpalus, Nearchus, Erigyius, Ptolemy   Harpalus and Ptolemy were Macedonians, the latter tied to the royal house through his mother. Nearchus, a self-proclaimed Macedonian, was in fact a native of Crete, while Erigyius was from Mytilene. The exile of Alexander's friends and the demand for Thessalus' extradition shows that Philip considered this an instance of high treason. Once aware of this confusion in the Macedonian royal house, Pixodarus withdrew altogether the offer of his daughter in marriage.

Pausanias   a jilted beloved of Philip's, according to Diodorus (16.93–94). Such homoerotic relationships were quite common, usually between an older man (the lover) and a youth (the beloved). The assassination itself was spectacular, occurring before a large crowd in a Macedonian theatre at Aegae, where Philip was receiving all the foreign dignitaries with great pomp. Alexander's Bodyguards apparently killed Pausanias immediately after the murder. Pausanias' death of course meant that he could not be interrogated, and this doubtless raised eyebrows. Justin, living sometime during the second to fourth centuries AD, composed a Latin epitome (summary) of the now-lost 'Philippic Histories' of Pompeius Trogus (c. first century BC to first century AD). Justin (9.6) records some suspicion that Olympias (still in Epirus) and even Alexander authored the assassination of Philip and its cover-up.

Cleopatra   Attalus' niece and Philip's most recent wife.

Alexander repeated this line from *Medea*: 'the father, the groom, the bride'. Still, Alexander searched out and punished **those complicit in the plot** and did express anger at **Olympias** for her ruthless handling of Cleopatra while he was away.

> • Macedonian nobles were highly educated in Greek culture and frequently quoted poetry in conversation. Who might Alexander be suggesting are the father, groom and bride? Who might be Medea?

Thebes: a warning to the Greeks

Alexander's situation after assuming the kingship was precarious. Both the barbarians to the north and the Greeks to the south saw Philip's assassination as an opportunity to revolt against their Macedonian oppressors. Alexander first defeated the barbarians, then in 335 BC marched on Thebes, whose citizens had revolted.

Plutarch 11 Even after Alexander had reached Thebes, he offered the city a chance to apologize for its actions, demanding that they hand over **Phoenix and Prothytes**, and promising immunity for those who would shift their allegiance to himself. But the Thebans demanded in response that Alexander hand over **Philotas and Antipater**, and they declared that those who wanted to liberate Greece were prepared to fight

---

Medea   tragedy by Euripides in which the hero Jason has abandoned his wife Medea to marry the daughter of King Creon. Medea responds by murdering the daughter, and, as it happens, Creon as well. In the quoted line (288), Creon tells Medea that he has learned of her threats against himself, his future son-in-law (Jason) and his daughter.

those complicit in the plot   officially determined through an ensuing investigation to be the brothers Heromenes and Arrhabaeus Lyncestes. Both were swiftly executed. A third brother, Alexander Lyncestes, was pardoned for his association with the family into which he had married and because he was the first to declare Alexander king upon Philip's assassination. Amyntas IV, the legitimate heir to the throne whom Philip had displaced, was soon made to disappear, and Attalus, abroad in Asia Minor at the time, was executed by Parmenion at Alexander's behest.

Olympias   she killed Attalus' niece Cleopatra and her infant daughter. According to Justin (9.7), Cleopatra was forced to hang herself after watching her daughter killed in her own arms. Pausanias (8.7) relates that Olympias had them roasted together over a brazier.

Phoenix and Prothytes   two men otherwise unknown to history.

Philotas and Antipater   according to Diodorus (17.8), Philotas was the commander of the Macedonian Guard in the Cadmeia, the Theban citadel, where Philip had earlier posted these troops to guarantee the cooperation of this powerful city. Antipater is the name of the Macedonians' chief general, but he was not present at the battle. It is possible that the Thebans refer to another man of that name, perhaps also in the Cadmeia.

alongside themselves. And so Alexander directed the Macedonians to battle. The Thebans fought then with a valour and zeal that surpassed their numbers, though they were arrayed against a foe that **outnumbered** them many times over. But when the Macedonian Guard, too, left the Cadmeia and attacked them from behind, most of the Thebans were surrounded and killed in the fighting itself. Their city was taken, thoroughly looted and then demolished, since Alexander fully expected that so great a disaster would intimidate Greeks elsewhere and cause them to cower in terror. But this move also enhanced his image by answering the complaints of his allies, the **Phocians and Plataeans** in particular, who had been denouncing the Thebans. After separating out the priests, all the *proxenoi* of the Macedonians, the descendants of **Pindar** and those who secretly opposed the ones who had voted to revolt, Alexander sold the rest – about 30,000 – into slavery. The slain numbered more than 6,000.

> 1 Why might Alexander have granted his allies the right to decide Thebes' fate, as Arrian records?
>
> 2 Why would it have been politically savvy for Alexander to spare Pindar's family?

Timocleia

The following episode features an act of clemency by Alexander during the sack of Thebes.

Plutarch 12 In the midst of the many terrible disasters that afflicted the city, some Thracians broke into the house of Timocleia, a highly respected and chaste woman. While the others were stealing her possessions, their leader raped her, and after disgracing her in this way demanded to know the whereabouts of any hidden gold

---

outnumbered all historical sources highlight the tenacity with which Greeks generally fight against numerical odds for their freedom. The failure by Darius and Xerxes to conquer Greeks during the Persian Wars doubtless contributed to the Greeks' powerful sense of superiority and courage.

Phocians and Plataeans two of the allies that fought with Alexander against Thebes. Other sources add the Thespians and Orchomenians to the list. All of them had bitter relations with Thebes. Diodorus (17.9) asserts that Alexander's rage drove him to sack the city, but Arrian (1.8) states that Alexander actually permitted Thebes' enemies to decide the city's fate.

proxenoi Theban citizens who officially represented Macedonian interests in Thebes. In exchange for the title of *proxenos* and other privileges, their duties would also have included hosting and entertaining the Macedonian visitors.

Pindar (*c.* 520–440 BC) the most famous composer of choral performances in celebration of victors at the Panhellenic athletic contests, including (allegedly) one in honour of the Macedonian king Alexander I (*c.* 498–454 BC).

or silver. She confessed to having some and led him alone into the garden. There she showed him a well where she said she had thrown her most costly possessions while the city was being taken. As the **Thracian** stooped down and inspected the spot, she shoved him from behind and killed him by hurling many stones down after him. When the Thracians brought her to Alexander with her hands tied, it was apparent from her look and walk that she was an honourable and high-minded woman, for she followed her escorts unshaken and unperturbed. Then, when the king asked who she was, she answered that she was a sister of Theagenes, the man who commanded troops against Philip for the freedom of the Greeks and who had fallen as general at Chaeronea. Alexander was so astounded then, at both her answer and her act, that he made her free, along with her children.

---

1 Why do you think Plutarch included this story about Timocleia in his biography of Alexander?

2 What is the relevance here of her brother's identity?

Diogenes and Delphi

The following general assembly, a meeting of the Corinthian League, was held at Corinth (a city located on the 'Isthmus', the strip of land connecting the Peloponnesus with the rest of Greece) in autumn 336 BC, soon after the assassination of Philip. In 338, Philip had been declared the leader of a proposed invasion of Persia; at this meeting, the League now officially recognized Alexander as commander-in-chief.

Plutarch 14 The Greeks held a general assembly at the Isthmus and voted to launch an invasion against the Persians with Alexander, who was declared its leader. When many statesmen and learned men then went to congratulate Alexander in person, he was expecting the same of **Diogenes** of Sinope, who was spending his time around Corinth then. But since this man had very little regard for Alexander and was instead dallying in **Craneion**, Alexander went to him. Diogenes happened to

---

Thracian this seems to be an error by Plutarch, who records in his own *Moralia* (259 D–260 D) that the man was a Macedonian who shared the same name as the king.

Diogenes important Cynic philosopher. The term Cynic, literally 'dog-like', may derive from a quotation ascribed to Diogenes himself: 'dogs bite their enemies, but I bite my friends – to save them.' Cynicism's central tenet was that self-sufficiency and happiness could be achieved through a virtuous life lived in accordance with Nature. This virtue required the rejection of things meaningless in the natural world (e.g. power, wealth and glory), since valuing these brings negative emotion and suffering. This tale of his meeting with Alexander is fictitious but famous.

Craneion suburb of Corinth.

be lying down in the sun, but he sat up a little at the approach of so many people and eyed Alexander, who greeted him and asked if he was in need of anything. 'Step a little to the side, out of my sun,' replied Diogenes. Alexander, they say, was so affected by his disdainful treatment and so awe-struck at the contempt and greatness of the man, that when his retinue were laughing and mocking Diogenes as they left, he said, 'I for one, if I were not Alexander, would be Diogenes.'

Since Alexander wanted to consult the god about the invasion, he went to Delphi, but it happened to be an ill-omened period during which it was unlawful to deliver oracles. First he sent for the **prophetess**, but when she cited the law and refused, Alexander himself went up and began dragging her to the temple by force. Then, as if broken by his will, she said, 'You are indomitable, child!' When he heard that, Alexander said he no longer needed the other oracle, since she had given him the response he wanted.

---

1 Although this assembly was held in 336 BC, prior to the sack of Thebes in 335, Plutarch reverses the order. What are some narrative effects of Plutarch's rearrangement of events?

2 Do you find any deeper significance in Diogenes' reply to Alexander?

3 What do you think Alexander means by his remark about Diogenes? What do Alexander and Diogenes have in common?

4 Why might Plutarch have chosen to include the story of the Delphic oracle immediately after that of Diogenes?

Invasion at all costs

Alexander is now poised to lead the Greeks against Persia, and Plutarch chooses to highlight the financial gamble in taking up this enterprise.

Plutarch 15   Regarding the **size of his army**, some say that it was as small as 30,000 infantry and 4,000 cavalry; others, as large as 43,000 infantry and 5,000 cavalry. According

---

prophetess   better known as the Pythia, she would normally deliver the oracle's prophecies in a trance inspired by Apollo. Oracles were issued only on specific predetermined days.

size of his army   Arrian (1.11) and Diodorus (17.17) agree that the infantry numbered 32,000 and the cavalry 5,100. As you will find, the number of soldiers varies considerably from source to source throughout the campaign, as does the number of those killed in battle. Plutarch here does not mention the more than 10,000 men who had already crossed the Hellespont under Parmenion in 336 BC to prepare the way for the coming expedition. If the number of talents at Alexander's disposal is correct, then this may be an improvement after his accession to the throne, when he inherited a treasury of 60 talents and a debt of 500. He had to borrow 800 talents then, and perhaps sold the Thebans into slavery in part because he needed the money.

to Aristobulus, Alexander had no more than 70 talents to supply those troops, which **Douris** describes as only enough provisions for 30 days; Onesicritus says that on top of this Alexander actually owed 200 talents. But although he was setting out with so few and scant resources, he did not board his ship until he had seen to the affairs of his **Companions**, giving farmland to one, a town to another and the revenue from a hamlet or port to a third. And when nearly all of the royal property had been used up or allotted, **Perdiccas** said, 'But, King, what are you leaving for yourself?' When Alexander answered, 'My hopes', Perdiccas replied, 'We too, then, who are marching with you shall share in those!' And once Perdiccas had declined the property allotted to him, some others of Alexander's friends did the same. Alexander, however, readily granted payment to those who accepted or requested it, and by distributing most of what was in Macedonia, he exhausted his resources. With this preparation and enthusiastic sense of purpose he crossed the **Hellespont**.

---

1   What specifically was Alexander trading for service to support the invasion?
2   What are the pros and cons of such a stratagem?

Douris (c. 350–260 BC) tyrant of the island of Samos who wrote philosophical and historical works, including a history of Macedonia. None of his writings is extant.

Companions   technical term designating a group of noble cavalrymen hand-picked by the Macedonian king.

Perdiccas   an important commander throughout Alexander's campaign. He was appointed regent over the empire at Alexander's death in 323 BC, but was assassinated three years later.

Hellespont   body of water connecting the Black Sea and the Mediterranean, and separating the continents of Europe and Asia. Xerxes famously bridged the Hellespont with ships during his invasion of Greece 150 years earlier.

Arrian's aims

Arrian (see Introduction, p. 5) begins his *Anabasis of Alexander* with this explicit discussion of his methodology.

Arrian,
Preface

Where **Ptolemy** son of Lagus and **Aristobulus** son of Aristobulus have both written the same things about Alexander son of Philip, I myself record them as entirely true. Where their accounts differ, however, I record the one I consider at once more believable and more worth relating. Others, granted, have written other things about Alexander; no one has been written about by so many, and no one has been the subject of more disagreement between writers. But I believe Ptolemy and Aristobulus are more trustworthy in their telling, since the latter shared in the invasion with King Alexander, while Ptolemy, in addition to his own participation in the invasion, was himself a king, so that it would have been more shameful for him to lie than for any other. Furthermore, both wrote after Alexander had died, and so were under no duress or payment to write anything other than what happened. Even so, I have also recorded some tales by others about Alexander, those that I thought worth relating and not entirely unbelievable. To those who might question why after so many have written about Alexander I mean to do the same, I say let them first read the works of those others and then turn to mine before putting such questions!

1 How convincing do you find Arrian's reasons for trusting the accounts by Ptolemy and Aristobulus? Why?

2 Based on this introduction as a whole, what qualities does Arrian believe set his work on Alexander apart from other accounts?

Ptolemy after serving as one of Alexander's generals, he went on to rule the kingdom of Egypt, initiating the Ptolemaic dynasty that lasted for three centuries until Cleopatra's suicide brought it to an end. Keenly interested in linking Alexander to his own Egyptian kingdom, Ptolemy successfully commandeered Alexander's corpse and brought it to Memphis for burial. The date of Ptolemy's account is unknown, but evidence suggests a point not long after Alexander's death. His work was not well known in antiquity, and Arrian's history appears to have been unique in part for its heavy use of Ptolemy's work.

Aristobulus Alexander's chief engineer throughout the campaign, who wrote an account that received far wider readership than Ptolemy's. The date of his account is no earlier than 301 BC, however – over 20 years after Alexander's death in 323. Consider as you read passages of Arrian whether he (a) faithfully notes all his departures from Ptolemy and Aristobulus, and (b) reveals every point where the two disagree.

2 Into Asia

The crossing

> The Persian navy was much larger than Alexander's, but an uprising in Egypt required the Persians' attention. This permitted the Macedonians to cross over into Asia uncontested.

Arrian 1.11 At the beginning of spring [334 BC] Alexander set out towards the Hellespont, after turning the administration of Macedonian and Greek affairs over to **Antipater**. He led little more than 30,000 infantry, including light-armed troops and archers, but more than 5,000 cavalry. He marched past Lake Cercinitis towards Amphipolis and the mouth of the Strymon River. After crossing the Strymon he passed by Mount Pangaeum towards Abdera and Maronea, Greek cities founded along the sea. From there he reached the Hebrus River, which he crossed easily, and then travelled through Paetice to the river Melas. After crossing the Melas too, he reached Sestus within 20 days of his departure from home. On coming to Elaeus, he sacrificed to **Protesilaus** at his tomb, because, of those Greeks who waged war with Agamemnon against **Ilium**, Protesilaus was thought to have been the first to step down from his ship into Asia. Alexander hoped by his sacrifice to secure a more fortunate landing than that of Protesilaus.

Parmenion was charged with overseeing the crossing of the cavalry and most of the infantry from Sestus to Abydos, and they used 160 triremes and many other cargo ships to accomplish this. The most common account holds that when

---

Antipater left as regent in Macedonia while Alexander led the eastern invasion. This was the typical Macedonian practice when the king went on campaign.

Protesilaus also the first to die – according to legend, he was killed immediately upon setting foot in Asia (*Iliad* 2.701–2). Still, Alexander assumes the role of Protesilaus himself later in this passage, though with a happier outcome. Herodotus (9.116) records that the Persian governor Artayctes plundered this sacred tumulus at the beginning of Xerxes' invasion of Greece in 480–479 BC.

Ilium another name for Troy, the city against which, according to legend, Agamemnon led an invasion as commander-in-chief of the Greek peoples.

Parmenion he crossed the Hellespont with over 10,000 men in 336 BC, but his expeditionary force had progressed no farther than the region just across the Hellespont. Here Parmenion is described as managing the crossing at the very point at which Xerxes crossed in the other direction in 480.

Alexander travelled from Elaeus to the **Harbour of the Achaeans**, he himself served as helmsman on the admiral's ship. When he was in the middle of the strait of the Hellespont, he slaughtered a bull to Poseidon and to Nereus, and poured a libation from a golden *phialē* into the sea. They say that he, too, was the first man bearing arms to step down from the ship onto Asian soil, and that he erected altars – to Zeus **Apobaterius**, to Athena and to Heracles – both where he had set out from Europe and where he landed in Asia. On going up to Ilium, he sacrificed to Athena of Ilium and dedicated his full armour in the temple there, taking in exchange some of the **sacred arms** still preserved from the Trojan expedition, which they say that the **Hypaspists** would carry into battle ahead of Alexander. Legend holds that Alexander sacrificed also to **Priam** at the altar of Zeus Herceius in the hope of mitigating the wrath of Priam towards the stock of Neoptolemus, from which he himself was descended.

---

1   What does the phrasing 'Macedonian and Greek' reveal about Macedonia's situation? What do you think might be one of Antipater's major concerns?

2   Athena was the patron goddess of Athens, and her temple there had been pillaged and destroyed by Xerxes in 480 BC. For this reason, Alexander led his war of revenge in that goddess's name. Why would Alexander have sacrificed to the other two?

3   This is the first example we have seen of Arrian's narrative. How does its style differ from Plutarch's? In what is Arrian interested? To what kinds of source does he appear to have access?

4   What evidence in his account suggests the importance of the Hellespont as a symbolic boundary? What past events is Alexander (or Arrian, or both) bringing to bear in this episode and how?

Harbour of the Achaeans   located at the mouth of the Scamander River, the point where the Greeks were supposed to have beached their ships in their invasion of Troy.

phialē   flat saucer used for drinking and for pouring drink offerings to the gods.

Apobaterius   cult epithet meaning 'of disembarkations'. It reflects the common practice of worshipping a deity under a specific identity appropriate to the situation.

sacred arms   although it would have been impossible for this to have been true, such stories were regularly believed in the ancient world.

Hypaspists   term here referring not to the infantry corps of that name, but to a small group of Companions who served as shield-bearers to the king in battle.

Priam   mythological king of Troy. When the city was sacked by the invasion led by Agamemnon, Achilles' son Neoptolemus brutally murdered Priam at the altar of Zeus Herceius. The title 'Herceius', meaning 'of the enclosure', highlights the violation of Zeus in his capacity as protector of the palace. This offensive act was one of the most famous war crimes by a Greek. Alexander traces his descent from Neoptolemus (and Achilles) through his mother Olympias, and so here is expiating his ancestor's notorious crime.

Arrian as author

Here, in his account of Alexander's visit to Troy, Arrian proudly justifies his role as Alexander's chronicler.

Arrian 1.12 Some say that Alexander also placed a crown on the very tomb of **Achilles** and that **Hephaestion** placed a crown on the tomb of **Patroclus**. And Alexander, as the story goes, called Achilles truly blessed, since he had been fortunate enough to have Homer proclaim his memory for posterity. In fact Alexander had no option but to admit that Achilles was blessed, for Alexander himself, despite all his other good fortune, has been overlooked in this regard, and his feats have not been imparted to humankind in a worthy manner – not in prose, really, nor has anyone set them to verse. He was not celebrated in lyrics, as were **Hieron**, **Gelon**, **Theron** and many others hardly comparable with him, and Alexander's feats are therefore far less known than the most trifling deeds of old. Furthermore, even the march of the Ten Thousand with Cyrus against King Artaxerxes, the sufferings of Clearchus and those captured along with him, and the Ten Thousand's return under **Xenophon's** leadership are because of Xenophon much better known to people than Alexander and Alexander's deeds are. And yet Alexander neither campaigned alongside another nor fled the **Great King**. Nor did he subdue only those who stood in the way of his march back to the sea. No, there is no other

---

Achilles, Patroclus Patroclus is a close and older friend of Achilles, the most formidable of the Greek heroes who fought at Troy. When the Trojan Hector kills Patroclus, Achilles returns to the war to avenge his friend's death. It is Homer's *Iliad* for which Alexander here envies Achilles. Although not indicated in the *Iliad*, the later Greek tradition, including that of Alexander's day, took the relationship between Achilles and Patroclus to be an erotic one.

Hephaestion boyhood friend of Alexander who continued to enjoy a particularly close relationship with the king.

Hieron, Gelon, Thelon kings of Sicily in the early fifth century BC. Hieron and Thelon commissioned the poets Pindar, Bacchylides and Simonides to celebrate their horse and chariot victories at Panhellenic games. A well-known poem of Pindar's grandly celebrates Gelon's military success against the Carthaginians.

Xenophon (c. 431–355 BC). He recounts these events – during which he himself was general – in his *Anabasis*. The Greek general Clearchus led 10,000 Greek mercenaries to battle alongside Cyrus the Younger (a Persian pretender to the throne) against the Persian King Artaxerxes II at Cunaxa on the river Tigris. They were victorious, but Cyrus was killed in battle. When Clearchus was then lured to a discussion of peace terms at which he was in fact executed, the Ten Thousand chose new leaders, including Xenophon, and these managed to lead the mercenaries through enemy territory all the way to the Black Sea. In Arrian's day Xenophon was generally acclaimed the foremost of the Greek prose historians, and Arrian imitates his style.

Great King the customary title of the Persian monarch.

single man who has performed feats so great, so magnificent in number or size, among Greeks or **barbarians**. For this reason I have set out to write this work, deeming myself not unworthy of making Alexander's feats known. Whatever else, I know this of myself: I need not record my name, for it is not unknown to men, nor is my fatherland, nor my people, nor the various offices I have held in my country. But I do write this: that my fatherland, my people, my offices cannot be separated from these tales; such has been the case since my youth. And for this reason I believe I do indeed deserve a place among the best writers in the Greek language, just as Alexander, too, was truly among the best in arms.

---

1 Which of the *Iliad*'s characters does Alexander resemble more, Agamemnon or Achilles? How? Why would it be in his interest to cultivate an association with the one over the other?

2 Arrian wrote during the Roman imperial period. Why do you suppose he did not compare or contrast Alexander's accomplishments with those of the Roman emperors?

3 In declining to give his name, country of origin and a summary of his career, Arrian breaks from the standard practice of his contemporaries. Why might he have chosen to do this? On what grounds, specifically, does Arrian believe his work superior?

4 How would you describe the relationship between Alexander and Arrian, as Arrian understands it?

Battle of the Granicus

With Darius far away, his generals had to decide how to cope with the initial Macedonian invasion into Persian territory.

Arrian 1.12   The **Persian generals** were Arsames, Rheomithres, Petenes and Niphates; Spithridates, satrap of Lydia and Ionia, and Arsites, hyparch of Hellespontine Phrygia, were with them also. They had already encamped near the city of Zelea with the barbarian cavalry and the Greek mercenaries, and the generals held a war-council after receiving word that Alexander had crossed over. **Memnon** the

---

barbarians   the Greek term *barbaros*, while not always flattering, is not as pejorative as our word 'barbarian'; it meant simply non-Greek.

Persian generals   those listed here were appointed by Darius, and were Persian satraps from Asia Minor, i.e. that portion of the empire most directly affected by Alexander's current invasion. These satraps were individuals typically appointed by the Great King himself to govern the empire's provinces ('satrapies'), which paid tribute to the king.

Memnon   married to Barsine, a daughter of a Persian noble, Artabazus. Memnon was Persia's head of operations against Macedonia, where he had in fact spent several years in exile. In this account, however, Memnon appears to have power over the other generals neither in the assembly nor during the battle.

Rhodian cautioned them not to risk fighting the Macedonians, whose infantry was far superior to their own. Furthermore, while Alexander himself was accompanying his own troops, the Persians were without Darius. Instead, Memnon argued, the Persians should march on, destroying the dried fodder by trampling it with their cavalry, and setting fire to the crops that were still in the ground. Nor should they spare the cities either. Alexander would then lack the supplies he needed and be unable to remain in the area. But Arsites declared, they say, that he would not allow a single house belonging to men under his command to be set alight, and the Persians in this council sided with Arsites, because they regarded Memnon with some suspicion, believing that he was wilfully postponing battle in the hope of winning honour from the king for himself.

1.13   In the meantime, Alexander began advancing to the **Granicus River** with his army arranged for battle. He had organized his ranks of **hoplites** into two rows and was leading the cavalry on the wings, with the **baggage train** following behind. Hegelochus led ahead some **sarissa**-bearing cavalry and as many as 500 light-armed soldiers to scout out the enemy's situation. Alexander was not far from the Granicus when some of these scouts rode up at a gallop, reporting that the Persians were arranged for battle on the far bank. He then immediately began organizing his whole army for battle, but Parmenion approached him and said: 'It seems sensible to me, King, under the present circumstances, to pitch camp on this bank of the river, just as we are. I do not think the enemy will dare to spend the night near us, since they are far inferior in infantry. By camping away from the river, then, they will allow our army to cross the ford at dawn with ease,

---

Granicus River   the modern Biga Çay, running from the Ida mountain range into the Propontis. The proximity to Troy here may still be felt, and those of Arrian's readers who were familiar with the *Iliad* would recall the importance of the Scamander River in that work.

hoplites   heavily armed infantry soldiers, most often arranged (as here) in a series of rows facing in the direction of the enemy. The Macedonians typically flanked this central infantry body with cavalry, which were one of the Macedonians' chief tactical advantages.

baggage train   the caravan of pack animals carrying necessary supplies and equipment for the army. As you continue to read, consider what this equipment must have included for various operations, and what sorts of non-fighting people were probably travelling with the baggage train as well.

sarissa   Macedonian pike remarkable for its great length (5–6 metres/15–18 feet). It was made of cornel wood and had a counterweight fixed to the butt to make it easier to manoeuvre. It was typically constructed of two pieces so that it could be taken apart for carrying. While the cavalry scouts carry it here, the sarissa was the primary weapon of the Macedonian infantry. The first three rows of a hoplite unit would lower their sarissae so that an approaching enemy would encounter three rows of these pikes before reaching the first row of Macedonian soldiers.

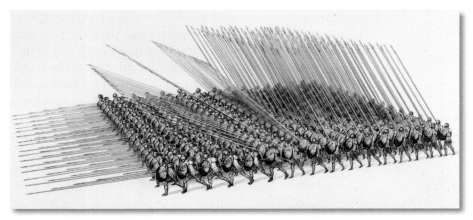

An artist's representation of the Macedonian phalanx, sixteen men deep and sixteen wide.

and we ourselves shall anticipate them by crossing before they can be drawn into formation. If we attempt an attack now, it will, I believe, be at no small risk; it is not possible to lead the army across the river while maintaining a solid front, since the river is visibly deep at many points, and, as you can see, the banks themselves are very high and precipitous. When our men emerge from the river in disarray, the enemy cavalry will already be organized into a front. They will charge us, then, while we are at our most vulnerable, with our flank forward. To lose this first battle would not be a mere momentary setback; it would prove detrimental to the outcome of the war as a whole.'

Alexander replied, 'I know this, Parmenion, but I would feel ashamed if I had easily crossed the Hellespont only to be stopped here by this tiny stream. (Thus did Alexander belittle the Granicus!) And that, I think, suits neither the Macedonians' reputation nor my own eagerness to tackle dangers. No, I think it would embolden the Persians to imagine themselves on a par with Macedonians, since they have suffered no immediate calamity to warrant any fear.'

1.14   After saying this, he sent Parmenion to command the **left wing**, while he himself went to the right. Philotas son of Parmenion was already stationed in front of

---

left wing   the left and right wings, and the centre, are the usual ancient terms for the three major portions of an army in battle formation. The terms 'left' and 'right' are applied from the perspective of the army described, so that an army's right wing faces its enemy's left, and vice versa. Parmenion, as Alexander's second-in-command, is in charge of the left, while the king himself, in accordance with Macedonian tradition, commands the right. In Arrian's ensuing record of the troop deployment (see plan on p. 36), he begins from the far right and moves left to the centre unit under Philip (son of Amyntas), and then from the far left to the centre (Philip again).

the right wing, in command of the **Companion Cavalry**, the archers and the **Agrianian** javelin-men. To Philotas' left was Amyntas son of Arrhabaeus, who was in charge of the sarissa-bearing cavalry, the **Paeonians** and the cavalry squadron of Socrates. Close beside them were the **Hypaspists** of the Companions, led by Nicanor son of Parmenion; next was the infantry battalion under Perdiccas son of Orontes; next, that of Coenus son of Polemocrates; then that of Amyntas son of Andromenes; and finally those commanded by Philip son of Amyntas. The **Thessalian cavalry**, led by Calas son of Harpalus, stood at the far end of the left wing. To their right was the **allied cavalry**, commanded by Philip son of Menelaus. Next were the **Thracians**, whom Agatho commanded, and holding close to them were the infantry, among them the battalions of Craterus, of Meleager and finally of Philip again, at the centre of the whole line.

The Persians' cavalry numbered about 20,000, while their **foreign mercenary infantry** numbered slightly fewer. Their cavalry was extended along the river's bank into a long battle-line, with the infantry behind them, since the ground atop the riverbank was high and defensible. Alexander himself was visible across from their left wing, thanks to the splendour of his arms and the enthusiasm of his retinue, and so the Persians arranged their squadrons of cavalry in close order opposite him.

Companion Cavalry   unit composed of elite Companions that fought alongside the king himself. The Macedonian nobility served in this unit, and you will note that Parmenion's son Philotas commands it, a reminder of the family's status among the Macedonians.

Agrianian   member of a Thracian tribe closely allied with Macedonia.

Paeonians   people of Paeonia, a region north of Macedonia that Philip II had incorporated into the Macedonian kingdom.

Hypaspists   members of the most respected infantry corps of Macedonians. Observe whose son commands this unit. Experience and good training were essential for the Hypaspists, since they stood next to the cavalry. Whenever the cavalry on the right charged ahead to strike the enemy, as it frequently did, the Hypaspists' own flank was exposed.

Thessalian cavalry   heavily armed horsemen of Thessaly equal in skill to the Macedonian Companion Cavalry.

allied cavalry   those men supplied by the Greek city-states participating in the Corinthian League.

Thracians   people of Thrace, a region north-east of Macedonia and invaded by Philip II, who founded the city of Philippopolis there, naming it after himself. The Thracian princes paid tribute to Philip and contributed soldiers to the Macedonian cause. Here Arrian refers to their cavalry unit.

foreign mercenary infantry   during this period, with relative stability within Greece, many Greek males with battle experience offered their service for pay. Of course, this meant fighting for states that were not one's own, including even the Persian Empire.

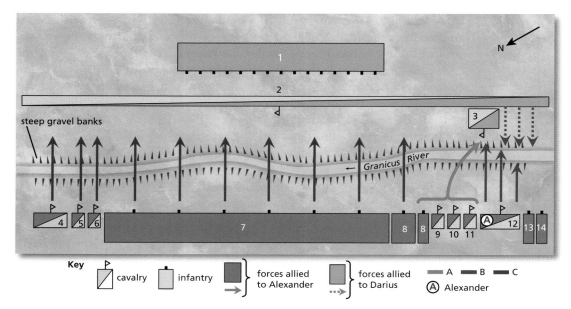

Key

cavalry   infantry   } forces allied to Alexander   } forces allied to Darius   ▬ A ▬ B ▬ C

Ⓐ Alexander

steep gravel banks

Granicus River

Forces allied to Darius
1 Greek mercenaries
2 Persian cavalry
3 best Persian forces and Persian generals

Forces allied to Alexander
4 Thessalian cavalry
5 Greek allied cavalry
6 Thracian cavalry
7 Macedonian infantry phalanx
8 Hypaspists
9 Socrates' squadron
10 Paeonian cavalry
11 sarissa-bearing cavalry (advance cavalry)
12 Alexander and Companion Cavalry
13 Agrianians
14 archers

The battle of the Granicus, May 334 BC, according to Arrian.
A) The Persian generals have placed themselves and their strongest cavalry force directly across from Alexander. He therefore sends a mixture of other cavalry and Hypaspists across the river first, to weaken this Persian force. B) Alexander himself leads the next charge, bringing his Companion Cavalry across the river at an angle. After hard fighting, Alexander's cavalry forces manage to rout the Persian cavalry. C) The rest of the Macedonian army crosses the Granicus and prepares to massacre the Greek mercenaries, who still stand in their original position on the Persian side.

1 Given that the Persian generals were also satraps in Asia Minor, which party do you suppose best represented Darius' interests, the generals or Memnon?

2 How would you characterize the very different solutions by Alexander and Parmenion to the problem posed by the Granicus? Whose approach to this problem would you argue is most strategically sound? Why?

3 In Diodorus' account of this battle (17.19), the Macedonians adopt the very tactic that Parmenion proposes in Arrian's account here. What possible reasons are there for such a striking difference between the historians' accounts?

4 That Greeks would fight alongside Persians against fellow Greeks might seem surprising. But can you think of any modern instances of people acting in their own (economic) interests even when these conflict with the best interests of their own country?

5 Why do you suppose Arrian offers no specific account of the Persian deployment of troops and commanders?

Arrian 1.14 For a time both armies hesitated on the edge of the river, uncertain of the future. They stood still, and there was heavy silence on both sides as the Persians waited for the Macedonians to enter the ford so that they could attack them as they emerged. Then Alexander leapt onto his horse. He enjoined those around him to follow and to prove themselves the noble men they were. He ordered Amyntas son of Arrhabaeus to charge first into the river with his advance cavalry, the Paeonians and one battalion of infantry. At the head of this charge he had placed Ptolemy son of Philip and the squadron of Socrates, which happened to hold **chief command** over the whole cavalry on that day. Alexander himself led the right wing amid trumpet blasts and war cries to **Enyalius**. He entered the ford, and as he did so, he kept stretching the line at an angle against the pull of the current, so that he himself could attack in as strong a formation as possible and prevent a Persian assault upon his flank.

1.15 The Persians struck at them from above, at the point where Amyntas' vanguard and Socrates reached the riverbank. Some hurled javelins into the river from the high ground along the bank; others rode along the lower stretches of the bank all the way to the water's edge. There was a great struggle between the cavalries, with one side trying to get out of the river and the other trying to stop them. The Macedonians fought with their lances under a great barrage of light javelins hurled by the Persians. But they were badly outnumbered and fared poorly in the first assault, since they were defending themselves on uneven ground and from the riverbed below, while the Persians fought from the higher ground of the bank. Furthermore, the strongest of the Persian cavalry were stationed here, and the sons of Memnon and even Memnon himself were risking their lives with them.

The first Macedonians to meet with the Persians were cut down, but they proved themselves noble men, those at least who did not fall back on Alexander as he drew near. He was already close by, bringing the right wing with him, and was the first among them to attack the Persians. He struck at that point where the whole mass of Persian cavalry was stationed, along with the commanders themselves, and intense fighting arose about him. By that point, battalion after battalion of Macedonians was now crossing with ease. Although this was a fight between cavalry, it seemed more like an infantry battle: horses locked with horses, men struggled with men, the Macedonians trying to push the enemy all the way from the riverbank into the plain, the Persians trying to prevent their landing and to press them back into the river again. A little later the advantage was now beginning to go to Alexander's men, thanks to their superior might and experience, but also because they were fighting with cornel lances against the Persians' light javelins. Just then, Alexander's lance splintered in the fighting. He called on his

---

chief command   here held by the squadron of Socrates, but apparently regularly passed from squadron to squadron, perhaps by lot.

Enyalius   epithet of Ares, the Greek god of war and battle-fury.

Royal Groom Aretas for another, but Aretas was in a bind, since his lance too had broken, although he still distinguished himself as he continued to fight with half his broken weapon. He showed it to Alexander and urged him to ask someone else. **Demaratus**, a Corinthian man and one of Alexander's Companions, then gave his own lance to Alexander, who took it and saw that Mithridates, the son-in-law of Darius, was riding far ahead of the others, leading the cavalry forward in a wedge formation. Alexander likewise charged ahead of his own men, then struck Mithridates in the face with his lance and threw him from his horse. Meanwhile Rhoesaces charged at Alexander, struck his head with a scimitar and chopped off part of his helmet. The helmet absorbed the blow, however, and Alexander unhorsed this man too, by driving his lance through Rhoesaces' breastplate and into his chest. Spithridates now had raised his scimitar behind Alexander, but **Cleitus** son of Dropides struck Spithridates at the base of his shoulder and lopped off the arm that held the weapon. Meanwhile, as cavalry units continually gained the riverbank, all those who were able were joining Alexander's force downstream.

1.16 And now from every direction the Persians were being struck in their faces with lances – they and their horses. They were driven back by the cavalry, but were sustaining severe damage also from the light infantry who were interspersed among the horse. Then the Persians gave way, first where Alexander was bearing the brunt of battle, but then, once their centre yielded, both wings of the cavalry broke also, and a desperate rout followed.

---

1   How precisely can the reader of Arrian's account here reconstruct the movement of troops and their formation when crossing the river?

2   Which does Arrian concentrate on in his battle narratives – the actions of the commanders or of the common soldiers? According to this account, what are the contributions of each (commanders and common soldiers) in the fighting?

Royal Groom   person in charge of helping the king mount his horse (Macedonians rode bareback) and who accompanied him in battle. He was probably a member of the Royal Pages, noble Macedonian youths who tended to the king's person and prepared his horse for battle.

Demaratus   possibly a relative of the Demaratus who urged Philip to restore Alexander from exile (see p. 21). As a Corinthian, he serves as a reminder that Alexander's Companions are now no longer exclusively Macedonians, as was traditional, but that this expedition, sanctioned by the Corinthian League, also incorporated soldiers from various areas of Greece.

Cleitus   elsewhere in the ancient sources he feels a strong allegiance to Alexander's father Philip, who probably appointed him as a Companion. The famous rescue of Alexander by Cleitus is described in various ways by the ancient sources. In Plutarch's version (16), for example, Cleitus pierces Spithridates with a spear.

Arrian 1.16   Around 1,000 of the Persian cavalry died, but the pursuit was not long, since Alexander next turned against the foreign mercenaries. That corps still stood where they had first been deployed, more from horror at the surprising outcome than from deliberate calculation. Alexander led his infantry line against them after commanding the cavalry to attack from every side. In this way he surrounded and slaughtered the **mercenaries**, so that no one escaped unless they had hidden among the corpses. Some 2,000 prisoners were taken alive. Persian commanders, too, were among the fallen: Niphates, Petenes, Spithridates, satrap of Lydia, Mithrobouzanes, hyparch of the Cappadocians, Mithridates, son-in-law of Darius, Arbupales, son of Artaxerxes' son Darius, Pharnaces, brother of Darius' wife, and Omares, the commander of the foreign mercenaries. Arsites fled the battle into Phrygia, but they say he committed suicide there because the Persians blamed him for the recent failure.

Of the Macedonian Companions, about 25 died in the first assault, and bronze statues of them stand in **Dium**. Alexander commissioned these from Lysippus, the only man he would permit to sculpt his own person. More than 60 of the remaining cavalry died, and the slain infantry numbered as many as 30. Alexander buried them all on the following day in full armour and other adornment, and he awarded exemption from land taxes and any other public duties or taxes on property to their parents and children. He gave considerable attention to his wounded, approaching them himself one by one. He examined their injuries, asked how each was wounded, and allowed them to describe their deeds and even embellish their accounts for him.

Alexander buried both the Persian commanders and the Greek mercenaries who had died fighting for the enemy. But he bound those Greeks whom he took alive as prisoners and sent them in fetters to Macedonia to do hard labour, since these Greek men had fought against their own people on behalf of barbarians, in violation of the **common resolution** passed by the Greeks. He also sent to **Athens** 300 Persian

---

mercenaries   according to Plutarch's account (16) of this battle, the Greek mercenary infantry hired by the Persians offered to negotiate terms of surrender once the Persians had fled. Alexander, however, attacked them in anger and the result was a protracted battle with heavy Macedonian losses.

Dium   site of an important sanctuary to Zeus at the foot of Mount Olympus.

common resolution   that is, the oath by member states of the League of Corinth.

Athens   Alexander sent these spoils to Athens as a political gesture, a reminder that his present invasion of Persia was an act of retribution for Xerxes' invasion of 480–479 BC. Alexander's campaign was the result of a decision by the Corinthian League of Greek city-states, of which Lacedaemonia was notably not a member. This explains the clause 'except for the Lacedaemonians'. The number 300 coincides with the number of Spartan (Lacedaemonian) hoplites who famously died in the battle of Thermopylae during Xerxes' invasion of Greece. This number therefore emphasizes the exclusion of the Lacedaemonians from Alexander's success, as the dedication honours Athens, Sparta's arch-rival throughout the Peloponnesian War.

suits of armour as a votive offering to Athena on the Acropolis, and ordered the following inscription: 'Alexander son of Philip and the Greeks (except for the Lacedaemonians) dedicate these spoils from the barbarians inhabiting Asia.'

Arrian 1.17   Alexander instated Calas as satrap of the province that Arsites had governed, and arranged that that province should pay the very same tribute it had paid to Darius. He also ordered the release, each to his own home, of all the barbarians who came down out of the hills and surrendered. And he cleared the Zeleans of responsibility, since he knew that they had been forced to fight with the barbarians. Parmenion was ordered to take control of Dascylium, and when he arrived he found the city already abandoned by its garrison.

---

1   Alexander did not free the Greek captives until after he had left Egypt and secured the entire Mediterranean seaboard. Other ancient sources state that only the Theban mercenaries were spared imprisonment. Why might they have received special treatment?

2   Could Alexander's massacre (of about 18,000) and imprisonment (of about 2,000) of these Greeks have been a matter of policy as well as rage? If so, what might be the rationale for such a policy?

3   Why would Arsites have been blamed for the Persian loss at the Granicus?

4   Why would only the 25 who died in the first assault be honoured with statues? What about their role in the battle would warrant such an honour?

5   What would be the effect on the local population of Alexander's demanding the same tribute that Darius had? What would be the effect of his clemency towards the barbarian fugitives and the people of Zelea?

The Gordian knot

After his victory at the Granicus, Alexander headed south and then east along the coastline of modern Turkey, taking any cities that resisted and securing for himself Lydia, Caria, Lycia and Pamphylia. From there he turned north, towards Pisidia and Phrygia, whose capital was Gordium.

Plutarch 18   After this, Alexander killed those of the Pisidians who resisted, and subdued Phrygia. And when he took the city of **Gordium**, reputedly the capital of King Midas in ages past, he saw the wagon bound with cornel-tree bark that everyone

---

Gordium   city once ruled by Midas, whose father Gordius had supposedly ridden into the town on this wagon, thereby fulfilling a prophecy that the future king would arrive in this way. The wagon is supposed to have been in the temple of Zeus Basileus ('Zeus the King') upon Alexander's arrival there. This is the same Midas whose touch, according to Greek legend, turned everything into gold. That tale, in fact, is a good reminder both of the wealth of eastern kings relative to Greeks, and of the Greeks' belief that such extraordinary wealth often came with a curse.

was talking about, and he heard the story about it that the barbarians believed to be true, that whoever loosened the bond was fated to become king of the **civilized world**. Now, the most common story goes that, since the bonds had their ends hidden within themselves and were woven through one another again and again in tangled convolutions, Alexander could not figure out how to loosen them, and so he cut the knot apart with his knife. (Once it was cut, many ends indeed were visible.) But **Aristobulus** records that loosening the knot was really very easy for Alexander, who pulled out from the wagon's pole the so-called *hestōr* that held the yoke-band together, and then simply slid the yoke free.

---

1 Gordium may have been a significant point of operations for Alexander early in this invasion; Parmenion met him there, as did reinforcements from Greece. Why would loosening the Gordian knot be a suitable endeavour under these circumstances?

2 Macedonian tradition held that Midas in fact came originally from Macedonia. How might this have contributed to Alexander's motivations here?

3 Which of Alexander's solutions to the knot is more in character?

4 The Gordian knot is still famous today. How is the term used nowadays?

Sickness at the Cydnus

In 333 BC Alexander left Gordium for Cilicia, where his advance was brought to a halt.

Plutarch 19   Darius was growing all the more confident, since he thought Alexander was staying so long in Cilicia out of cowardice. In fact, Alexander lingered there because he was ill. Some attribute his illness to exhaustion, but others say that he grew sick from bathing in the icy waters of the Cydnus River. In any case, no doctors dared to help, since they thought his sickness was stronger than any cure and they were afraid that the Macedonians would level allegations against them in the event of their failure. **Philip** the Acarnanian, however, saw the suffering of the king

---

civilized world   the stated prize only in Plutarch. Every other source names 'Asia', which could refer either to Asia Minor or to the contemporary Persian Empire.

Aristobulus   Plutarch's source for this and the Timocleia tale, he was Alexander's chief engineer. He is the only source for this alternative version.

hestōr   Plutarch probably gets this technical term directly from the engineer Aristobulus. The *hestor* was the peg connecting the end of the wagon pole to the yoke. The top of this peg was fixed with a ring through which the inner reins passed.

Philip   originally from Acarnania in western Greece (west of Aetolia, see map on p. 11) and a friend of Alexander's since boyhood.

---

and trusted in his friendship with him. Even though it meant exposing himself to danger, he thought it a base thing not to bear his share of risk by helping to the fullest extent of his knowledge. He therefore prepared a drug and persuaded Alexander to drink it if he was truly eager to restore his fighting strength.

Meanwhile, however, Parmenion had sent a **letter** from camp claiming that Alexander should beware Philip, whom Darius had persuaded to murder Alexander, promising Philip magnificent gifts and a daughter in marriage. Alexander read the letter, but told none of the **Friends** and slipped it beneath his pillow. When the time came, Philip entered along with the Companions, carrying the drink in a cup. Alexander gave him the letter while he himself took the **drug** eagerly and without suspicion. The result was a marvellous and stage-worthy spectacle, with one man reading as the other drank, and then both at once looking at one another, though not in the same way. Alexander expressed his goodwill and trust towards Philip through his relaxed and beaming countenance, while Philip, appalled at the accusation, now called upon the gods with hands extended to the heavens, now encouraged Alexander to take heart and follow his instructions. At first the drug overpowered Alexander's system, as if it were repelling his strength and burying it deep within him. His voice abandoned him and his perception completely clouded over and he became faint, until he lost consciousness. But thanks to Philip, he regained his senses and, once recovered, presented himself to the Macedonians, who would not be reassured until they had seen Alexander.

> 1 Remember that Plutarch is most interested in Alexander's character. What qualities does this episode highlight?
>
> 2 How else might Alexander have handled the situation with Philip? Why do you think Alexander handled the situation in this way? What did he stand to gain by taking this risk?

letter sent from a different camp. Parmenion had probably been sent ahead when Alexander first fell ill.

Friends Alexander bestowed the formal title 'Friend' on a select number of his Companions, apparently in imitation of Persian custom.

drug the Greek word *pharmakon* was used of medicine as well as poison.

3 Issus and Egypt

Speech before battle

Alexander was on the move again. He marched to Issus and then south along the coast, on the west side of the Amanus mountain range, expecting to meet Darius. Darius, however, had marched north on the eastern side of the same range, then crossed west at the Bahçe pass, and doubled back south on Alexander's tail (see the inset map on p. 44). By all accounts, Alexander was surprised to discover that Darius was behind him, and in fact Darius' presence there was quite a threat, for it effectively cut off the Macedonian supply lines. Alexander had even left behind his wounded at Issus, and Darius' army slaughtered these. On learning of Darius' presence, Alexander quickly turned to attack him in the narrow land between the mountains and the sea. According to Alexander's court historian Callisthenes, the battle took place in an area only 14 stades (about 2.6 km/1.6 miles) wide, bounded by the sea to the west and the Amanus Mountains to the east. Alexander delivers the following speech not to the army as a whole but to his officers. These were his immediate audience, but in giving the speech Alexander is at the same time feeding his officers material for their own speeches to the individual battalions.

Arrian 2.7 Alexander convened his generals, the squadron commanders and the leaders of the allies. He called on them to take courage, reminding them that they had already overcome grave dangers before, that this would be a battle between proven conquerors and men already conquered; he told them that Zeus was already conducting the war in their interest, since he had put it into Darius' mind to lead his force out of a wide open space and into a narrow one. There the terrain offered the perfect area for the Macedonians to deploy their phalanx, while the enemy's vast numbers would be rendered useless in battle. Furthermore, the enemy was nowhere near a match for the Macedonians in either body or mind. Macedonians would be fighting with Persians and **Medians** in a battle between men long weakened by luxury and those whom previous danger had already accustomed

---

Medians strictly the people of Media, a region south-west of the Caspian Sea. Tradition held that when the Persian Cyrus conquered the Medians, many of their political institutions were incorporated into the Persian Empire. To the Greek mind, therefore, the Persian Empire represented a combination of the two peoples and their traditions.

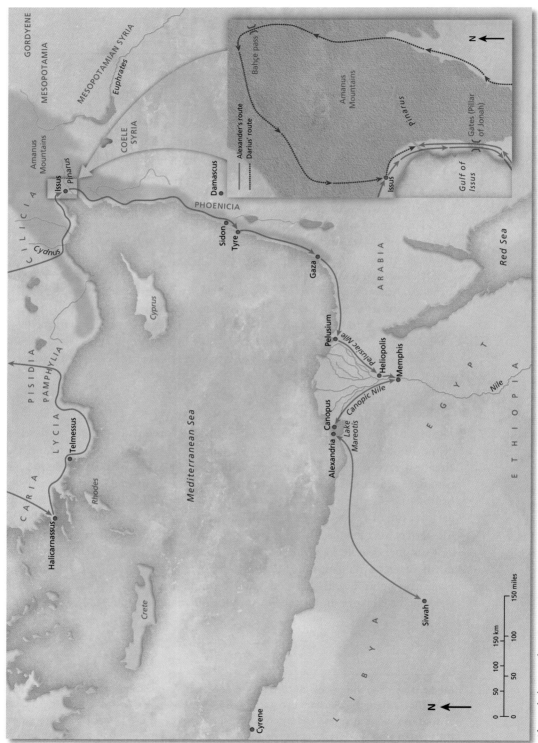

Alexander's route from Issus to Egypt

to the toils of war. It would be a battle, in short, between **slaves and free men**. And while Greeks would be pitted against Greeks, the two sides would not be fighting for the same reasons. Those with Darius were facing dangers in return for pay, and not much pay at that, while **those with the Macedonians** were of their own free will avenging themselves for Greece's sake. And the allies – Thracians, Paeonians, Illyrians and Agrianians – were the toughest in all Europe. These most warlike men would be marshalled against the softest and most indolent races of Asia. And on top of this, they would have an Alexander commanding opposite a Darius. In addition to laying out the advantages that would be theirs in the contest, Alexander pointed to the great rewards that they would gain from the dangers. It would not be the satraps of Darius they defeated now, nor the cavalry marshalled at the Granicus, nor the 20,000 mercenary soldiers there, but the best of the Persians and Medians, all the other peoples subject to the Persians and Medians who dwell in Asia, and the Great King himself. Nothing would be left for them to do after this contest but to rule all Asia and to put an end to their many labours. In addition to these things, he recalled those deeds already so brilliantly accomplished for the common good; he named the men who had shown themselves to be remarkably daring and praised their actions, while recounting his own risks in battle as modestly as possible.

It is said that Alexander also made mention of Xenophon and the Ten Thousand who accompanied him. They could not compare to the Macedonians in number or any other respect, and yet with no cavalry – none of the Thessalians, Boeotians, Peloponnesians, Macedonians, Thracians, nor with any of the other cavalry that were now in their ranks – and with no archers or slingers (aside from a few **Cretans and Rhodians** that Xenophon enrolled on the spot in the midst of danger), they defeated the king and all his force at Babylon itself and were victorious against all the peoples along the way down to the Black Sea. And Alexander spoke all the

---

slaves and free men the rhetoric here exploits well-developed Greek stereotypes regarding the Persians. As early as the eighth century BC, the various city-states had begun identifying formally what they considered a common ethnic identity, based primarily on shared customs and language. Being 'Greek', for example, was early on a prerequisite for participation in the Olympic games. During the Persian Wars, these city-states saw their freedom threatened by a vast empire under the firm control of a single king, and the Greeks naturally hailed their success in thwarting the Persian invasions as the cooperation of free and independent city-states in defeating a king's army of slaves. Such Panhellenism, famously advanced by the Athenian orator Isocrates (436–338 BC), proved crucial to the enterprises of both Philip and Alexander, who found it in their interest to promote the concept.

those with the Macedonians including mercenaries. According to Diodorus (17.17), there were 5,000 Greek mercenaries at the crossing to Asia, and a mere 7,000 Greeks enrolled by member states of the Corinthian League.

Cretans and Rhodians in fact served Xenophon as a unit of slingers throughout the expedition.

other words of encouragement **that one would expect** from a good leader rallying good men under such circumstances prior to battle.

At this point they all crowded around Alexander. They shook the hand of their king, shouted words of encouragement and demanded that he lead them forward at once.

---

1   Consider Alexander's reported reasons why the Macedonians should take courage against the numerically superior force of Darius. How would you characterize his approach to the problem?

2   Which of Alexander's reasons would have appealed to the soldiers' emotions rather than their rational beliefs?

3   How does the reported speech represent the enemy? Do you believe it wiser prior to battle to cast an enemy as a strong or a weak adversary?

4   Recall Arrian's earlier reference to Xenophon in addressing his authorship of this work (p. 31). What features do these accounts of Xenophon share with one another?

The battle of Issus

Arrian 2.8   Alexander then ordered them to eat dinner and sent a few from the cavalry and the archers on to the **Gates** to investigate the road behind them. During the night, Alexander took the army as a whole and marched to regain the Gates. By about midnight he had re-established control of the passes, and then, after setting up carefully selected lookouts, he rested the army on the rocks for the remainder of the night. At about dawn he took the road down from the Gates. So long as the terrain was narrow on all sides he marched the army in column formation, but when it began to open out he kept unfolding the column into a **phalanx** by bringing one battalion of hoplites after another out to the sides, towards the mountain on the right and towards the sea on the left. Up to that point his cavalry was stationed behind the infantry, but once they marched ahead to open ground he immediately

---

that one would expect   Arrian's account of Alexander's speech is traditional in that it is reported, i.e. not quoted directly. The reconstruction of speeches such as these was part of the art of the historian, who could exercise considerable freedom and even showcase his own rhetorical talent. Thucydides, in his history of the Peloponnesian War (1.22), acknowledges the difficulty of preserving speeches accurately. His solution was to keep as close as possible to the sense of what was said, while including what he thought the given circumstances demanded of the speaker.

Gates   a ridge of land identified with the Pillar of Jonah/Yunus, about 100 metres (330 feet) high. By seizing it quickly Alexander was able to ensure that a battle would occur in the narrow coastal plain to the north.

phalanx   this formation, according to Callisthenes (Polybius, *Histories* 12.19), was originally 32 ranks deep on the march. As the terrain widened, the infantry line was extended so that the formation was only eight deep. The usual Macedonian file was 16 deep.

The northern coastal plain, as seen from the Pillar of Jonah.

organized the army into **battle formation**. The Royal Guard and Hypaspists, led by Nicanor son of Parmenion, were the first of those infantry deployed on the right wing, towards the mountain. Next to them was Coenus' battalion and after them that of Perdiccas; these forces extended from the right all the way to the centre of the hoplites. From the left wing, the battalion of Amyntas came first, Ptolemy's next, and then Meleager's. Craterus had been assigned command of the left infantry, while the left wing as a whole was led by Parmenion, who was under orders not to leave the sea and allow the barbarians to encircle them, for the enemy sought to use their numbers to outflank the Macedonians on all sides.

When he received the report that Alexander was advancing against him in battle formation, Darius moved about 30,000 of his cavalry across the **Pinarus River** and around 20,000 of the light infantry with them, so that he could deploy the rest of his force with ease. He stationed his Greek mercenaries, approximately 30,000, in front of his hoplite force and opposite the Macedonians' phalanx. Next to these, on either side, were 60,000 other hoplites, the so-called **Cardaces**; the limited space permitted only this many in a single phalanx. He also stationed about

---

battle formation   would have included the cavalry on either side of the infantry, the deployment seen previously at the battle of Granicus.

Pinarus River   the actual location of the battle. The battle of Issus is so called for the town of Issus that lay nearby, to the north. The precise location of Issus and identification of the Pinarus have long been the subject of debate. Based on the ancient description of the river's banks and the distance between the sea and the Amanus mountains, general consensus identifies the Pinarus with the modern Payas.

Cardaces   probably an elite infantry body from Persia proper (roughly modern Iran).

20,000 on the mountain to their left, opposite Alexander's right, and a number of these men actually found themselves behind Alexander's army. (This was because the mountain curved inland to afford an open, bay-like area of land at its foot, but then came back around behind the location of Alexander's right wing.) The remaining mass of Darius' light-armed troops and hoplites were arranged according to nationality into deep ranks, and were therefore of no use, because they were standing behind the Greek mercenaries and the barbarian force assigned to the phalanx. Darius' total force was said to have been about 600,000 soldiers.

As the land continued to widen with his advance, Alexander brought the cavalry out to the sides. He deployed the so-called Companion Cavalry and the Thessalian cavalry on the right wing with himself and sent the cavalry from the Peloponnesus and the other allied horsemen to Parmenion on the left wing.

Darius, as soon as his phalanx was deployed, signalled for the return of the cavalry that he had stationed in front of the river to ensure the secure deployment of his army. He placed most of them on his right wing near the sea, opposite Parmenion, since the land there was more suited to cavalry action, but he also sent a portion of them to the left wing, towards the mountains. When it seemed, however, that the narrow space there would render cavalry useless, he ordered most of them, too, to ride over to the right. **Darius** himself occupied the centre of the whole force as custom ordained for Persian kings. (**Xenophon** son of Gryllus has recorded the rationale for this formation.)

2.9   When Alexander saw that all but a few of the Persian cavalry had been moved towards the sea, against his left, where only his Peloponnesian and the other allied cavalry were deployed, he immediately sent his own **Thessalian cavalry** to the left, but gave them orders not to ride in front of the whole force. Instead, they were to pass unobserved behind the phalanx, so that the enemy would not notice their change of position.

Darius   he occupied the centre, according to Arrian and Callisthenes, but Curtius (3.9) places him on the Persian left. If at the centre, he would have been located with his cavalry guard behind the Greek mercenaries. If on the left, he would probably have been near the mercenaries (arguably still near the army's centre) and flanked by his guard.

Xenophon   according to Xenophon (*Anabasis* 1.8), the Persian kings kept to the centre of their army in the belief that this was the safest position and the most efficient location from which to issue orders to all the troops.

Thessalian cavalry   apparently still behind the infantry as the army marched slowly forward towards the Persians. The position of the Thessalian cavalry would therefore be apparent to Darius only as the land widened and the cavalry moved forward to flank the infantry on either side. The long Macedonian sarissae would probably have served as a screen to obscure the movements of Alexander's cavalry troops behind the infantry phalanx. Alexander's movement of the Thessalians is here a response to the deployment of Darius' cavalry, carried out in secret so as to gain the advantage of surprise.

Alexander sent the advance cavalry led by Protomachus to the right of the cavalry on the right wing, along with the Paeonians led by Ariston. To the right of the infantry he placed the archers commanded by Antiochus, and he deployed the **Agrianians** under Attalus and some of the cavalry and archers at an angle, to face the mountains at his rear. The result was that on his right the phalanx extended into two wings: one facing Darius and all the Persians across the river, and the other facing the enemy soldiers deployed on the mountain behind his own men. Next to the infantry on the left side came the Cretan and Thracian archers commanded by Sitalces, and next to them the cavalry of the left wing. The **mercenaries** were deployed in support of everyone.

Alexander decided that the formation of the **phalanx** was not tight enough on his right wing and that the Persians might outflank him there, and so he ordered two squadrons of the Companions (the Anthemusian squadron commanded by Peroedes son of Menestheus, and the so-called Leugaean squadron under Pantordanus son of Cleander) to pass unobserved from the middle to the right wing. And by bringing the archers, too, and a portion of the Agrianians and Greek mercenaries, over to his right wing, he extended the phalanx beyond the Persians' wing. The Persian soldiers positioned up the mountain did not come down; when Alexander ordered the Agrianians and the few archers to charge against them, they were easily driven back from the foot of the mountain and fled to the summit. Given this, Alexander decided he could use the troops originally set against those men to complete his phalanx instead, and so he was content to assign 300 cavalry to face the Persians on the mountain.

---

1 What makes the land nearest the sea better suited to cavalry action?

2 Consider how differently Alexander and Darius manage the deployment of their troops. What precautions does each commander seem to be taking in the lead-up to the battle? Based on these precautions, what does each side appear to fear most from the other?

Agrianians   these and others here apparently presented a line at roughly a right angle to the Macedonian front. According to Xenophon (*Anabasis* 1.8), this formation resembled the Greek letter *gamma*: Γ.

mercenaries   these troops remained in reserve to provide support in the event of a break in the front line. The 7,000 conscripts from the Corinthian League mentioned by Diodorus (17.1) were probably in reserve with them.

phalanx   in this context the word clearly refers to the front line, not strictly to an infantry formation. The movement of the two Macedonian squadrons strengthened the line, while the forces gathered from the archers, the Agrianians and mercenaries extended the front line to the right along the Pinarus up into the foothills. Note that this would effectively have cut off those Persian troops on the mountain behind them.

Arrian 2.10 Alexander gradually led his army forward in this formation for some time and with rests, so that his advance seemed altogether relaxed. After first deploying his barbarians, Darius had made no further advance, remaining instead on the bank of the river, which was steep at many points and which he had fortified with a palisade where access seemed easier. This made it immediately clear to Alexander and his men that Darius was already defeated in mind.

When the armies were now close, Alexander rode along every part of his force and challenged his men to be good soldiers. He not only called out the names of his commanders, honouring them appropriately, but also named the squadron leaders and captains, and even those mercenaries who were well known for their reputation or some particular act of bravery. A cry then arose from all sides, that Alexander stop delaying and attack the enemy. And yet even then, although he now had Darius' force in his sights, he kept leading the army in formation and at a walk, so as not to disrupt the phalanx and throw it into disorder by a more intense pace. But on coming within shooting range, Alexander led a sudden charge of those with him on the right wing into the river, to throw the Persians into a panic and to reduce casualties from the archers.

Things turned out just as Alexander had predicted. As soon as the armies met, those on the Persians' left wing were routed, and there Alexander and his men were winning in splendid fashion. But the right wing of the Macedonian **phalanx** had been broken and the gap there was widening. This was because, while Alexander had energetically charged into the river, fighting at close quarters and already driving back the Persians, the Macedonians in the centre had not leapt to action with the same spirit. On running up against the riverbank, which was steep at many points, they had found themselves unable to keep the formation of the phalanx's front line intact, and the Greek mercenaries with Darius were attacking the Macedonians where they saw their phalanx most disrupted. The fighting was ferocious at that spot; the Persians were struggling to push the Macedonians back into the river and salvage the victory in spite of those on their own side who were already fleeing, while the Macedonians were striving to equal Alexander's obvious success and to keep intact the reputation of their phalanx, which had so far been roundly declared invincible. And on top of this, something of a rivalry had taken hold of the Greek and Macedonian races. Here Ptolemy son of Seleucus fell, after proving himself a noble soldier, along with about 120 other distinguished Macedonians.

2.11 At that point, when the battalions of the right wing saw that the Persians who faced them had now been defeated, they turned left against the foreign mercenaries

---

phalanx in what follows, Plutarch explains how the Macedonian infantry phalanx becomes broken towards its right wing. As those to the right advanced along with Alexander's successful cavalry charge, those at the centre of the phalanx met with more difficult terrain and great resistance from Darius' Greek mercenaries. The natural result was a deadly rift in the line that Darius' mercenaries were keen to exploit.

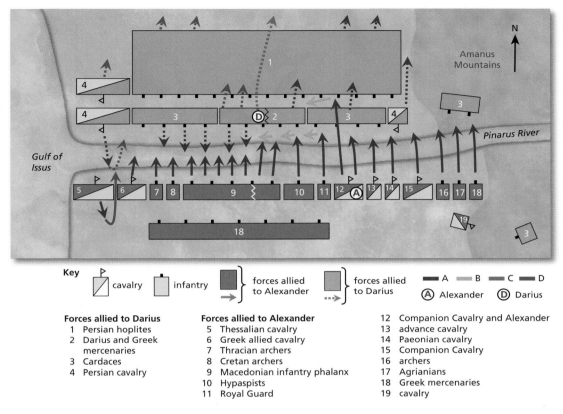

Key
△ cavalry   ▢ infantry   ▨ } forces allied to Alexander   ▢ } forces allied to Darius   ▬A ▬B ▬C ▬D
         →   ⇢   Ⓐ Alexander Ⓓ Darius

Forces allied to Darius
1 Persian hoplites
2 Darius and Greek mercenaries
3 Cardaces
4 Persian cavalry

Forces allied to Alexander
5 Thessalian cavalry
6 Greek allied cavalry
7 Thracian archers
8 Cretan archers
9 Macedonian infantry phalanx
10 Hypaspists
11 Royal Guard

12 Companion Cavalry and Alexander
13 advance cavalry
14 Paeonian cavalry
15 Companion Cavalry
16 archers
17 Agrianians
18 Greek mercenaries
19 cavalry

The battle of Issus, November 333 BC, according to Arrian.
A) On coming within bowshot, Alexander's army charges forward. The right wing successfully crosses the Pinarus and quickly routs the Persian left. At the same time, the cavalry of the Persian right charge across the river and push back Parmenion and the Thessalian cavalry. The swift forward movement of the Macedonian right meanwhile creates a break in the infantry phalanx, whose centre is unable to press forward so quickly. B) Because Darius' Greek mercenaries have the upper hand there, the forces of Alexander's right turn to help the centre. C) On seeing his left wing in disarray, Darius flees from the battle in his chariot. D) Once the initially successful Persian cavalry see Darius flee, they lose their resolve and are routed with the rest of the Persian army.

where their own side was struggling. They pushed the mercenaries back from the river, flanked the disrupted portion of the Persian army, attacked them from the side and immediately began cutting the mercenaries down.

Meanwhile, the Persian cavalry deployed opposite the Thessalians had not remained on the other side of the river once the battle began, but had **crossed in force** and

crossed in force the Persian cavalry on the right actually charged across the Pinarus. While in Arrian's account the cavalry withdraw on learning of Darius' defeat, Curtius (3.11) records that the Thessalians suffered a serious setback under the Persian attack, but were able to retreat, regroup and drive back the Persians on their own.

Detail from the famous Alexander Sarcophagus of c. 325–300 BC from the Royal Necropolis of Sidon, showing Alexander (far left) fighting on horseback at the battle of Issus. This is not the sarcophagus of Alexander, but of either Abdalonymus, king of Sidon, or Mazaeus, governor of Babylon. Alexander wears a helmet modelled on the lion skin that his mythical ancestor Heracles wore.

attacked the Thessalian squadrons. Here the cavalry fighting was ferocious indeed, and the Persians did not relent until they learned that Darius had fled and that the mercenaries had been separated from them by the onslaught of the Macedonian phalanx. Then, however, there was a sudden and overwhelming rout. The Persians' horses were particularly hard hit in the rout, since they were carrying heavily armed men, and the cavalrymen themselves, retreating in panicked chaos through narrow paths, suffered as much harm from trampling each other as they did from the pursuing enemy. And the Thessalians continued to press them hard, so that in the rout there was as much slaughter of cavalry as infantry.

As soon as Darius saw that Alexander had thrown his left wing into a panic and had severed it from the rest of the army, he **immediately took flight** in his chariot, just as he was, and was among the first to do so. As long as he came across level terrain, Darius fled in the safety of his chariot, but when he struck gullies and other rugged areas, he abandoned the chariot, and with it his shield, his ***kandys***, and even

immediately took flight   Curtius (3.11) and Diodorus (17.34) speak of fierce fighting around Darius. They state that the king fled only when he was about to be overwhelmed and captured. Alexander's chamberlain Chares asserted in his *Histories of Alexander* that Darius actually wounded Alexander in the thigh, but this combat between the rival kings is almost certainly romantic invention. Arrian's depiction of Darius' early flight is probably the product of propaganda under Alexander himself, designed to portray Darius as a coward and unfit to rule the Persian Empire.

kandys   the royal tunic, long-sleeved and purple.

This opposite side of the sarcophagus shown on p. 52 depicts Macedonians and Persians cooperating in a lion hunt.

his bow, then mounted a horse and continued his flight. It was in fact the onset of night soon afterwards that prevented his capture by Alexander, for Alexander kept up the pursuit with all his strength as long as it was light, but when it was already growing dark and the way ahead was obscured, he turned back towards camp. (He did take Darius' chariot, however, along with his shield, *kandys* and bow.) Alexander's pursuit had in fact been delayed because, when the phalanx had first broken formation, he had wheeled round to help it, and he did not head off in pursuit of Darius until he had seen that the foreign mercenaries and the Persian cavalry were pushed back from the river.

Among the Persian casualties were Arsames, as well as Rheomithres and Atizyes, both of whom had been cavalry commanders at the Granicus. Also Sauaces the satrap of Egypt and Boubaces were among the Persian noblemen who died. As many as 100,000 of the Persian rank and file perished, including more than 10,000 cavalry. There were so many dead that **Ptolemy** son of Lagus, who was with Alexander at the time, records that when those accompanying them in pursuit of Darius came to a ravine during the chase, they crossed it on corpses.

Darius' camp was taken immediately by storm, and his **mother**, his wife (who was also his sister) and his infant son were seized. Two daughters of his were captured,

---

Ptolemy an important source for Arrian (see p. 28), and here we have a direct reference to what he wrote. Ptolemy's claim here is almost certainly impossible, since Ptolemy and Alexander were at the head of the rout, so that there would have been no one ahead of them to kill these Persians. What might this suggest about the nature of Ptolemy's history?

mother Darius' mother is elsewhere called Sisygambis, and his wife Statira. Reported names for his daughters are Statira (also called Barsine) and Drypetis, and Curtius (4.11) names a six-year-old son, Ochus. It was not uncommon for members of the Persian royal family to marry their sisters.

too, and with them a few wives of high-ranking Persians; the rest of the Persians had sent their wives and baggage to **Damascus** when Darius had transferred there most of the money and all the other items that accompany a Great King to furnish the lifestyle of extravagance that he maintains even when going to war. For this reason, no more than 3,000 talents were seized from the camp. But even the money in Damascus was captured soon after by Parmenion, who was sent there for this express purpose. This, then, was how that battle ended, fought during the archonship of **Nicocrates** in the month of Maimacterion.

---

1   What psychological effect on the waiting Persians do you suppose Alexander's frequent stops at the beginning of **2.10** might have had?

2   Do you believe that Darius' refusal to advance (**2.10**) really indicates that the Persian king was indeed 'defeated in mind'? Why or why not?

3   Why in most battles would the casualties among routed infantry be far higher than those of the cavalry?

4   How important did it seem to Alexander, according to Arrian, to capture Darius? Do you agree? Why or why not?

5   Can you think of any leaders now or in recent history who escaped capture by their enemy? What has been the result of their escape?

6   Consider Arrian's account of the battle of Issus from start to finish. What are some of the factors that may have contributed to Alexander's reputation as a great general?

7   What has Arrian focused on in his account of the battle of Issus? Is he more interested in providing the tactics of the battle, the psychologies of the armies or colourful vignettes about its leaders? Is there a difference in emphasis at different points in the account?

8   Does Arrian give even-handed treatment of Greeks and Persians, or does he show bias?

Damascus   a prosperous city in modern Syria, roughly 300 kilometres (190 miles) south of the battle. Because battle was imminent, Darius had sent the camp followers and all valuables there for safekeeping.

Nicocrates   methods of dating varied from *polis* to *polis* in Greece, and there were considerable differences between their calendars, intercalary months and days, etc. By Arrian's day, however, years were defined by the name of the Athenian archon, the city's chief official. (Arrian himself was elected archon at Athens, though this was by that time really only an honorific title.) Nicocrates was archon at Athens in 333/32 BC, and the Macedonian month Maimacterion would have fallen somewhere between late October and late December of that year.

After Issus

Arrian 2.12   On the following day, although he had been injured in the thigh by a sword, Alexander visited the wounded, gathered up the dead, and conducted a magnificent funeral with the entire army marshalled as splendidly as possible in battle formation. In his speech he called attention to everyone who had performed some outstanding deed that he himself had witnessed or that was attested by the accounts of others, and he honoured each man with wealth to match his deserts …

Nor did Darius' mother, wife and children go uncared for. Rather, many of those who wrote about Alexander record that during the night, when he returned from pursuing Darius and entered Darius' tent, which had been reserved for him, he heard the wailing of women and other such clamour coming from nearby. When Alexander then asked who the women were and why they had been quartered so near, someone replied, 'King, Darius' mother, wife and children are mourning his death, because they received word that you had his bow and royal *kandys*, and that even his shield had been captured.' When Alexander heard this, he sent Leonnatus, one of the Companions, with orders to tell them that Darius lived, that he left his weapons and *kandys* on his chariot when he fled, and that these items were all that Alexander had captured. Leonnatus entered the tent and told them this, adding that Alexander would grant them a royal retinue and the rest of their honours, including the name of queen, since his war against Darius did not stem from personal hatred, but had been pursued lawfully for the sake of the empire of Asia.

This is what Ptolemy and Aristobulus record. There is also the story that on the following day Alexander himself went inside, accompanied by Hephaestion alone of the Companions. Darius' mother was uncertain which of the two was king, since both wore the same attire, and so she approached Hephaestion and performed *proskynēsis* because he looked taller. When Hephaestion shrank back from her and one of her attendants pointed out the real Alexander, she withdrew in shame at her error. Alexander, however, said that she made no error, since Hephaestion too was an **Alexander**. I have recorded these things neither as true nor entirely unbelievable. If this really happened, I applaud Alexander for taking pity on the women and for trusting and honouring his companion. And if it seems plausible to the historians that Alexander would have done and said these things, for that reason, too, I applaud Alexander.

---

proskynēsis   literally 'the bestowing of a kiss', the term refers to a range of acts, from kissing one's fingertips to bending forward prostrate upon the ground. Greeks associated such behaviour with the worship of a god, but the Persians regularly performed *proskynesis* as an act of respect towards social superiors.

Alexander   his name may be interpreted to mean 'defender of men' in Greek, and ancient authors often suggest that a name may hint at a quality of its bearer. This may be the sense behind the comment here, but there is also a philosophical tradition at least as old as Aristotle that a true friend was a second self. As Arrian suggests, the episode stresses not only Alexander's generosity towards Sisygambis, but also his respect for Hephaestion.

1   Curtius (3.12), Diodorus (17.38) and Plutarch (21) record also that Alexander permitted the women to choose which of the dead they wanted buried in the Persian style. What benefits did Alexander have to gain by treating Darius' family as royalty even after the Great King's defeat?

2   Consider carefully the explanation that Leonnatus gives for the royal honours. Is the reason given for Alexander's invasion different from what you have previously encountered? If so, how do you account for this?

3   Arrian appears to doubt the story of Alexander's encounter with Sisygambis. Why does he depart from his regular practice of following the histories of Ptolemy and Aristobulus? Interpret the episode's final sentence to support your answer.

Alexander and sex

Alexander's brilliant and decisive victory over Darius and the subsequent seizure of Damascus brought the army into contact with tremendous wealth and the opportunity to pursue a more luxurious lifestyle. Plutarch recounts the following episodes to illustrate Alexander's self-restraint in contrast to that of his army.

Plutarch 21   But Alexander's greatest and most kingly expression of kindness towards these noble and chaste captive women was his ensuring they neither heard of nor suspected – nor expected – any shameful action against them. It was as if they were not held in an enemy camp, but protected in sacred and hallowed **maidens' quarters** where they could not be seen or talked about by men, even though they say that Darius' wife was by far the most attractive of all the royal women. (Darius himself was likewise the most handsome and tallest of men, and his daughters resembled their parents.) But Alexander, it seems, thought that showing mastery over himself was more kingly than conquering his enemies, and he neither touched these women nor slept with any others prior to marriage, except **Barsine**, who had been widowed after the death of Memnon and was captured

---

maidens' quarters   Alexander's treatment of Darius' wife and daughters reflects not only Persian royal honours, but also Greek values. While the precise customs differed considerably from state to state in Greece, women were generally kept out of the public eye for the sake of their reputation. In Greek homes, women's quarters were separate from the men's, either in the rear of the house or on the upper floor. Such social conventions were viewed by members of the culture as a respectful preservation of feminine virtue.

Barsine   in fact not the name of Memnon's widow and daughter of Artabazus, but of Darius' eldest daughter, whom Alexander ultimately married in Susa. (Barsine, like Memnon's widow, was captured at Damascus.) The relationship described here with Memnon's widow does not appear to be a true, formal marriage.

near Damascus. She had received a Greek education and showed decorum, and her father, Artabazus, was son of a king's daughter, so that at Parmenion's urging Alexander attached himself, as Aristobulus records, to this refined and noble woman. When he saw these other captives of outstanding beauty and stature, Alexander would say in jest, 'They torture the eyes, these Persian women!' But he responded to their physical form by demonstrating the beauty of his own self-control and moderation, passing by them as one would lifeless statues.

22 **Philoxenus**, general of the forces along the coast, once wrote to Alexander that he had with him one Theodorus of Tarentum who was selling two boys of magnificent beauty, and he asked whether Alexander would buy them. Alexander was enraged, and cried out repeatedly to his Friends, demanding to know what disgraceful act of his Philoxenus had ever witnessed that would make him waste time proposing such a shameful arrangement. As for Philoxenus, Alexander chastised him severely in a letter and ordered him to banish to hell both Theodorus and his wares. Alexander berated **Hagnon**, too, for writing that he wanted to purchase and deliver to him Crobylus, a favourite youth in Corinth. Furthermore, when Alexander learned that Damon and Timotheus, Macedonians fighting under Parmenion, had raped some of the mercenaries' women, he wrote to Parmenion, ordering that, if convicted, the two should be punished and slain like wild beasts destructive to humankind. He even wrote of himself specifically in this letter. I quote: 'I for one can be found neither to have seen Darius' wife nor to have wanted to see her, nor even to have enjoyed the talk of those commenting on her beauty.' Alexander used to say, too, that he recognized his mortality most clearly in sleep and intercourse, since both pain and pleasure originate from a single innate weakness.

> 1 Which of Barsine's qualities make relations with this non-Greek acceptable to Alexander? What do the three youths whom Alexander rejects have in common? What sort of heterosexual and homosexual relations might Alexander have found acceptable?
>
> 2 What is the 'innate weakness' **(22)** to which Plutarch refers here?

Philoxenus an important general, apparently trusted by Alexander. He served as treasurer in 333 BC, and then became one of the major tax collectors two years later.

Hagnon one of Alexander's Companions. His offer to purchase the most beautiful boy in Corinth for the king would not have been surprising in fourth-century Greece, where men regularly found youths sexually attractive. While the youth on offer here is a slave, pederasty between a man and a free youth was in many places a social norm. Alexander's father Philip, you will recall, was assassinated by the noble youth Pausanias, a Bodyguard who was no longer receiving the king's erotic attentions (p. 22).

Alexander and food and drink

Plutarch 22 Alexander had remarkable control over his appetite, too, as he proved in many ways, including by what he said to **Ada**, whom he had called 'Mother' and appointed queen of Caria. Out of affection she had begun sending many delicacies and pastries to him daily, and finally even cooks and bakers famous for their expertise. But Alexander said he needed none of them, since Leonidas his tutor had already given him better cooks: a night-march for breakfast and a light breakfast for dinner. 'And this same man,' Alexander said, 'would even come and search the blankets and clothes in my chest to make sure that my mother had not slipped into it some dainty or other luxury for me.'

23 Wine, too, appealed to Alexander less than was thought, a misconception that arose from the amount of time which he would spend over each cup – not so much drinking as conversing, invariably giving a dramatic speech – whenever he had plenty of spare time. For when he had work to do, he differed from other generals in that nothing stood in his way – not wine, not sleep, not games, not marriage, not spectacles. His life – which, though certainly brief, he filled with numerous and colossal achievements – proves this. During times of leisure he would first get up and sacrifice to the gods, then immediately sit down to breakfast. Next he would pass the day hunting, deciding cases, arranging some military affair, or reading. When making a march that was not particularly pressing, along the way he would practise archery or mounting and dismounting from a moving chariot. And often for sport he would hunt foxes and birds, as can be seen in his *Ephēmerides*. At the end of a day's march, when he was bathing or oiling up, he would enquire of his head bakers and cooks whether preparations for dinner were under way. But it was late (after dark, in fact) before he would lie down on a couch and begin eating. And then it was amazing how observant he was, watching the table closely to ensure that no one was served a portion too large or too small. And he would draw out the drinking, as I said, to get his fill of talk. But at those times, while he was the sweetest of all kings to associate with in other respects, and while he lacked no courtesy, his bouts of boasting made him unpleasant and

---

Ada exiled by her brother Pixodarus, the satrap of Caria. You will recall that this Pixodarus had planned to marry his daughter to Philip's son Arrhidaeus (p. 21). This would have meant an alliance between Macedonia and Caria, but after Alexander's attempts to marry her himself, Pixodarus had doubts about the stability of the Macedonian royal court and allied himself with Persia instead. When Alexander took Caria, he instated the exiled Ada as its ruler and even adopted her as 'Mother'.

Ephēmerides the daily records of the king's actions. The question for historians is how authentic these records were. Our knowledge of them comes only by way of second-hand sources, as here, all of which do accept the *Ephēmerides* as a faithful record of royal activity.

too soldier-like; and in addition to sinking to such boastfulness of his own accord, he also let his flatterers **ride him like a horse**. This galled the more refined guests, who wanted neither to compete with the flatterers nor to praise Alexander any less than they did; the first option seemed shameful, the second was dangerous.

> 1 What sort of information do the *Ephemerides* appear to contain? What do you think would have been their purpose?
>
> 2 What do you imagine the atmosphere was like at these dinner parties?
>
> 3 Why does Plutarch attempt to discredit the notion that Alexander drank to excess?
>
> 4 What does Plutarch criticize in Alexander instead? In what other episodes have we seen Alexander exhibit this quality?

Macedonians and luxury

Plutarch 24   After the battle at Issus, Alexander sent ahead to Damascus and confiscated the treasure, the baggage and the children and wives of the Persians. It was the Thessalian cavalry that profited most in this, since Alexander sent them with the intention that they would reap profits in measure with the outstanding valour they had displayed in the battle. But the rest of the army, too, was steeped in **wealth**. And once the Macedonians had got their first taste of gold, silver, women and barbaric life, they began to pant for the chase like dogs fixed on a scent, raring to hunt down the Persians' wealth.

> 1 For what demonstration of valour is Alexander rewarding the Thessalian cavalry?
>
> 2 Can you think of modern cases in which people have identified wealth and luxury as both a source and a symptom of moral corruption within the richest and most powerful nations?
>
> 3 Note that this representation of the Macedonians after Issus follows the focus on Alexander himself in the two previous passages. How does Plutarch's arrangement of these passages affect your perception of the relationship between Alexander and his Macedonians?

---

ride him like a horse   recall that Plutarch earlier used managing a horse as philosophical metaphor for self-control (see p. 15). Here the metaphor highlights the mastery of Alexander by flatterers.

wealth   along with the dichotomy of free Greeks versus Persian slaves described previously (p. 45), came the Greeks' belief that the Persians were morally corrupted by the vast amount of wealth at their disposal. General Greek wisdom valued moderation and considered love of excess (*koros*) morally depraved, so that even the acquisition of Persian wealth might readily bring dangers with it. Greek philosophy generally defined humans by their ability to control their appetites, in contrast to animals, which were slaves to their impulses. The depiction of Macedonians as dogs is therefore particularly damning.

Tyre

> After Darius' defeat at Issus and Parmenion's capture of Damascus, all the Phoenician cities except Tyre came over to Alexander's side between November 333 and January 332 BC. Tyre, a Phoenician island-city about 800 metres (half a mile) off the coast of modern Lebanon, was the powerful and prosperous trade centre that looms large in the Hebrew scriptures. It was well fortified, with walls extending all the way down to the sea, and also enjoyed a powerful and adept naval force to protect those walls. Aware of Alexander's approach by land (he had disbanded his fleet by this point), the Tyrians had already secured a promise from Carthage (a Tyrian colony founded in modern Tunisia) to help in the event of a siege. Tyre therefore had every reason to believe it was impregnable, and in its determination to remain neutral in the war between the Greeks and Persians, the city had declared publicly that it would permit neither party to enter it. Unfortunately for Tyre, the Carthaginians never came, and the island of Cyprus allied itself with Alexander, giving him access to its powerful navy.

Plutarch 24 Alexander decided first to secure the lands along the sea. Right away, the kings came and handed Cyprus over to him, and all Phoenicia, too – except for Tyre. While he was laying siege to Tyre for **seven months** with moles and engines of war, and with 200 triremes by sea, Alexander dreamt that **Heracles** was extending his right hand towards him from the wall and beckoning him. **Apollo** appeared to many of the Tyrians in their sleep as well, and said that he was going over to Alexander's side because he disapproved of what they were doing in their city. In response, they seized Apollo's colossus as if it were a man deserting to the enemy;

---

seven months a remarkably long time (January–July 332 BC) for Alexander to spend at one location. Recall that Alexander only began the invasion in earnest in 334. His assault on the city involved constructing a mole of timber and rocks across the deep water from the mainland to the city, and he suffered a series of setbacks in the process as the Tyrians responded with remarkable ingenuity. Arrian (2.16–24) and Curtius (4.2–4) both offer lengthy and exciting descriptions of this siege and are well worth the read.

Heracles this 'Heracles' was Melcarth, the primary deity of Tyre, and equated with Syrian Baal and Babylonian Bel. According to other accounts, the Tyrians had refused to permit Alexander to sacrifice at the temple to Melcarth, which was located inside the city. Alexander enjoyed a special connection with Heracles as Macedonian royalty (p. 9).

Apollo as the god of prophecy, Apollo was particularly able to predict the future. That the statue of a deity actually embodied the deity itself was a belief common to ancient Mediterranean religions. Binding a statue to prevent the protective deity's desertion appears to have been regular ancient practice. One might wonder about the authenticity of such stories, particularly the Tyrians' dreams; they may well have been propaganda designed to confirm Alexander's divine mandate.

The island-city of Tyre is now connected to the mainland, thanks to the silting that has occurred around Alexander's siege mole.

they bound it with chains and nailed it to its base, dubbing it an Alexandrist. And Alexander had another dream. A satyr appeared jeering at him from a distance, and whenever he tried to grab it, it kept slipping away. But in the end, after repeated begging and chasing, the satyr let itself be caught. Alexander's seers divided the name 'satyr' in two and concluded convincingly, 'Tyre will be yours!' Still today, in fact, people point to the spring where Alexander dreamt he saw the satyr …

25   The siege ended as follows. While Alexander was resting most of his force after their earlier efforts, and led only a few soldiers to the walls – enough to prevent the enemy from relaxing – Aristander the seer made a sacrifice. After inspecting the signs, he declared rather rashly to those near him that within the month the city would surely be taken. This led to joking and laughter, since it was in fact the last day of the month. But the king always tied his own endeavours to Aristander's prophecies and so, when he saw that Aristander was perplexed, he ordered the day be changed from the thirtieth to the twenty-eighth. Then, with the signalling

---

satyr   one of the mythological male creatures of the wild that often accompanied Dionysus in his retinue. They are anthropomorphic, but frequently sport the tails, ears and legs of a horse or goat. Known for their passion for food, drink and sex, they are also endowed with great wisdom. According to legend, King Midas captured one such creature in his garden in Macedonia, and was rewarded with divine knowledge. That this satyr comes to Alexander willingly is particularly striking. The Greek word for satyr, *satyros*, can be divided into two words, *sa Tyros*, or 'your Tyre'. The hidden meanings of words and names had mystical significance for the ancient Greeks, in contrast to modern notions of punning and wordplay as rather frivolous.

blast of a trumpet, he assailed the walls more vigorously than he had originally planned. The assault went splendidly; even those back in camp did not hold back, but came running *en masse* to help. The Tyrians surrendered, and the city did in fact fall to Alexander on that very day.

1　Why do you suppose that capturing Tyre would have been so important to Alexander?

2　A change to the calendar was a significant act, in part because it was fundamentally a religious schedule. It is possible that Alexander would have continued to add days to the month until Tyre fell. Do you recall any other instance of Alexander fiddling with the calendar to his advantage?

3　Are we to admire Alexander for his boldness, or do accounts such as these suggest that he is overstepping the mark?

4　What does this episode suggest about the role of Aristander in Alexander's expedition?

Memphis and Alexandria

Alexander next headed south towards Egypt, only to meet resistance from the city of Gaza, which he took by siege (September–October 332 BC). Taking Egypt next would secure that corner of the Persian Empire, but Alexander appears to have had other goals in mind as well.

Arrian 3.1　Alexander was marching towards Egypt, his original destination, and he reached Egyptian **Pelusium** on the seventh day out of Gaza. The fleet had been sailing alongside him towards Egypt from Phoenicia, and he met them already moored in Pelusium. The Persian **Mazaces**, appointed satrap of Egypt by Darius, had learned of the battle at Issus and of Darius' shameful flight, and knew that Phoenicia, Syria and most of Arabia now belonged to Alexander. And because he had no Persian force with him, he welcomed Alexander warmly into the cities and the land. Alexander garrisoned Pelusium and ordered the fleet to sail up the river all the way to Memphis, while he himself marched towards Heliopolis, keeping

---

Pelusium　located on the Egyptian coast, on the eastern edge of the Nile delta. It represented the gateway to Egypt and was well fortified against invaders on its eastern flank. That Alexander's fleet was already moored there ahead of his land force appears to indicate that he had already previously negotiated his entrance into Egypt. The fleet had sailed along with the march from Gaza to Pelusium, probably to provide resources to the army when necessary. The fleet would serve as the swiftest and most practical means of troop transport in Egypt, whose cities were located along the Nile or in the river delta.

Mazaces　a freshly appointed satrap, officially replacing Sauaces, who had taken his army to Issus and died in the battle there.

Worship of Apis continued under Macedonian and Roman rule of Egypt, centuries after Alexander's death, but as the incarnation of Serapis (bottom left) rather than Ptah. This basalt statue of Apis was commissioned by the Roman emperor Hadrian (ruled AD 117–138) for Alexandria's Serapeum. The disc between the bull's horns emphasizes the animal's connection to the sun, while the uraeus (the rearing cobra within the disc) symbolizes divine sovereignty.

the river Nile on his right. He took possession of all the lands along the way as their inhabitants surrendered, and then crossed the desert to Heliopolis. From there he crossed the ford and came to **Memphis**, where he sacrificed to all the gods – and Apis in particular – and held athletic and musical **contests** between the most notable competitors in these fields, for they had come to join him from Greece. From Memphis Alexander began sailing downriver towards the sea, after taking on board the Hypaspists, archers, Agrianians and the Royal Squadron of Companion Cavalry.

Memphis   the capital of Egypt at this time. After Alexander's death, the Egyptian coronation of the Ptolemaic kings took place here, in the temple to Ptah. Apis was regularly identified by the Greeks with Epaphus, a legendary king of Egypt and son of Zeus and Io. The Egyptians recognized the Apis bull as a manifestation of their creator-god Ptah. Two Persian kings, Cambyses and Artaxerxes III Ochus, were traditionally thought to have slain Apis bulls. Alexander's sacrifice to the bull was particularly remarkable, for it was the first time that he honoured a foreign deity not already directly equated with a Greek god.

contests   such musical and athletic contests were by this time regularly sponsored by wealthy patrons such as Alexander. The cost of such productions was steep, for top performers were professional members of guilds and commanded quite a sum, not unlike those of our own day. Sponsorship was therefore not merely a religious and civic duty as it had been in classical Athens; it was a spectacular demonstration of wealth and power. A contemporary contest might have included athletic entertainment (e.g. footraces, wrestling, boxing, horseracing or chariot races) and musical entertainment (e.g. dancing, comedies, tragedies, singing to the lyre, piping or rhapsodic performances of epic poetry).

When he had come to **Canopus** and sailed over Lake Mareotis he disembarked where the city of **Alexandria**, named for Alexander, now stands. The site struck him as perfect for founding a city, and a prosperous one at that. Seized by a longing to carry out the deed, he himself laid out the city plans: where the marketplace should be built, how many temples and to what gods (both Greek gods and Egyptian **Isis**), and where the wall should circle the city. With this in mind he made sacrifices, and they proved auspicious.

3.2   A certain story is told roughly as follows, and I do not doubt its truth. Alexander wanted to leave behind the plans of the walls for the builders, but there was no way of marking the earth. Then one of the builders had an idea. He gathered together all the **grain** that the soldiers were carrying in their containers and poured it along the ground precisely where the king instructed. In this way he marked the ring of the outer wall that Alexander was planning for the city. After pondering over this, the seers – in particular Aristander the Telmessian who was said to have given many other true predictions for Alexander – declared the city would be prosperous in all things, but especially in the fruits of the earth.

---

1   Why would Alexander have been so keen to honour Apis publicly?

2   Do you believe that Ptolemy or Aristobulus recorded the tale at **3.2**? Why or why not?

Canopus   city situated at the mouth of the Canopic branch of the Nile, just as Pelusium sat at the mouth of the Nile's easternmost, Pelusiac, branch.

Alexandria   the city was indeed founded here, on the narrow strip of land only about 7 stades (1.3 km/0.8 miles) wide, between the Mediterranean Sea and Lake Mareotis near the small fishing village Rhacotis. Within two centuries, Alexandria grew into the largest city in the world. It is not clear whether Alexander expected the city to become the intellectual centre it did, with its famous library and Museum. The other cities founded during his campaign served primarily military functions, and Alexandria's location on the western edge of the delta may have been meant to defend the region in that direction, much as Pelusium guarded its eastern side.

Isis   important Egyptian goddess, associated with the annual flooding of the Nile, and therefore with rebirth and renewal. The historian Herodotus equated her with the Greek Demeter, goddess of grain and the harvest, but Alexander here apparently means to honour her in her native Egyptian guise.

grain   according to Curtius (4.8), it was a Macedonian custom to trace the lines of the foundations in grain. In other ancient accounts a flock of birds devours the grain and inspires the prophecy of Alexandria's future prosperity.

Pharos and Homer's *Iliad*

> The following tale recorded by Plutarch offers a somewhat different version of Alexandria's founding, pointing to literary and mystical reasons for choosing the site.

Plutarch 26   Those who handled Darius' wealth and baggage brought Alexander a **chest**, which they considered Darius' most precious possession. Alexander then asked his Friends which of his own possessions they thought most worthy of placing in it. They named all sorts of things, till he himself declared he would keep his *Iliad* safe inside it. A number of trustworthy accounts testify to this, and if what those Alexandrians who believe **Heracleides** say is true, it was no idle or grudging Homer that seemed to join Alexander's expedition. They say that after he subdued Egypt Alexander wanted to leave behind a great and populous Greek city founded in his name. He had not yet begun measuring and walling the site recommended by his architects, but while asleep one night he saw a wondrous vision. A man with very grey hair and a majestic appearance stood beside him and said the following:

> An island lies in the wave-filled sea
> in front of Egypt, and they call it Pharos.

Alexander then got up immediately and began walking towards Pharos, which was still an island then, a little above the Canopic mouth, though now it is connected to the mainland by a mole. He saw that the place was exceptional for its natural qualities: the narrow strip of land was like an isthmus, separating a large lake from the sea, which formed a great harbour. He said that Homer, amazing in many ways, was certainly the wisest of architects, and he ordered that they design the city's plan to suit the site.

---

chest   Plutarch here refers to an incident that followed the battle of Issus and the capture of Darius' possessions there. According to Plutarch, Alexander chooses the *Iliad* because it is a prized possession of his own. While the *Iliad* treats events that took place during the Trojan War, it is a poor resource for military strategy. Its focus, however, upon the godlike Achilles could surely have provided a wealth of inspiration for military valour (pp. 16, 31).

Heracleides   this man's identity is uncertain, but there was a scholar from Alexandria called Heracleides Lembus who is credited with writing histories and a book on Homer. The quoted lines come from the *Odyssey* (4.354–5), where Menelaus recounts for Odysseus' son Telemachus how he was stranded on Pharos on his way home from the Trojan War. It is on this island of Pharos, in fact, that Menelaus captures the sea divinity Proteus and forces a prophecy from him about his journey home. The Greeks probably thought that the island itself had prophetic associations, therefore, and the later Ptolemies – if not Alexander himself – doubtless capitalized on this by encouraging stories such as these.

Alexander goes to Siwah

Plutarch 26   Alexander himself set out for the oracle of **Ammon**, a long journey of many troubles and sufferings, but with two dangers in particular. First, a lack of water turns the land into a desert for days on end; second, a south wind can violently assail men travelling through deep and boundless sand, as they say may have happened long ago to the army of **Cambyses**, when the wind whipped up a great wave of sand that washed over the plain and engulfed his 50,000 men, killing them all. Nearly everyone enumerated all these perils, but it was hard to dissuade Alexander from something he was inspired to do, since **Luck** herself was giving in to his designs and thereby making his mind obstinate. In fact the passionate spirit behind his every effort invariably paved the way for his indomitable desire to rival all, so that he not only subjugated his enemies, but also flouted the constraints of space and of time.

27   At any rate, the divine aid that he received in times of difficulty during this journey is certainly more believable than the oracle's responses later, but in some sense this aid lent credibility to those oracles, too. First of all, Zeus sent plenty of water in the form of lasting showers; these erased any fear of thirst and quenched the sand's dryness, dampening and compacting it so that the air became more pure and fresh. Then, when the landmarks their guides used proved perplexing, and

---

Ammon   Egyptian god whom the Greeks identified with Zeus (see p. 12). The oracle of Zeus Ammon, which rivalled the oracles at Dodona and Delphi, was situated in the oasis of Siwah, in western Egypt near the modern border with Libya. Plutarch's version of the journey to the oracle is highly dramatic, as are the other extant accounts of it. According to Arrian, for example, Ptolemy wrote that a pair of snakes led the expedition to the oracle and back. The oracle of Ammon was a famous one, and there was a road to it from the Nile, along the north coast of Egypt and then south-west. This is the way Alexander took, and the modern paved road still follows the same route.

Cambyses   Persian invader of Egypt who was said to have sent a force to destroy the oracle of Ammon in 525 BC. Recall that Alexander had already paid honours to the Apis bull that this same Cambyses had reportedly killed (p. 63). Together with his journey to Siwah, this may well represent a conscious effort by Alexander to contrast his own rule with Egypt's former domination by Persia.

Luck   *Tyche* in Greek, the personification of good fortune. This deity was regularly represented as being crowned by city battlements, so that her mention in connection with Alexander's conquests is particularly suggestive.

Temple of the Oracle of Ammon, Siwah oasis.

the party got lost and separated in their confusion, ravens appeared and took over the job of leading the march; they would fly ahead, urging them to follow, and would wait for them when they straggled behind. What was most amazing of all, however, was that, as **Callisthenes** records, the ravens would with their cawing call back those who strayed during the night and set them once again on the route of the march.

After crossing the desert Alexander came to the oracle, and the prophet of Ammon bid him welcome from the god as if from a father. When Alexander asked whether any of his father's murderers had escaped him, the prophet cautioned him to speak with reverence since his father was not mortal. Alexander then asked instead whether he had avenged all of Philip's murderers, and then enquired about his rule, specifically whether the god would grant him dominion over all humankind. When the god responded both that he granted this and that Philip was fully avenged, Alexander presented splendid offerings to the god and money to the people. This is what most sources say about the oracle's responses, but Alexander himself says in a letter to his **mother** that he was given certain secret prophecies that he would tell to her alone in person on his return. Others say the prophet wished to address Alexander in Greek with the friendly greeting

---

Callisthenes a philosopher, and nephew of Aristotle. He served as Alexander's official court historian.

mother this letter to Olympias, if genuine, corroborates other ancient accounts indicating that at least part of Alexander's consultation with the oracle was private.

ō paidion, but his barbarous accent added an 's' to the ends of his words, so that he said *o paidios*, using 's' instead of 'n'. This mistake in pronunciation pleased Alexander, and the story spread that the god had addressed him as son of Zeus.

They say that in Egypt Alexander listened attentively to **Psammon** the philosopher, too, and especially approved of his argument that all people are under the sovereignty of a god, since within every person the governing and ruling element is divine. But Alexander himself speculated even more philosophically on this matter, saying that while being father of all people alike, that god adopts the most noble as his very own.

28   On the whole, Alexander treated the barbarians haughtily, as if fully convinced of his origin and birth from a god, but he made himself a god only rarely in front of the Greeks, and then with discretion. One exception was his letter to the Athenians about **Samos**, in which he said, 'I for my part would not have granted you that free and famous city, but you have received it from your former lord and my reputed father' – that is, Philip. But later when he had sustained an arrow-wound and was in a state of agony, Alexander said, 'this stuff that flows, Friends, is blood, and not "**ichor**, which courses through the blessed gods".' Once, when a thunderclap threw everyone into a panic, **Anaxarchus** the sophist was present and said to Alexander, 'As son of Zeus, can you not thunder like that?' Alexander laughed and said, 'I do not wish to terrify my Friends as you encourage me to do by despising my dinner when you see fish and not the heads of satraps on the tables!' It is true that Anaxarchus is supposed to have said this when the king had sent small fish to Hephaestion, but Anaxarchus' statement then was meant to denigrate and lampoon those who seek universal admiration through danger and great hardship and yet enjoy little or no more pleasure or benefit than the rest of humankind. It is clear, then, from what has been said that Alexander was hardly afflicted with a delusional belief in his own divinity; on the contrary, he used it to enslave all others.

ō paidion   another example of mystical wordplay (cf. p. 61). *o paidion* means 'little child', while *o pai Dios* means 'son of Zeus'.

Psammon   not otherwise known. The striking similarity in name to Ammon suggests that this figure and the conversation may well be an invention.

Samos   island lying off the western coast of Turkey. The letter, if genuine, was probably written in 323 BC, so that the wound must in fact have pre-dated the letter to the Athenians.

ichor   substance which is the equivalent for the gods of blood for mortals. The quotation comes from Homer, *Iliad* 5.340. There, during the fighting outside Troy, the mortal Diomedes pierces the goddess Aphrodite, who bleeds ichor from her wound. Alexander received his wound in 327 BC at the Assacenian capital of Massaga.

Anaxarchus   a man who generally receives a negative portrayal in the Alexander sources, mainly as a luxury-loving sycophant in contrast to Callisthenes.

1. What do the responses of the oracle's prophet (27) imply about Alexander's parentage?

2. There were very good reasons for Alexander to spend as little time in Egypt as possible. Darius was gathering a new force to the east, and while Alexander remained in Egypt his supply lines were vulnerable to a westward movement by Darius. What various motives, then, do you suppose led Alexander to take the time to visit this oracle?

3. What does this account indicate about how Alexander wished the journey to be seen?

4. What are some fundamental differences between the philosophical statements of Alexander and this Psammon? In what way does Alexander's suit his current situation?

5. What message do you think Lysimachus was trying to send by representing Alexander in the guise of Ammon on the coin depicted below?

This coin depicts Alexander with the horns of Ammon and was issued by Lysimachus, king of Thrace and Asia Minor, c. 300 BC (Alexander died in 323 BC).

4 Gaugamela to the death of Darius

Darius' letter

While Plutarch states that the following letter reached Alexander on his return to Tyre after his visit to Egypt, Arrian (2.25) and Curtius (4.5) record that Alexander received it during the siege of that city.

Plutarch 29   Darius sent Friends with a letter to Alexander begging him to accept 10,000 talents in exchange for the Persian prisoners, and to become Darius' Friend and ally. They offered all the land that lay west of the Euphrates and one of Darius' daughters in marriage. When Alexander shared this offer with his Companions, **Parmenion** said, 'If I were Alexander, I would accept these terms.' 'I, too, by Zeus,' replied Alexander, 'if I were Parmenion!' Instead, he wrote back that Darius would not fail to find good treatment if only he would come to Alexander; if not, Alexander would march against him at once.

> 1   What might have led Alexander to refuse this offer and press on against Darius?
> 2   Has Alexander thus far achieved his professed goal, to avenge Persia's conquest of Greece?

Approaching Gaugamela

Alexander left Egypt in late spring 331 BC, returned to Tyre and then headed inland to Damascus. From there, he marched north and east and crossed the Euphrates, the very river that Darius had suggested be the new western boundary for his Persian Empire. Darius had not been idle in the meantime. After the overwhelming defeat at Issus, Darius had called for new recruits, and these had been supplied by satrapies throughout the Persian Empire, the farthest forces coming from locations more than 2,000 kilometres (1,200 miles) away. The battle would occur at Gaugamela, roughly 50 kilometres (30 miles) east of the Tigris River, on 1 October 331.

Parmenion   another example of Parmenion's advice not taken. The offer would certainly have been tempting. A marriage would have sealed a truce, while the Euphrates River offered an easily defensible boundary.

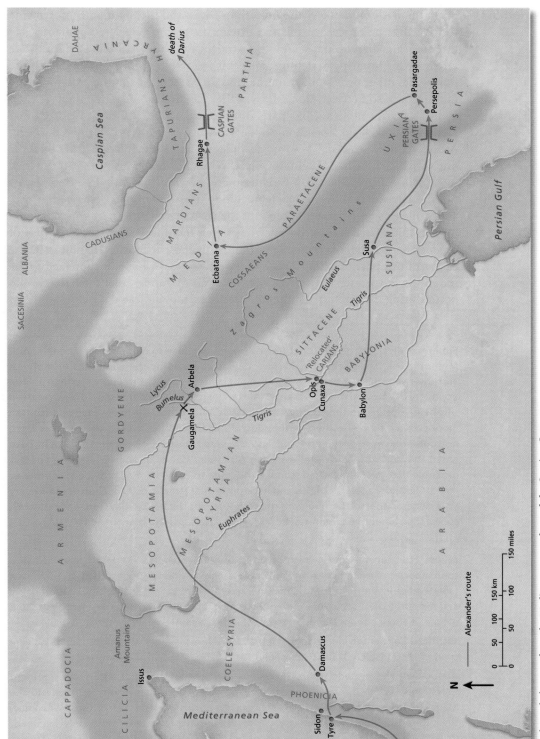

Alexander's route from the Mediterranean to beyond the Caspian Gates

Arrian 3.7 From there Alexander kept the **Euphrates River** and the mountains of Armenia to his left as he proceeded inland through the region called Mesopotamia. He did not leave the Euphrates and head straight for Babylon, because things were far easier for his army marching along this road: there was green fodder for the horses and other provisions from the land for the taking, and the scorching heat did not burn so fiercely. Along the way they captured some of the men sent out from Darius' army to various parts on reconnaissance, and these reported that Darius had taken up a position on the Tigris River and was determined to stop Alexander if he crossed. They said also that he had a much larger army than the one with which he had fought in **Cilicia**. When Alexander heard this, he hurried towards the Tigris River. On arriving there, however, he found neither Darius nor the garrison that Darius had left behind. Instead, Alexander crossed the ford, and while this was difficult because of the current's swiftness, no one was there to stop him. Then he rested his army. When there was a near-total **eclipse** of the moon, Alexander **sacrificed** to Moon, Sun and Earth, who are said to be the causes of this phenomenon. **Aristander** declared that what had happened to the moon was auspicious for the Macedonians and Alexander, that the battle would occur during that month and that the sacrifices, too, indicated a victory for him.

Euphrates River large river that flows through Baghdad in modern Iraq. The region of Mesopotamia, 'Land between the Rivers', was bounded by the Euphrates to the west and the river Tigris to the east. Recall that Darius proposed the Euphrates as a shared boundary of empire in his letter sent to Alexander (p. 70), a deal that would have reserved this highly fertile land for Darius. The great fertility of the soil there made agriculture more possible than elsewhere in the rugged region, and the rivers themselves provided not only sources for irrigation, but also the easy transport of goods. This would have eased the task of feeding and watering Alexander's army in enemy territory, but it is probable that the Persians had stripped the route to Babylon of all provisions in order to direct Alexander towards Darius and his army at Gaugamela instead. There is in fact very little water in the northern regions of Mesopotamia. The land is hilly, too, and not much cooler than along the Euphrates. In August the average high is about 104° F (40° C).

Cilicia satrapy in which Issus was located.

eclipse this lunar eclipse, which occurred on 20 September 331 BC, is described in a contemporary astronomical diary kept by Babylonian priests and recorded on cuneiform tablets now in the British Museum. The account records the inauspicious astronomical and meteorological conditions during the eclipse, as well as the occurrence of deaths and plague. It also mentions Darius' subsequent defeat and Alexander's entry into Babylon.

sacrificed ancient evidence suggests that Macedonians regularly worshipped the divine triad of Moon (Selene), Sun (Helios) and Earth (Ge).

Aristander this episode recalls Herodotus (7.37), where the sun and moon represent Greek and Persian interests respectively. There, however, it is a solar eclipse, and the Mages interpret it as an omen of Xerxes' success against the Greeks. For those who knew their Herodotus, this lunar eclipse could readily have represented not only imminent Greek success, but success in direct response to the Persian invasion of Greece by Xerxes.

Alexander headed out from the Tigris and travelled across Assyria, keeping the Gordyenian mountains on his left and the Tigris on his right. On the fourth day from the crossing-point, the advance guard reported that enemy cavalry were visible throughout the plain but that it was impossible to estimate their number. Alexander therefore drew up his army and advanced in battle formation. Then others of the guard galloped up. They had observed things more closely and declared that in their opinion there were no more than 1,000 enemy cavalry. Alexander quickly advanced with the Royal Squadron, one Companion squadron and the Paeonian advance guard, but ordered the rest of the army to follow at a march. When the Persian cavalry saw Alexander and his men approaching swiftly, they fled with all speed, and Alexander pressed them in pursuit. The majority escaped, but some of those whose horses tired in the flight were killed, while others were taken alive along with their mounts. The Macedonians learned from these captives that Darius was not far off and had a large army with him.

1 Would the report that Darius was prepared to stop the Macedonian advance by holding the other side of a river have surprised Alexander? Refer to the earlier battles of Granicus (p. 33) and Issus (p. 47) to explain why or why not.

2 Recall Alexander's surprise before the battle at Issus on finding Darius at his rear (p. 43). What does the early interaction between the armies here reveal about the difficulties of reconnaissance in antiquity?

3 Although Arrian offers us little from the perspective of the Persians, which army appears to have the upper hand in gathering intelligence? Explain your reasoning.

Gaugamela

Arrian 3.8 Those who had come to the aid of Darius were the Indians that neighboured the Bactrians, the Bactrians themselves and the Sogdianians, all commanded by Bessus, satrap of Bactria. These were followed by the Sacians, a tribe of those Scythians inhabiting Asia. These mounted archers were not subject to Bessus, but came because of an alliance with Darius, and Mauaces commanded them. Barsaentes, satrap of the Arachotians, led the Arachotians and the Indian hill-people, as they were called. The Arians were led by their satrap, Satibarzanes. The Parthians, Hyrcanians and Tapurians – all cavalry – were led by Phrataphernes. The Medians were commanded by Atropates, and the Cadusians, the Albanians and the Sacesinians were marshalled along with them. Those neighbouring the Persian Gulf […] were mustered by **Orontobates, Ariobarzanes and Orxines**.

Orontobates, Ariobarzanes and Orxines   these men in fact did not lead those near the Persian Gulf. There is probably a lacuna (i.e. gap) in the text of Arrian, indicated here by the ellipsis. The Persian Gulf peoples were probably led by Astaspes, satrap of Carmania, while Orontobates, Ariobarzanes and Orxines led the contingents from Persia proper, and the Mardian and Cossaean allies.

The Uxians and the Susianians were under the command of Oxathres son of Abulites. Bupares commanded the Babylonians, the **relocated Carians** and the Sittacenians. The Armenians were led by Orontes and Mithraustes, and Ariaces led the Cappadocians. The Syrians from Coele Syria and those of Mesopotamian Syria were led by **Mazaeus**. The whole of Darius' army was said to comprise as many as 40,000 cavalry, 1,000,000 infantry and 200 **scythe chariots**. There were a few **elephants** – the Indians from the near side of the Indus had approximately 15.

Together with this force Darius was camped in Gaugamela near the river Bumelus, some 60 stades [11 km/7 miles] away from the city of Arbela and on ground that was level all around; even those places previously not level enough for riding the Persians had now made suitable for driving chariots and riding on horseback. This was because some had convinced Darius that the narrowness of the land had in fact put him at a disadvantage in the battle at Issus; and Darius was easily persuaded of this.

3.9   When the captured Persian scouts reported these things, Alexander remained for four days at the place where he had received the news. He rested his army from its march and fortified the camp with a ditch and a palisade, since he had decided to leave behind the pack animals and those soldiers who were unfit, while he himself together with his able-bodied men would go to battle carrying nothing but their arms. And so he set out with his force during the night, at about the second watch, intending to meet the barbarians at dawn. When the report reached Darius that Alexander was already advancing, he marshalled his army for battle. Alexander was leading his force in battle formation, too, and the armies were in fact no more than 60 stades [11 km/7 miles] apart, though they had not yet spotted one another, since hills stood between them.

When Alexander was some 30 stades [5.5km/3.5 miles] away and his army was already coming down from the hills, he spotted the barbarians and halted his army. He then called together the Companions, generals, squadron commanders and the

---

relocated Carians   otherwise unknown, they probably inhabited an area on the Tigris' east bank, next to Sittacene.

Mazaeus   satrap of Cilicia and/or Syria. According to other sources, Darius had sent him west to oppose Alexander at his crossing of the Tigris, but he did not manage to do so.

scythe chariots   these had long blades extending outward from the wheels that were meant to cut down any soldiers (and horses) in the chariot's path. According to Xenophon, they were first used by Cyrus the Great (*Cyropaedia* 6.1).

elephants   these generally terrified horses unfamiliar with their sight and smell, and threatened to trample infantry as their riders hurled javelins or shot arrows at them from above. Arrian's numbers for the enemy are the highest recorded from antiquity, just as they were at Issus. Diodorus (17.53) lists 800,000 infantry and 200,000 cavalry while Plutarch (31) refers to one million in all. Curtius (4.12) offers a far lower count: 200,000 infantry and 45,000 cavalry. This latter figure is strikingly close to Arrian's cavalry count.

commanders of the allies and of the foreign mercenaries, and considered whether he should advance his force from there immediately, as most urged him to do, or do as Parmenion thought best: pitch camp then and there to thoroughly scout out all the land and see whether any of it looked perilous or impassable – whether there were ditches anywhere or hidden stakes driven into the earth – and to examine more precisely the arrangement of the enemy forces. Parmenion's opinion **won out**, and they pitched camp there in the same formation that they had assumed for battle. Alexander took the light-armed troops and the Companion Cavalry and moved about the area, examining the whole of the terrain where he intended to fight.

When he returned and called the same leaders together again, he declared that they did not need him to incite them to battle, since they were used to rousing themselves by their own courage and their frequent and splendid deeds. He did think it important, however, that each of them inspire his own men – each infantry commander his infantry, each squadron commander his squadron, each battalion commander his battalion, and the generals of the infantry the division assigned to each – since in this battle they would be fighting not over Coele Syria or Phoenicia, nor over Egypt, as before, but over the whole of Asia. Then and there it would be decided who was destined to rule it. There was no need for long-winded speeches urging the men to noble action, since this trait was already theirs by nature. But it was vital in the heat of battle for each and every man to maintain his position with care, to keep strict silence when there was call to advance silently, or to give a loud shout when it was right to shout, and a terrifying war cry whenever the moment should demand that. The commanders themselves needed to listen sharply to those delivering orders and to pass them on directly to their respective units. Furthermore, each and every man had to remember that if he was negligent he could endanger the entire enterprise, but if he executed his orders carefully the result would be a triumph for all.

3.10   When Alexander had incited his leaders with this and other brief speeches, they offered a rousing response that inspired his confidence in them, and so he ordered the army to eat and rest. **Parmenion**, they say, came to Alexander in his tent and recommended carrying out a night attack against the Persians, who, he argued, would be taken by surprise in disarray and be more frightened in the dark. But because there were others listening closely to their conversation, Alexander replied

---

won out   an instance where the advice of Parmenion, Alexander's second-in-command, wins approval. At most other points in the historians his advice is rejected, as you have seen in Arrian's account of the battle of Granicus (pp. 33–4) and Plutarch's description of the arrival of Darius' letter (p. 70).

Parmenion   now we have an example of Parmenion's advice rejected soon after his earlier counsel had won out. Variations of this story appear in other accounts as well, and they are possibly the result of Callisthenes' negative portrayal of Parmenion in his court history.

that it was shameful to steal victory, and that he would win his victory in the open and without guile. This lofty speech of his appeared to be not so much arrogance as confidence in danger. I personally think he made a shrewd calculation along the following lines. Many night missions have not gone according to plan, irrespective of whether the troops were adequately or inadequately prepared for battle; the stronger side has failed and the victory been handed to the weaker, contrary to the expectations of both. Even to Alexander, then, who often took chances in battle, the night seemed perilous. Besides, should Darius lose once again, he could deny the actual inferiority of himself and his men by citing the underhanded nature of the night attack. But if some disaster befell the Macedonians contrary to plan, their enemies would find friendly support in the region while they themselves, who did not know the land, would be in unfamiliar territory and surrounded by enemies, a large proportion of whom were their own prisoners, who would surely attack them at night not only if the Macedonians lost, but even if they seemed to win by a narrow margin. For these calculations I praise Alexander, and I praise him no less for his apparent arrogance.

1. How does the composition of Darius' army differ from that of the one he led at the battle of Issus (see pp. 47–8)?

2. Does Arrian appear to believe that Darius was at a disadvantage at Issus? Why would Darius have been 'easily persuaded' (**3.8**) that he had been?

3. There seem to be some difficulties with Arrian's account. What detail in Arrian's narrative (**3.9**) seems oddly inconsistent with a night march? At what point in the narrative do you envision dawn to arrive?

4. Observe who is the immediate audience of Alexander's speech here and who is the intended secondary audience. Why does Alexander here and prior to the battle of Issus (pp. 43–6) not address the rank and file directly?

5. How does Alexander's speech (**3.9**) contribute to Arrian's narrative and the reader's experience?

6. The presence of others within the tent leads Alexander to make a show of his conversation with Parmenion (**3.10**). Do you believe this is an example of good generalship? Why or why not? How does this exchange characterize Alexander?

7. Arrian's analysis of Alexander's strategy suggests that a night attack might improve the odds of the weaker side. Is Arrian assuming that Darius' side is weaker than Alexander's?

Arrian 3.11   Darius and his army remained during the night in the same formation they had assumed at the beginning, because they had no real camp about them and were afraid that the enemy might make a night attack. This, more than anything else, made matters worse for the Persians at the time; holding that position for so long under arms meant that the fear that normally arises in the face of great dangers did not occur on the spur of the moment, but was nursed over a long time and enslaved their minds.

Darius' army was organized as follows, for a written copy of his troop deployment was later captured, as **Aristobulus** records. The Bactrian cavalry held his left wing and with them the Dahae and Arachotians. To their right the Persians were marshalled, with both the cavalry and infantry mixed together, then the Susians next to the Persians, and next to the Susians the Cadusians. This was the arrangement of the left wing all the way to the middle of the entire battle-line. On the right were marshalled the soldiers from Coele Syria and Mesopotamia. Also on the right flank, from right to left, were the Medians, the Parthians and the Sacians, then the Tapurians and the Hyrcanians, then the Albanians and the Sacesinians, whose forces extended to the centre of the entire battle-line. At the centre, where King Darius was, were marshalled the king's **Kinsmen**, the Persian *Mēlophoroi*, the Indians, the so-called 'relocated' Carians and the Mardian archers. Behind these, the Uxians, the Babylonians, those neighbouring the Persian Gulf and the Sittacenians were drawn many ranks deep. Next, on the left wing and across from Alexander's right, were marshalled the **Scythian** cavalry, as many as 1,000 Bactrians and 100 scythe chariots. The elephants were stationed in front of [Darius'] Royal Squadron, along with 50 chariots. On the right were marshalled the cavalries of the Armenians and Cappadocians and 50 scythed chariots. The Greek mercenaries, who flanked both sides of Darius himself and those Persians with him, were positioned right across from the Macedonian phalanx as the only ones able to counter that force.

Alexander's army was arranged as follows. The Companion Cavalry held his right wing, and next to them was the Royal Squadron, whose commander was Cleitus son of Dropides. To its left was the squadron of Glaucias, next to that the squadron of Aristo, then that of Sopolis son of Hermodorus, then of Heraclides son of Antiochus, next Demetrius son of Althaemenes, after that Meleager, and then the last of the squadrons, whose commander was Hegelochus son of Hippostratus. Philotas son of Parmenion was in charge of the whole Companion Cavalry. In the Macedonian phalanx, immediately next to the cavalry was stationed the Hypaspist Guard, and to its left the rest of the Hypaspists, who were led by Nicanor son of Parmenion. Next was the battalion of Coenus son of Polemocrates, and after

---

Aristobulus apparently claimed to have had access to the list of Persian troop deployments. This was not the case at Issus or the Granicus, where Arrian records the arrangement of Persian troops in considerably less detail.

Kinsmen according to Diodorus (17.59), the Royal Kinsmen were an elite Persian cavalry squadron 1,000 strong. Though not necessarily blood-relatives of the king, they were members of the noblest class. Only the Kinsmen were permitted to kiss the king when performing *proskynesis* before him.

Mēlophoroi literally the 'apple-bearers', a group of 1,000 infantry selected from the so-called Immortals, the regular Persian infantry corps of 10,000. Each *melophoros* carried a spear with a golden apple on the butt as counterweight and butt spike.

Scythian Arrian here begins his description of the forces in front of the main line.

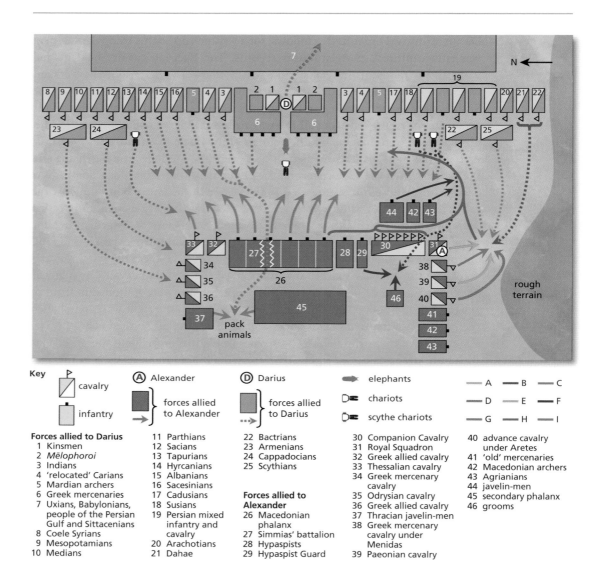

Key

cavalry

infantry

(A) Alexander

(D) Darius

forces allied to Alexander

forces allied to Darius

elephants

chariots

scythe chariots

— A — B — C
— D — E — F
— G — H — I

Forces allied to Darius
1 Kinsmen
2 *Mēlophoroi*
3 Indians
4 'relocated' Carians
5 Mardian archers
6 Greek mercenaries
7 Uxians, Babylonians, people of the Persian Gulf and Sittacenians
8 Coele Syrians
9 Mesopotamians
10 Medians
11 Parthians
12 Sacians
13 Tapurians
14 Hyrcanians
15 Albanians
16 Sacesinians
17 Cadusians
18 Susians
19 Persian mixed infantry and cavalry
20 Arachotians
21 Dahae
22 Bactrians
23 Armenians
24 Cappadocians
25 Scythians

Forces allied to Alexander
26 Macedonian phalanx
27 Simmias' battalion
28 Hypaspists
29 Hypaspist Guard
30 Companion Cavalry
31 Royal Squadron
32 Greek allied cavalry
33 Thessalian cavalry
34 Greek mercenary cavalry
35 Odrysian cavalry
36 Greek allied cavalry
37 Thracian javelin-men
38 Greek mercenary cavalry under Menidas
39 Paeonian cavalry
40 advance cavalry under Aretes
41 'old' mercenaries
42 Macedonian archers
43 Agrianians
44 javelin-men
45 secondary phalanx
46 grooms

The battle of Gaugamela, 1st October 331 BC, according to Arrian.
A) The two armies face one another, when Alexander suddenly leads his cavalry right, towards terrain too rugged for Darius' scythe chariots. B) Darius responds by sending some cavalry to counter this movement. C) Alexander counters Darius' counter-movement with his Greek mercenary cavalry. D) Darius then sends additional cavalry forces to the spot, and these easily repel the outnumbered Greek cavalry. E) Another charge by the Greek mercenaries, this time with the Paeonians, proves successful at first, but the Bactrians regroup and rally the others, who still outnumber those cavalry fighting for the Macedonian side. F) Darius sends his scythe chariots directly against Alexander and the Companions, but the javelin-men and Agrianians intercept most of them. The rest pass through the lines and are destroyed by the Hypaspist Guard and the grooms. G) Darius' whole army now advances, and Alexander sends Aretes and his advance cavalry in support of the other cavalry already fighting on the right. H) The fighting on the Macedonian right has caused a break in Darius' cavalry. Alexander swiftly exploits the resulting gap. I) The Macedonian infantry phalanx breaks as its left side offers support to Parmenion's cavalry. Some of Darius' cavalry punch through this gap and ride all the way to the pack animals, only to find the reserve phalanx and the Thracians turning towards them. Meanwhile, Darius flees.

them that of Perdiccas son of Orontes, then of Meleager son of Neoptolemus, next Polyperchon son of Simmias, and then the battalion of **Amyntas** son of Philip. But **Simmias** led this battalion since Amyntas had been sent to Macedonia to enlist more men. The left of the Macedonian phalanx was occupied by the battalion of Craterus son of Alexander, the same Craterus who was in charge of the left half of the infantry. Next to it was the allied cavalry led by Erigyius son of Larichus. Extending from them all the way to the end of the left wing were the Thessalian cavalry, which Philip son of Menelaus commanded. The whole of the army's left wing was led by Parmenion son of Philotas, and about him ranged the Pharsalian cavalry, the strongest and most numerous of the Thessalian horse.

3.12   This is how Alexander had arranged his front line, but he also deployed a **second line** so that he would have a phalanx facing both directions. He had ordered the commanders of the forces positioned there that, if they saw their own troops being surrounded by the Persian army, they should turn towards them and take on the barbarians at the rear. In case the phalanx should need to be extended or tightened, half of the Agrianians were stationed on the right wing, at an **angle** to the Royal Squadron. Attalus led these, and with them were the **Macedonian archers** whom Brison commanded. Next to the archers were the so-called '**old' mercenaries**, led by Cleander. The advance cavalry and the cavalry of the Paeonians, commanded by Aretes and Ariston respectively, were stationed next to the Agrianians and the archers. And marshalled ahead of them all were the **mercenary cavalry** that Menidas commanded. In front of the Royal Squadron and the rest of the

---

Amyntas, Simmias Amyntas was in fact son of Andromenes. Simmias was Amyntas' brother. Other ancient sources record that Philippus son of Belacrus commanded this battalion. Neither Philippus nor Simmias is well known, but Ptolemy appears to have been the only source that gave Simmias a role.

second line this would have included infantry sent by members of the Corinthian League, and some mercenary troops. As at the battle of Issus (p. 49), these troops are kept in reserve, so that the Macedonian infantry with their long sarissae comprise the front.

angle it appears to have been a right angle. Curtius (4.13) describes the overall Macedonian formation as rectangular. The Agrianians and the following troops composed the right side of that rectangle, and the order of those contingents runs from right to left (i.e. back to front, towards the front line). Likewise, the troops on the left side of the rectangle are listed from left to right, again from the army's rear to the front.

Macedonian archers not mentioned anywhere else in the ancient sources. Curtius (4.13) records that these archers were Cretan, and it may be that there were no Macedonian archers at all.

'old' mercenaries presumably members of the mercenary corps of Alexander's father Philip II.

mercenary cavalry the forward-most of those forces deployed at an angle on the Macedonian right (i.e. on the rectangle's right side).

Companions were the other half of the Agrianians and the archers, as well as the javelin-men of Balacrus. These had been positioned across from the scythe chariots. Menidas and his men had been ordered that, if the enemy rode around their wing, they should attack them in the flank once the enemy had wheeled round. This is how Alexander arranged the forces on the right wing. Along the left wing at an angle were stationed the Thracians that Sitalces led and next to them the allied cavalry that Coeranus commanded. Next were the Odrysian cavalry led by Agathon son of Tyrimmas. Here in front of everyone was stationed the foreign cavalry of the mercenaries, commanded by Andromachus son of Hieron. The infantry from Thrace were set on guard duty over the **pack animals**. The entirety of Alexander's army comprised as many as 7,000 cavalry and around 40,000 infantry.

---

1   Why do you suppose Darius placed elephants and chariots in front of his Royal Squadron (**3.11**)?

2   The organization of Arrian's catalogue of Darius' forces ends climactically with a focus on Darius in the Persian centre and on the Greek mercenaries between him and the Macedonian phalanx. How did the Greek mercenaries fare against this phalanx at their last meeting (see p. 50)?

3   One modern theory proposes that because the sons of Andromenes opposed Ptolemy in 321 BC, Ptolemy may have made Simmias commander in his history so that the blame for what occurs in the battle itself would rest on him. How does this square with what Arrian says about Ptolemy's reliability as a source back in his introduction (p. 28)?

4   Military strategy aside, might there have been political reasons for Alexander's keeping the Corinthian League forces out of the immediate action, i.e. in the secondary phalanx?

Arrian 3.13   When the armies were beginning to close on each other, Darius was visible, as were those with him: the Persian *Melophoroi*, the Indians, the Albanians, the 'relocated' Carians and the Mardian archers. All these were drawn up **opposite Alexander himself** and his Royal Squadron. But Alexander began leading his men to the right instead, and the Persians started to shadow his movement, far outflanking the Macedonians with their own left wing. And now Darius' Scythian cavalry, in riding along the battle-line, were making contact with those forces stationed in front of Alexander's line, but still Alexander continued to shift his men to the right, and they were close to moving beyond the terrain that the Persians had

---

pack animals   located at the rear of the whole fighting force.

opposite Alexander himself   dramatic exaggeration. Arrian has already set Darius, flanked by the Greek mercenaries, directly in front of the central Macedonian phalanx (see pp. 77, 78). Alexander, the Royal Squadron, the Agrianians and the javelin-men of Balacrus stand opposite the scythe chariots on Darius' left wing.

levelled for riding. Consequently, Darius feared that if the Macedonians advanced onto the rough terrain the Persians' chariots would be rendered useless, and so he ordered those positioned ahead of his left to ride around the Macedonians' right wing, where Alexander was leading them, so that his men would not be able to move this wing any further forward. When they did this, Alexander ordered his mercenary cavalry under Menidas to attack them. The Scythian cavalry in turn charged at these forces, along with those Bactrians who had been deployed with the Scythians, and they, enjoying great numerical superiority, drove back Alexander's mercenaries, who were few in number. Alexander then ordered both the Paeonians with Ariston and the mercenaries to attack the Scythians, and the barbarians gave way. The Paeonians and mercenaries, however, were then assaulted by the Bactrians, who redirected back into battle those who were retreating on the Persian side, and kept the cavalry fighting going. Alexander's men were sustaining the greater casualties, because of the barbarians' numbers and because the Scythians and their horses wore better-fitting armour. But even despite this, the Macedonians withstood their attacks, attacked vigorously themselves, and pressed them out of formation.

By this point the barbarians had launched their scythe chariots against Alexander himself in the hope of throwing his line into disarray. This effort, however, was utterly foiled. As soon as the chariots drove forward, the Agrianians and Balacrus' javelin-men, who were positioned ahead of the Companion Cavalry, hurled their javelins at them. Next they started to grab the reins, pull down the drivers, and surround and cut down the horses. Some chariots did hurtle all the way through the Macedonian lines, which had orders to part wherever the chariots attacked. This was mainly why the chariots passed through untouched and without harming those they drove against. The grooms of Alexander's army and the **Royal Hypaspists** overpowered these chariots.

3.14   Darius now began to attack the Macedonian front as a whole, and Alexander ordered Aretes to charge against those cavalry that were attempting to encircle the Macedonian right wing. For a while Alexander himself continued to lead those with him towards the wing. But when the cavalry sent as reinforcements against those encircling the right wing broke the barbarians' front line a little, Alexander turned towards the opening. He arranged the Companion Cavalry and the adjoining phalanx into a **wedge** formation, and with a great battle cry led it forward at a run against Darius himself. There was hand-to-hand combat for a brief period. But then Alexander and his cavalry started to press with

---

Royal Hypaspists   also called the Royal Guard or the Hypaspist Guard, they were typically deployed between the Companion Cavalry and the Hypaspists proper.

wedge   formation in the form of an upside-down 'V'. Alexander and his Companions led the charge, at the wedge's apex.

determination, thrusting their shields forward and spearing at the Persians' faces. Then the Macedonian phalanx, compact and bristling with sarissae, approached the Persians. When Darius, who was already filled with dread, beheld all these horrors at once, he himself was the **first** to turn and flee. Meanwhile, the Persians riding to encircle the Macedonian right were terror-stricken, too, since Aretes and his men continued to assault them with resolve.

In this part of the battlefield the Persians were utterly routed, and the Macedonians pursued and slaughtered them as they fled. But Simmias and his infantry battalion could no longer keep up with Alexander in his pursuit. He had halted his phalanx and was fighting it out there, because the Macedonian left was reported to be in distress. Its formation had been broken, and some of the Indians and Persian cavalry burst through the opening and made straight for the Macedonians' pack animals. The situation there was truly critical, since the Persians were boldly attacking men who were largely unarmed and not expecting any enemies to break through the two-fold phalanx and attack them. Furthermore, once these Persians did attack them, the barbarian **prisoners** also joined in. The commanders of the reinforcements to the front phalanx, however, quickly learned of the incident. They turned their battalion around – just as they had been ordered – and attacked the Persians' rear. They slaughtered many of those Persians as they crowded around the pack animals, though some of them did turn and flee. Those on the Persian right wing, however, had not yet heard of Darius' flight. They had ridden around Alexander's left wing and were attacking Parmenion's men.

3.15   At this point, since the Macedonians were at first surrounded on both sides, Parmenion sent a messenger to Alexander with the urgent report that his flank was in distress and needed help. When this news reached him, Alexander turned back from pursuing the Persians further, and instead wheeled round with his Companion Cavalry and charged the barbarians' right wing at a gallop. He attacked first those of the enemy cavalry who were fleeing: the Parthians, some Indians, and Persians, the enemy's most numerous and strongest force. In fact

---

first   Arrian is the only source that accuses Darius of initiating the flight. Plutarch (33) writes that Darius fled when his own men were being pressed back upon him, while Curtius (4.15) and Diodorus (17.60) record that Darius' driver was killed in hand-to-hand combat, and that the Persians then began to flee because they thought the fallen man was Darius himself. You will recall that in the battle of Issus, too, Arrian has Darius initiating flight, while Diodorus and Curtius present a Persian king who is slower to flee (see p. 52 and note).

prisoners   it appears to be a base camp that is under attack, since there are prisoners of war as well as pack animals. Arrian recorded previously (p. 75) that Alexander's army set up camp a good distance from the battlefield. This apparent contradiction is difficult to resolve.

this cavalry action turned out to be the most hard-fought of the whole battle. The barbarians were drawn up as squadrons in deep ranks and began to rally. They met Alexander's men head-on, and no longer used the javelin or the wheeling of horses typical of cavalry action. Instead, each on his own struggled to break through, as though this was his only hope for survival. They dealt wounds and took them freely, no longer fighting for someone else's victory, but for their own lives. Around 60 of Alexander's Companions fell there. Hephaestion himself was wounded, as were Coenus and Menidas. Yet Alexander overpowered these enemies too.

All the Persians who did break through Alexander's men fled headlong. Alexander was now on the verge of engaging with the enemy's right wing; but meanwhile the **Thessalian** cavalry had fought splendidly and were not outdone by Alexander in combat, so that those from the barbarian right wing were in fact already fleeing when Alexander engaged them. He therefore turned back once again to the pursuit of Darius, and kept up the chase as long as there was light.

Parmenion's men followed their own enemies in pursuit as well. When Alexander crossed the river **Lycus** he made camp there to rest his men and horses a little, while Parmenion took the barbarian camp, along with its pack animals, elephants and camels. After Alexander had rested his cavalry till midnight, he began advancing again with all speed towards Arbela, to capture Darius there, along with his property and the other royal equipment. He reached Arbela on the following day, after a total pursuit of well up to 600 stades [110 km/70 miles] from the site of the battle. But he did not seize Darius in Arbela, for he was fleeing with no rest whatsoever. Darius' property was recovered, however, along with his royal equipment; his chariot was captured **a second time**, his shield a second time, and his bow and arrows, too.

Nearly **100** of Alexander's men died, and more than 1,000 horses, nearly half of them from the Companion Cavalry, perished from wounds and the intense stress of the chase. There were reports of up to 300,000 barbarian corpses, but far more

---

Thessalian   while they commend the Thessalian cavalry's success, both Curtius (4.16) and Diodorus (17.60) credit the victory to the withdrawal of Mazaeus on learning of Darius' flight.

Lycus   river (the Great Zab) lying about 32 kilometres (20 miles) from the site of the battle.

a second time   this chariot and shield are of course not the same as those captured previously at Issus.

100   as usual, Arrian's number of Macedonian dead is the lowest of the ancient sources. Compare that with 500 (Diodorus 17.61) and 330 (Curtius 4.16). Likewise, Arrian gives the highest number of dead on the Persian side. Curtius records 40,000 and Diodorus 90,000.

The famous Alexander Mosaic of c. 100 BC, from the House of the Faun at Pompeii, is a copy of a Greek painting of the fourth century BC. Alexander (left) charges on Bucephalas, perhaps at Gaugamela. The dead tree in the background appears to symbolize the coming death of Darius and the end of the Achaemenid dynasty. It bears a haunting resemblance in form to Darius and his charioteer, who wheels the horses around to flee.

men were captured than killed. The elephants, too, were taken, as were all the chariots that were not cut to pieces in the battle. This is how the battle ended, during the archonship at Athens of Aristophanes, in the month of **Pyanepsion**. Indeed, Aristander's prophecy was fulfilled, that during the same month as the lunar eclipse Alexander would triumph victoriously in battle.

1　How do you think the Persian contingent's attempt to shadow Alexander's movement towards the right (**3.13**) would have affected the Persian line?

2　Curtius (4.16) does not record Parmenion's message to Alexander (**3.15**), and Diodorus (17.60) records that the attempt to get a message to him was unsuccessful. Which do you believe is more likely to be true? What evidence can you find to support your answer?

3　How many of Arrian's 100 Macedonian casualties (**3.15**) are mentioned in his description of the battle itself?

4　Aristander predicted a schedule of Alexander's victory for Alexander on a previous occasion, at the siege of Tyre (pp. 61–2). What might have been Alexander's purpose in having a seer place such time constraints upon his own military actions?

Pyanepsion Macedonian month spanning October/November. The eclipse and the Babylonian record (see p. 72 and note) confirm Plutarch's date of 1 October, one month earlier than Arrian's date here.

Alexander arrives in Babylon

After his success at Gaugamela Alexander marched on Babylon, the administrative capital of the Persian Empire.

Arrian 3.16   Immediately after the battle, Darius rode towards Media by way of the Armenian mountains. He was joined in his flight by the Bactrian cavalry, who had been stationed next to him during the battle, as well as by some Persians, specifically the Royal Kinsmen and a few of the so-called *Melophoroi*. During the flight, up to 2,000 foreign mercenaries joined him, led by Patron the Phocian and Glaucus the Aetolian. Darius fled to Media because he thought Alexander would take the road to Susa and Babylon after the battle for the following reasons: the entire length of the route was populated, the road was not difficult for pack animals, and at the same time Babylon and Susa were clearly the prize of the war. The road to Media, in contrast, was not easy for a large army to take.

Darius was not mistaken: Alexander did set out at once from Arbela and advance towards Babylon. He was already close to Babylon and leading his force in battle formation when the entire populace of Babylon, including their priests and leaders, came out and offered him their city, its governance and its treasure. Once Alexander entered Babylon, he commanded the Babylonians to rebuild

Glazed-brick wall decor from the palace of Darius I at Susa, c. 500 BC. The winged disc of Ahura Mazda, god of wisdom, appears above a pair of griffons.

all the temples that Xerxes had demolished, especially the temple to **Bel**, whom the Babylonians honoured most among the gods. Alexander appointed **Mazaeus** as satrap of Babylon, Apollodorus of Amphipolis as commander of the soldiers left behind with Mazaeus, and Asclepiodorus son of Philo to collect the revenue. He also sent Mithrenes, who had surrendered the acropolis at Sardis to him, to Armenia as satrap. Alexander actually met with the **Chaldaeans** at Babylon as well, and did everything they recommended regarding the temples there, including offering sacrifices himself to Bel under their direction.

---

1   Recall that Bel-Marduk was identified with the Tyrian Melcarth (p. 60 and note). With what Greek hero was this god identified? What was his significance to Alexander?

2   Why might Alexander have promised to rebuild this temple in particular?

3   Why might Alexander have appointed a Persian (Mazaeus) as satrap of Babylon? Are the Persians not the enemies of the Greeks and Macedonians?

4   What do you imagine might have been the relationship between Mazaeus and the two Macedonians appointed to other important offices at Babylon?

5   Alexander underwent a coronation in Egypt, and sacrificed in accordance with local tradition there as well (p. 63 and note). Why is Alexander taking special care to involve himself in such foreign rites as these?

Bel   this temple to Bel, or Bel-Marduk, was a step pyramid eight storeys high with a temple complex to the south. The Greek historian Herodotus visited Babylon and described the temple as still intact long after Xerxes' death. He mentions only the absence of the cult statue, which Xerxes did in fact remove. Any destruction of the temple that Alexander found, therefore, could not have been the doing of Xerxes. Babylonian tradition, however, did remember Xerxes as a destructive tyrant.

Mazaeus   this is the first instance of Alexander appointing a Persian satrap. The Macedonians Apollodorus and Asclepiodorus have important positions, too, and according to Diodorus (17.64) and Curtius (5.1) the Macedonian Agathon was appointed *phrurarch*, commander of the palace citadel itself.

Chaldaeans   when the Persians absorbed the Chaldaean Empire into their own, the term Chaldaean ceased to refer to the people of Babylonia, and was applied instead to a learned priestly class, strictly priests of Babylonian Bel, famed for their knowledge of the magical arts and their prophetic wisdom. The rite described was probably a coronation ceremony, traditionally performed in Bel's sanctuary. This is supported by the fact that in cuneiform documents Alexander's name is accompanied by the traditional Babylonian royal title 'King of Lands'.

Persepolis

After visiting Babylon, Alexander advanced east to Susa. The people there had opened the gates to him and offered him Darius' treasure, a reported 50,000 talents. The city also contained treasures that Xerxes had taken from Greece in his invasion of 480–479 BC, and Alexander returned bronze statues of Harmodius and Aristogiton (see p. 113) to Athens. Fresh troops, too, arrived at Susa from Macedonia, and Alexander marched into Persia itself in early 330. After taking the Persian Gates through a brilliant surprise manoeuvre, he marched on to Persepolis, the ceremonial capital of the Persian Empire, and captured the treasure there, variously reported at 40,000 talents in coin alone (Plutarch 37) and 120,000 talents in all (Diodorus 17.71; Curtius 5.6). Yet another source (Strabo 15.3) values the combined treasure of Susa and Persepolis at only 40,000 or 50,000 talents.

Plutarch 37   Alexander gazed upon a giant statue of Xerxes that had been inadvertently overturned by a mob of those crowding into the palace, and he addressed it face to face as if it were alive: 'Should I pass you by as you lie here because of your invasion against the Greeks, or should I raise you from the ground for your **greatness of mind** and your excellence in other respects?' In the end, after pondering to himself for a long time in silence, Alexander walked on.

He spent four months there because it was winter and he wished to rest his soldiers. And they say that when he sat down for the first time on the royal throne with its golden canopy, **Demaratus** the Corinthian, a kind man and a friend of Alexander's through his father, wept like an old man and said that those Greeks who had died before seeing Alexander seated on Darius' throne had been robbed of a great pleasure.

38   After this, when Alexander was preparing to march against Darius, he once indulged in some drunken amusement with his Companions. There were women too, who had come to join their lovers, and took part in the drinking and revelry. By far the most famous of these women was Thais, the courtesan of the future king Ptolemy and an Athenian. She combined appropriate praise of Alexander in certain things with comments that poked fun at him for others, and in her drunkenness she was inspired to deliver a speech suited to the character of her

---

greatness of mind   the Greek word (*megalophrosynē*) implies not intellectual acumen, but aristocratic ideals and lofty liberality. Alexander appears to see in Xerxes some of his own ambitions.

Demaratus   the same man who fought as a Companion at the battle of the Granicus (p. 38). According to Demosthenes, he was one of the Macedonian party leaders at Corinth during the reign of Philip, so that it is perhaps no surprise that he here speaks highly of Alexander's accomplishment on behalf of all Greeks.

This frieze from an audience hall built for Darius I (c. sixth century BC) in Persepolis depicts envoys bringing gifts to the Great King of Persia in an annual rite that reaffirmed the monarch's reign.

fatherland but too grand for her lowly station. On that day, she said, she received recompense for the suffering she had endured as she wandered throughout Asia, since she was now revelling in the magnificent luxury of the Persian palace. But it would be sweeter still, she said, to stop revelling and set fire to the house of that **Xerxes** who burned Athens to the ground. She herself, in fact, should start the fire while the king looked on, so that people would tell the following story: more so even than the famous generals by sea and by land, the mere women in Alexander's train punished the Persians for the sake of Greece! This speech was met with immediate and boisterous applause, and the Companions urged him on relentlessly. The king was won over. He leapt to his feet, torch in hand, and led the way wearing a garland. Those following on his heels surrounded the palace with shouting and revelry, and as other Macedonians learned what was afoot, they began to run up with torches of their own and join in the celebration. They were hoping for their own sakes that the burning and destruction of the palace meant that Alexander's mind was intent on home, and that he did not mean to live among the barbarians. Some say that the fire started this way; others, that it was a deliberate plan. But there is agreement that Alexander soon changed his mind and ordered the flames extinguished.

Xerxes   the palace was indeed constructed by Xerxes, so that the Greeks would readily have associated its burning with the devastation suffered by Greece during Xerxes' invasion in 480 BC. Most notable, and certainly on the mind of Thais, was the destruction by Xerxes of the old temple to Athena on the Acropolis during his sack of Athens. Greek culture deemed women as inherently inferior to men, so that Thais' proposal to start the fire represents for her audience the utter emasculation of Xerxes. Arrian notably does not mention Thais at all. He (3.18) glosses over the entire event and records only that Alexander meant to punish the Persians for destroying Greek temples by fire.

1. What does the toppled statue of Xerxes symbolize here?

2. Can you offer a modern example of a toppled statue and discuss its significance?

3. If you were Alexander, would you have let the statue of Xerxes remain?

4. It is always worth considering how certain tales come to be more well known than others. What factors do you imagine might have led the Corinthian Demaratus' remark to become widespread?

5. Although Plutarch sets the tale of Xerxes' statue at Persepolis in this account, he elsewhere locates it at Susa, as do Curtius (5.2) and Diodorus (17.66). It may have been a slip on Plutarch's part, but locating the event at Persepolis does permit the natural grouping of these three episodes (Xerxes' statue, Demaratus, and Thais). What does Plutarch achieve by grouping them so? What do they tell us about Alexander's character?

6. What does this episode have in common with Plutarch's representation of Alexander's retributive sack of Thebes (pp. 23–4)?

The extravagance of Alexander's men

Alexander remained with his army in Persepolis from January to May 330 BC, and Plutarch uses this pause in the campaign to contrast the behaviour of Alexander and his generals, now that Persia itself and all its wealth were in their hands.

Plutarch 40 Alexander saw that his retinue had given themselves completely over to **luxury** and were enjoying a lifestyle so base and extravagant that Hagnon wore boots with silver nails, that numerous camels were transporting dust from Egypt for **Leonnatus'** work-out, and that Philotas' hunting nets were 100 stades [18.5 km/11.5 miles] long. Whenever they exercised and bathed, they used myrrh instead of olive oil, and they took around with them masseurs and butlers. Alexander reprimanded them in a gentle and philosophical manner, professing his amazement that men who had fought in so many contests had forgotten that

---

luxury Plutarch offers specific examples of luxuries that a Greek audience would have deemed moral corruption by eastern influence. Myrrh, for example, was a perfume associated with Africa and the East, while the olive was native to Greece and its oil was regularly used in bathing and exercise there. The use of myrrh then compromises and softens the Greek tradition of gymnastics as a method of exercise that served to toughen the body and prepare it for battle. Hunting nets were regularly used; several were put together to form a perimeter enclosure into which assistants would drive the quarry, but 100 stades (18.5 km/11.5 miles) was absurdly long for a single one of these nets.

Leonnatus one of Alexander's Bodyguards, he has a reputation in other ancient sources for delighting in Eastern luxury. He was one of the men to kill Pausanias, who assassinated Philip II, and was the one to reassure Darius' captured family after the battle of Issus (p. 55).

Remains of the palace complex at Persepolis.

victors who toil sleep more sweetly than those who are toiled for – for these men did not even recognize by comparing the Persians' lives with their own how very slavish a life of luxury is and how kingly is the life of labour. 'And what's more,' he would say, 'how could a man groom his horse on his own or lift a spear or wear a helmet if he is no longer used to handling his own person? Do you not know that the key to conquering is to behave differently from the conquered?'

And so Alexander threw himself all the more into military expeditions and hunting, enduring hardship and exposing himself to danger, so that a Spartan ambassador who was at hand when Alexander took down a great lion said, 'Valiantly, Alexander, have you vied with this lion for the kingship!' This was the hunt that **Craterus** commemorated with a memorial at Delphi, a commission in bronze of the lion, the dogs, the king in combat with the lion, and of himself coming to help. Lysippus cast some of them; **Leochares**, the others.

Craterus his dedication was actually discovered at Delphi around the end of the nineteenth century. The inscription on it made clear that the dedication was made not by Alexander's general Craterus, but by Craterus' son (also named Craterus) in the early third century BC.

Leochares he also made gold and ivory sculptures of the Macedonian royal family for the Philippeion at Olympia (Pausanias, *Description of Greece* 5.20).

This pebble mosaic of the fourth or third century BC was found in the Macedonian capital Pella and is believed to depict a helmeted Alexander on the verge of slaying a lion in the hunt. Some speculate that the figure on the right is Craterus, and that the mosaic is inspired by the episode described by Plutarch.

1 Hagnon makes Alexander an offer in a previous episode (p. 57). Does his offer there square with the way Plutarch represents him in this passage?

2 What is the significance of Plutarch's using the word 'philosophical'?

3 How are Alexander's (and perhaps Plutarch's) own cultural biases revealed in this episode?

4 What does Alexander's definition of the 'key to conquering' suggest about his intentions with regard to the Persian Empire?

5 The lion hunt was an important symbol of royalty in the Near East and Macedonia. But what do you imagine was the tone of the Spartan ambassador?

6 Why might a life of luxury be seen as slavish?

The pursuit of Darius

In May 330 BC Alexander advanced in pursuit of Darius, who was still capable of raising yet another army from those parts of his empire that remained loyal to him.

Arrian 3.19   Alexander set out towards Media, having learnt that Darius was there. Darius' plan was that, if Alexander stayed in the area of Susa and Babylon, he himself would remain among the Medians in case some mutiny burst out in Alexander's camp. If Alexander marched out against him, however, he himself would head up to Parthia and Hyrcania, the whole way to Bactra, destroying all the land and thereby making the journey forward impossible for Alexander. He sent the women, the rest of the property still in his possession and the covered wagons to the so-called **Caspian Gates**, while he himself remained in Ecbatana with what forces he was able to cobble together from those at hand.

When Alexander heard this, he set out towards Media, subdued the Paraetacenians by invading their land and instated as their satrap Oxathres son of Susa's satrap Abulites. When it was reported along the way that Darius was resolved to engage him in battle and put him to the test once more – now that Scythian and Cadusian allies had joined him – Alexander commanded the pack animals and their guards to follow behind with the rest of the property, and led the remainder of the army forward in battle order. Eleven days later he arrived in Media, where he learned that Darius' force was not battle-ready, and, in fact, no Scythian or Cadusian allies had joined him. Rather, Darius had decided to flee. Alexander pressed on then with even greater haste, and when he was about three days away from Ecbatana, **Bisthanes**, son of the Ochus who had ruled the Persians before Darius, met him and reported that Darius had fled four days earlier, taking with him his Median treasury of up to 7,000 talents and an army of no more than 3,000 cavalry and 6,000 infantry.

When he reached Ecbatana, Alexander sent the **Thessalian** cavalry and the other allies back to the sea after paying them in full their agreed-upon wages and an extra **2,000 talents**. He then instructed any of them who still wished of his own volition to serve as a mercenary to enlist, and there were many who did so. He appointed Epocillus son of Polyides to command those returning to the sea, with other cavalry to protect them, since the Thessalians had sold their horses there. And he ordered Menes to see that when they reached the sea they would be carried on triremes to Euboea.

Caspian Gates   term referring to present-day Sar-i Darreh, a narrow and well-watered region south of the Caspian Sea. Alexander legend later misapplied the name to the passes on the Caspian's west side, and this has been a source of great confusion. Although Alexander never actually visited the latter location, later legend held that he walled this pass with God's help, to keep out the supposedly unclean barbarians to the north. It is this western pass, also called the 'Gates of Alexander', that becomes a popular subject of travel literature (e.g. *The Travels of Marco Polo*) in later times, and should not be confused with the original Caspian Gates, the pass through which Alexander actually travelled.

Bisthanes   his appearance here as a son of Ochus is a surprise, for according to Diodorus (17.5), Ochus' line had been entirely wiped out. It may be that he was the son of a royal concubine and therefore not technically a legitimate son of the former king.

Thessalian   this cavalry and other allies here discharged by Alexander include all the non-Macedonians in the army. Some of the Thessalians clearly did not choose to stay on, and required an escort and transportation back to their homeland. It is very probable that they were forced to 'sell' their horses to Alexander before returning home.

2,000 talents   this amount was spread over the cavalry only, 1 talent apiece. The infantry received 10 minae each (1 mina = 1/60 talent). Many of the Greeks accepted Alexander's offer to become mercenaries, and according to Diodorus (17.74) Alexander offered each a 3-talent bonus to do so – quite an incentive.

Alexander ordered Parmenion to deposit the treasure brought from Persia in the citadel at Ecbatana and to hand it over to Harpalus, whom Alexander left behind in charge of the treasure, along with 6,000 Macedonians to protect it, both cavalry and a few light-armed troops. **Parmenion** himself was to take the foreign mercenaries, the Thracians and all cavalry other than the Companion horse and lead them past the Cadusian territory into Hyrcania. Alexander ordered Cleitus, commander of the Royal Squadron, when he reached Ecbatana from Susa – for he had been left ill in Susa – to take those Macedonians left in charge of the treasure there and to head for Parthia, where Alexander planned to go himself.

---

1   Have we seen any hint that the sedition Darius hopes for might occur?

2   Curtius (5.8–13) relates the account of Darius' flight largely from Darius' perspective here. How does Arrian's choice of perspective affect the experience of the reader?

3   Alexander's dismissal of his allies appears to indicate an end to the war of Greek revenge that he has waged thus far under the auspices of the Corinthian League. How specifically do the changes in enlistment redefine Alexander's relationship with those Greeks who had served under him? What do you think is the purpose of Alexander's campaign now?

Arrian 3.20   Alexander then took the Companion horse, the advance cavalry, the mercenary cavalry commanded by Erigyius, the Macedonian phalanx (excluding those stationed at the treasury), the archers and the Agrianians, and marched them in pursuit of Darius. Because of the swift pace of the march, many of his soldiers were left behind exhausted, and his horses were dying. He pressed on despite this, and reached **Rhagae** on the eleventh day. That place is a day away from the Caspian Gates for someone advancing at Alexander's pace, but Darius had already managed to pass within those Gates. Of those fleeing with Darius, many abandoned him during the flight for their respective homes, and more than a few actually turned themselves over to Alexander. Since he had given up hope of capturing Darius in hot pursuit, Alexander remained there for five days. He rested his army and appointed **Oxydates** as satrap of Media, a Persian man who happened to have been arrested by Darius and held in Susa. For Alexander, this

---

Parmenion   his route from Ecbatana to Hyrcania, a route different from Alexander's, was meant to exert influence among the Cadusians, loyal allies of Darius, and to prevent a Persian retreat through that region. When this plan was cancelled, Parmenion remained behind to garrison Ecbatana and control Media with the original mercenaries (i.e. not those newly enrolled) and the Thracian and Odrysian cavalries.

Rhagae   a city (now Rey) over 80 kilometres (50 miles) east of the Caspian Gates. Alexander's mix of cavalry and infantry could not have covered the distance in a day.

Oxydates   another Persian appointed to a satrapy, this one a prisoner sentenced to death under Darius, according to Curtius (6.2).

was reason enough to trust him, and he pressed on towards Parthia. On the first day he set up camp at the Caspian Gates, and on the second he passed within the gates as far along as it was populated. He had heard that the land beyond was desert, and so he sent **Coenus** to forage with cavalry and a few of the infantry in order to stock up with provisions from the area.

3.21   At that time Bagistanes, a Babylonian man of noble status, and with him Antibelus, one of the sons of Mazaeus, arrived from Darius' camp. They reported that Nabarzanes, **chiliarch** of the cavalry fleeing with Darius, Bessus, the satrap of the Bactrians, and Barsaentes, the satrap of the Arachotians and Drangians, had captured Darius. When Alexander heard this he pressed on at a still greater pace, taking with him the Companions and the advance cavalry, as well as the toughest and most agile from the infantry. He did not wait for Coenus to return from his foraging. He set Craterus over those left behind and ordered him to follow at a normal march. Those with Alexander carried only their weapons and food for two days. He journeyed the entire night and the following day until noon before resting his army a short time and once again marching all night long. At dawn he reached the camp from which Bagistanes had set out in the other direction, but failed to catch up with the enemy. He did learn, however, that the captive Darius was being transported on a covered wagon. Bessus was now in charge rather than Darius. He had been named commander by the Bactrian cavalry and by the barbarians who had fled with Darius. Only Artabazus, the sons of Artabazus and the Greek mercenaries remained loyal to Darius, but because they were not able to prevent what was happening, they turned from the highway and headed to the hills on their own, playing no part in what Bessus and his men did. Those who had seized Darius had decided that, if they heard that Alexander was pursuing them, they would hand Darius over to Alexander and win his goodwill towards them. But if they heard that Alexander had turned back, they would gather as large an army as they could and preserve their rule together. **Bessus** was in charge for the time being because of his relationship with Darius, and because this action had been taken during his satrapy.

Coenus   his orders here are a good reminder of the logistical difficulties involved in a swift march by thousands. An army on such a march moves too quickly for the supply lines to provide for it. Observe that Alexander remains in a populated area of the Gates.

chiliarch   literally 'commander of 1,000', this term is regularly applied to Greek cavalry commanders of approximately 1,000 men, but it was also used, as here, of the Persian second-in-command, whose title referred to that officer's original role as chief of the Persian palace guard, apparently 1,000 strong.

Bessus   his precise relationship to Darius is not certain. The satrapy of Bactria/Sogdiana was an important one, and its previous satraps had been members of the royal family. It is therefore quite possible that Bessus was in fact related to Darius. It was quite common for Persian satraps to rise up against Persian kings, and a tie to the royal house would have given Bessus a special claim to the throne.

When Alexander heard this, he decided on a full pursuit. Both his men and his horses were already exhausted from the constant hardships, but he pressed on nonetheless. He covered much ground marching through the night until noon the next day, at which point he reached a certain village where those conducting Darius had camped only the day before. There he heard that the barbarians had decided to make the journey by night, and so he asked those who lived there whether there was any short cut to the fugitives. They said they knew one, but that it was devoid of any water. Alexander ordered that they lead him that way regardless, and when he saw that the infantry would not follow him at a swift pace, he removed as many as 500 of the cavalry from their horses. He then selected those of the **infantry** who were still strong, and ordered them and the infantry officers to mount the horses fully armed. He ordered Nicanor, commander of the Hypaspists, and Attalus, commander of the Agrianians, to lead those men who had been left along the road that Bessus and his men had taken. These were to be outfitted as lightly as possible, and he ordered the rest of the infantry to follow in formation.

1	Why do you suppose Alexander gave up the pursuit on arriving at Rhagae? What has changed?
2	Why might Antibelus (**3.21**) have naturally defected to Alexander?
3	Arrian offers us the thoughts of the men who arrested Darius. How might Arrian have had access to this information? Do the men in fact follow through with their plan?
4	What does Alexander appear to be doing with the men who have defected from Bessus?
5	Given the amount of food Arrian reports was available to Alexander's party, at what point in the pursuit should it have run out?

infantry foot-soldiers travelling on horseback in full armour is a striking and ingenious response to the need to transport them quickly. Alexander is credited with inventing a corps of *dimachae*, men trained to serve as both infantry and cavalry. A body of skilled infantry was vital during this pursuit, in case of a battle. A cavalry force is incapable of charging successfully against a line of infantry in good formation; foot-soldiers must engage an enemy infantry first, so that the cavalry can then flank them without the risk of running onto their readied spears.

The death of Darius

Arrian 3.21 Alexander himself began advancing during the afternoon and pressed on at a run. He covered as much as 400 stades [74 km/46 miles] during the night, and at dawn came across the barbarians marching in disarray and unarmed. As a result, only a few of them tried to defend themselves while the majority, as soon as they saw Alexander in person, fled without fighting. And those who did turn to fight also fled after a few of them were killed. Bessus and those with him were still transporting Darius in the covered wagon, but, now that Alexander was upon them, Satibarzanes and Barsaentes wounded Darius and left him there, while they themselves fled with 600 cavalry. Darius died from the wound a little later, before Alexander saw him.

3.22 Alexander sent the body of Darius to Persepolis and ordered that it be buried in the royal tombs just as the other kings before Darius had been. He gave the satrapy of Parthia and Hyrcania to Amminapes the Parthian, one of the men who along with Mazaces had handed Egypt over to Alexander. Tlepolemus son of Pythophanes, one of the Companions, was appointed with him to supervise affairs among the Parthians and Hyrcanians.

This was the end of Darius, during the archonship of Aristophon in Athens, in

An Iranian storyteller performing the end of Darius, as described by the medieval Persian poet Firdowsi. Ultimately, the tale comes from one preserved also in the Alexander Romance (2.20), in which Alexander witnesses Darius' death.

the month of **Hecatombaeon**, the end of a man more cowardly and incompetent than any other when it came to war, though in other matters he did nothing indecorous, or had no chance to, at least, since as soon as he attained the kingship he happened to be attacked by the Macedonians and Greeks. It was no longer possible for him, therefore, to abuse his subjects had he wanted to, since he was in greater danger than they. While he lived, one catastrophe after another befell him from the moment he **acceded to the throne**. Right away the cavalry disaster of the satrapies at the Granicus occurred. Then immediately both Ionia and Aeolis were taken, as were both Phrygias, Lydia and all Caria save Halicarnassus. A little later, **Halicarnassus** too was captured, and next all the seaboard to Cilicia. Then came his loss at Issus, where he saw his mother taken as a prisoner of war, along with his wife and children. After that, he lost Phoenicia, and all Egypt. Next he himself was shamefully among the first to flee at **Arbela**, and the army he lost was the largest of all the barbarian race. A wandering refugee fleeing his own empire and handed over to the worst of fates by his own attendants, a king and prisoner in one, he was led away amid dishonour only to die a death plotted by those closest to him. These sorts of things befell Darius in his life, but on dying his burial was kingly. Alexander reared and educated Darius' children as if Darius were still king and had Alexander himself for his **son-in-law**. When the end came, Darius was about 50 years old.

---

1   The brief and matter-of-fact description of Darius' death comes as a huge anticlimax after the excitement of the long chase. Why do you suppose Arrian gives greater attention to Darius' pursuit than to his death?

2   Why would Alexander have given his enemy Darius a royal burial?

3   Is there anything complimentary in Arrian's obituary of Darius? How fair a treatment of Darius is it?

4   How does the passage reflect on Alexander?

Hecatombaeon   this Greek month sets the date roughly in July of 330 BC. It is possible that Arrian is off by one month, as he was in dating the battle at Gaugamela, and that Darius died in August.

acceded to the throne   in 336 BC.

Halicarnassus   this city in fact continued to serve as a Persian naval base even after the battle of Issus.

Arbela   the largest city in the vicinity of Gaugamela. The ancient sources therefore frequently refer to that battle as the battle of Arbela. Arrian refers to the site as Gaugamela elsewhere, and the slip here is striking. As his tone and style shift here, so does his concern for accuracy.

son-in-law   Alexander did in fact become Darius' son-in-law through his later marriage to Barsine at Susa in 324 BC.

5 East to India

Alexander wears barbarian attire

Alexander's soldiers hoped that the death of Darius would mean the end of campaigning, but Alexander had other plans. He delivered an inspiring speech, persuading his troops to advance further east from Hyrcania. With Darius' death, Alexander could now claim sovereignty over the former Persian Empire, and the selection below discusses his decision to assume more native attire.

Plutarch 45 Alexander headed into Parthia, and during a break in that journey he wore barbaric dress for the first time. He did so perhaps to link himself to the local traditions, believing that shared customs and a common nationality were important means of civilizing people. Or perhaps this was some covert attempt to introduce *proskynesis* among the Macedonians, to accustom them gradually to his own new behaviour and to change in general. But at least he did not adopt the Median style of dress, which is utterly barbaric and foreign. Nor did he wear trousers or a ***kandys*** or a tiara, but created a good combination of Persian and Median style, more modest than the former and more stately than the latter. In the beginning he wore this attire when giving audience to the barbarians or in the company of his Companions, but later everyone saw him riding around and conducting matters of state in this dress. The sight upset the Macedonians, but since they admired his excellence in other areas, they thought they would compromise on a few things that brought him pleasure and fame. After all, on top of everything else, an arrow had struck his shin, so that the shattered bone of his tibia protruded from the wound, and a stone had hit him in the back of the neck with such force that it clouded his vision for some time. Yet even so, he never stopped risking his

---

kandys purple long-sleeved woollen shirt, which, like the tiara, was of Median origin and indicated royalty (see pp. 52, 55). Such Median and Persian clothing implied luxury to a Greek audience, and Plutarch appears to be discussing Alexander's choice of clothes as a moral issue, believing that to some extent one's clothes reflect oneself.

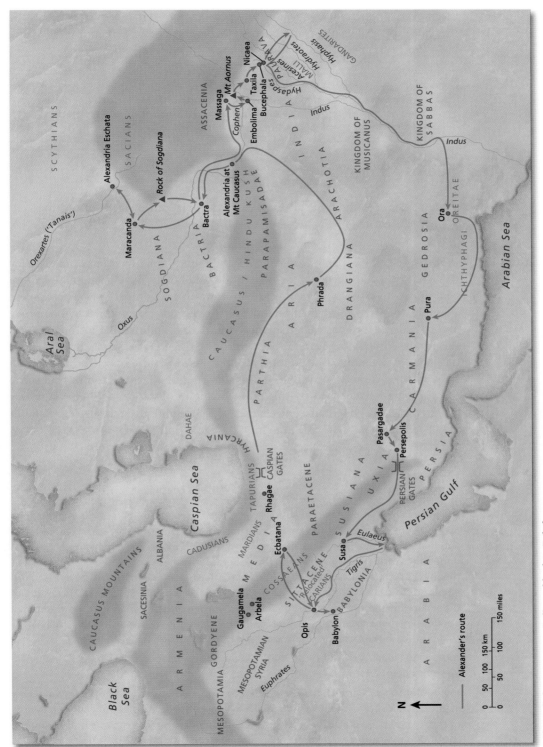

Alexander's route east to India and back to Babylon

life at every opportunity. In fact he [later] even crossed the **Orexartes** (which he thought was the Tanais), routed the Scythians and pursued them for 100 stades [18.5 km/11.5 miles], though afflicted all the while with diarrhoea.

> • Plutarch appears here to distinguish between the Companions (most of whom were Macedonian) and the Macedonians. Does Plutarch imply that the two groups might have viewed Alexander's adoption of Persian dress differently? If so, what might account for this?

The Philotas affair

> Alexander continued his advance east into Aria and then south to Phrada, where he learned of an alleged plot against his life.

Plutarch 48

Philotas, son of Parmenion, enjoyed a lofty status among the Macedonians; they thought him a **courageous man** of fortitude, and no one but Alexander was more generous with gifts or more affectionate towards his companions. There is, for example, the story that when one of his close friends asked Philotas for money and he ordered it to be granted, his accountant told Philotas that he did not have the funds. Philotas replied, 'What are you saying? Have we no drinking-cup or cloak to give him?' But Philotas also possessed a sense of self-importance, a huge fortune, a preoccupation with his person and a lifestyle **too burdensome** for a private citizen. And by this point his pompous and lofty behaviour was disagreeable: his boorish pretence lacked elegance and fostered suspicion and ill will. Even Parmenion once said to him, 'Be more humble, my son, please!'

Orexartes river also known in antiquity as the Jaxartes, the modern Syr Darya (see map on p. 99). The Greeks had not explored the northern reaches of the Aral and Caspian seas, and many in fact believed that the Caspian was a gulf of Ocean, the mythical river that ringed the world. Such ignorance of the geography of these northern lands led to other theories as well, including the identification of the Orexartes with the river Tanais, which empties into Lake Maeotis, north of the Black Sea (see p. vii). Strabo (11.7) considered the linking of the two rivers propaganda by Alexander; the Tanais was the traditional boundary between Europe and Asia, and by equating it with the Orexartes Alexander could establish the latter as a northern limit to his campaign against all Asia.

courageous man you will recall that Philotas has commanded the Companion Cavalry up to this point (see pp. 34–5, 77).

too burdensome Plutarch here refers to a common Mediterranean notion of kingliness in antiquity. Not only should a king (a divinely sanctioned status) rightly adopt a degree of stately pomp; he is also, because he is a king, inherently more capable of resisting the corruption that such grandeur can work upon an ordinary man, such as Philotas.

For some time, too, Alexander had been hearing accusations against Philotas. After the defeat of Darius in Cilicia and the confiscation of the treasure in Damascus, many prisoners were brought to the Macedonian camp, and among them was a good-looking woman from Pydna named Antigone. Philotas got her as his courtesan and, just as any youth, especially when drinking, will boast openly to his mistress about his glorious military exploits, so Philotas would tell her of his greatest feats, and of his father's. But he would describe Alexander as a mere child who enjoyed a nominal rule that Parmenion and himself had won for him. Antigone passed these words on to one of her friends, who naturally told another, until eventually the tale reached Craterus. He arrested the courtesan and escorted her in secret to Alexander, who heard her speak and ordered her to continue seeing Philotas as before, but also to come and report to him all that she heard him say.

49   Since Philotas was ignorant of these arrangements, he often enjoyed Antigone's company, and out of anger and pride he would sound off and make inappropriate remarks against the king. Still, despite the convincing evidence against Philotas, Alexander restrained himself and kept his silence, either because he was sure of Parmenion's goodwill towards himself, or because he feared the prestige and power of the father and son. **At this time**, a Macedonian from Chalaestra named **Limnus** plotted against Alexander. Limnus asked one of the youths, Nicomachus, a man with whom he was amorously involved, to take part in the deed. Nicomachus did not agree to it, and instead told his brother Cebalinus about the plan. Cebalinus approached Philotas and demanded that he bring them before Alexander, saying they needed to meet with him regarding some great and pressing news. For some reason that remains unclear, however, Philotas refused to take them to Alexander because, as he said, the king was occupied with other more important business. In fact Philotas denied their requests on two occasions. They then grew suspicious of Philotas and turned to **someone else**, who did escort them to the king. In telling

---

At this time   this episode took place in 330 BC. According to Arrian (3.26), both Ptolemy and Aristobulus recorded that Philotas' treason had been reported to Alexander back in Egypt, but that Alexander disbelieved it because of their long friendship and because Alexander had been so generous towards Philotas and Parmenion. Plutarch, however, states elsewhere (*Moralia* 339 F) that Alexander had suspected Philotas for seven years.

Limnus   his actual name was Dimnus, as it appears in Curtius and Diodorus. This error reminds us of our dependence upon centuries of scribes for the manuscripts we have in our possession today. Because of the similarity between the Greek letters Δ and Λ (our D and L), a scribe mistakenly copied the name Dimnus (ΔΙΜΝΟΣ) as the more familiar Limnus (ΛΙΜΝΟΣ). The error appears in all the extant manuscripts of Plutarch's *Alexander*, so that it must have occurred very early, perhaps even in a source used by Plutarch when composing this biography. It is unlikely that this figure, otherwise unknown and from the small town of Chalaestra, would have masterminded a conspiracy.

someone else   Metron (Curtius 6.7), one of the Royal Pages.

Alexander about Limnus' plans, they revealed in passing that Philotas had twice dismissed their request for a meeting. This fact already disturbed Alexander a great deal, but he was all the more upset when Limnus was killed while resisting arrest, for he believed that proof of the conspiracy had now eluded him.

Because Alexander had bitter feelings towards Philotas, he gathered together men who had long hated the man, and these now openly declared that the king was naive to think that Limnus, a man from Chalaestra, would attempt so bold an act all on his own. Instead, they argued that he was a mere stooge, probably an instrument under the command of someone more powerful. Any inquest, therefore, must focus upon those most interested in concealing the matter. The king offered a ready ear to such talk and suspicion, and so **these men** next presented countless accusations against Philotas. He was then arrested and interrogated. The Companions stood by during his torture, while Alexander himself listened from behind a tapestry hung for the occasion. They say that as Philotas implored Hephaestion and his men with pitiful cries and grovelling supplications, Alexander remarked, 'Were you this soft and cowardly, Philotas, when you undertook so great an enterprise?'

Right after Philotas was put to death, Alexander sent men to Media to kill **Parmenion**, too. He was a man who had often assisted Philip in his achievements and who had been the only one of Alexander's older Friends – or at least the most vocal – to encourage Alexander to cross into Asia. But now, after seeing two of his **three sons** die earlier in the invasion, he himself was eliminated with the third. These acts made Alexander a source of fear for many of the Friends, especially Antipater, who actually sent an embassy to the Aetolians and forged a secret alliance with them.

---

these men cannot be identified for certain, but Curtius (6.8) gives the names of those who arranged the arrest: Craterus, Leonnatus, Hephaestion, Coenus, Erigyius and Perdiccas. According to Curtius, it was Craterus who convinced the other Companions of Philotas' guilt. Recall that it was Craterus also who had reported to Alexander Philotas' boasts to Antigone (see p. 101).

Parmenion a very popular general, and Alexander's second-in-command, who had been left in Ecbatana with control over the treasury there as well as the communication and supply lines to Alexander and his troops.

three sons Parmenion's youngest son Hector died after falling from a capsized boat on the Nile and swimming ashore. Nicanor, Parmenion's second eldest son and the commander of the Hypaspists throughout the expedition, grew ill and died on the journey east from Hyrcania. With the death of Philotas and Parmenion, the entire family of high-ranking generals was extinguished.

Bessus' mutilation

Alexander learned that after Darius' murder Bessus had changed his name
to Artaxerxes, declared himself king of Asia and started wearing the royal
Persian garb. Bessus furthermore had the support of Persians who had escaped
after Gaugamela, as well as Bactrians, and he was expecting reinforcements
from Scythia. Alexander secured Drangiana and Arachotia, and in 329 BC
marched north into Bactria, crossing the Hindu Kush. Bessus retreated to
Sogdiana under Alexander's advance, but was eventually found and captured
by Ptolemy. Alexander had Bessus tortured and sent to Bactra for execution.
He next advanced north across the Orexartes and routed the Scythians
(see p. 100). In the episode below, Arrian discusses Alexander's treatment of
Bessus on his return to Bactra.

Arrian 4.7   Then Alexander convened a **meeting** of those present and brought Bessus before
them. After accusing him of betraying Darius, he ordered Bessus' nose to be
cut off, along with his ear lobes, and that he be taken to Ecbatana for execution
there at an assembly of Medians and Persians. I for my part disapprove of Bessus'
punishment as excessive, for I consider the **mutilation** of extremities barbaric.
I agree that Alexander had been brought to the point of emulating Median and
Persian luxury and that style of rule characteristic of barbarians, namely the
regular treatment of attendants as subservient. Furthermore, I in no way approve

meeting   probably a public assembly of the people in Bactra. After this show before
the Bactrian people, the spectacular execution would be held before the Median and
Persian peoples in Ecbatana. The ancient sources differ remarkably in their accounts of
Bessus' execution. Curtius (7.5) records the mutilation Arrian describes, but also that he
was shot with arrows while crucified. According to Diodorus (17.83), Alexander had the
corpse dismembered and scattered, while Plutarch (43) models the execution on Theseus'
mythical execution of Sinis, who was tied to two bent saplings that tore him apart when
they were released.

mutilation   a practice generally frowned upon in Greek culture. According to Persian
tradition, however, a mutilated man could not become king.

of the fact that, though a **descendant of Heracles**, he traded his Macedonian attire for **Median dress**; he was not even ashamed to wear the tiara of the conquered Persians in place of what he himself had long worn as conqueror. I approve of none of these things. But, I think, surely Alexander's great deeds more than anything offer clear proof that even if someone possessed a strong body, a distinguished lineage and success in war surpassing Alexander's own – even if he circled Libya by sea to Asia, just as Alexander had intended, and took them both, even if he added Europe as a third domain to Asia and Libya – none of these could further the happiness of one who achieves superficial greatness, but lacks self-control.

---

1   Why might Alexander have mutilated Bessus so publicly?

2   Why do you suppose Arrian deemed the episode of Bessus' punishment the proper place to express his own disapproval of Alexander's attire?

3   This episode's final moralizing sentence suggests a loss of self-control in Alexander. Are you convinced that Alexander's punishment of Bessus, treatment of attendants and choice of clothing show a loss of self-control? Why or why not?

4   While this final sentence ostensibly criticizes Alexander, how does it manage to praise him as well?

The murder of Cleitus

Even after Bessus' capture, Alexander was forced to continue campaigning in Bactria and Sogdiana. The following incident occurred at Maracanda in autumn 328 BC.

---

descendant of Heracles   Heracles was generally recognized as a Greek culture hero, associated with colonization and the spreading of Greek customs. Arrian here suggests that Alexander's adoption of Median dress represents an inversion of his ancestor's role.

Median dress   Arrian nowhere distinguishes Median dress from Persian. The tiara to which he refers was indeed the tall, conical headdress of the Persian kings, but it was technically Median in origin. Plutarch (p. 98, *Moralia* 329) and others (Diodorus 17.77; Strabo, *Geography* 11.13) record that Alexander avoided Median dress such as the tiara, trousers and the *kandys*. According to Eratosthenes (Plutarch, *Moralia* 330), he combined traditional Macedonian clothing with select Persian attire such as the white-striped tunic, the girdle and the diadem. While the Persian kings typically wore the diadem (a purple ribbon with a white stripe) around the Median tiara, Plutarch and others (Diodorus 17.77; Curtius 6.6; Justin 12.3) make clear that Alexander wore the diadem not around the tiara, but around the *kausia*, the felt hat that Macedonian kings traditionally wore.

Arrian 4.8   There was a day sacred to Dionysus among the Macedonians on which the king sacrificed annually to the god. On this occasion, they say, Alexander overlooked Dionysus and for some reason decided to sacrifice to the **Dioscuri** instead. Alexander had already adopted **new drinking habits** that tended very much towards the barbaric. The drinking continued at length, and the conversation turned to the Dioscuri, in particular how their parentage had been stripped from Tyndareus and given to Zeus. Some of those present – the sort who are always corrupt and cause trouble for kings – were flattering Alexander and claimed that Polydeuces and Castor could hardly be compared with him and his deeds. Others in their drunkenness said the same of Heracles, insisting that envy alone deprived the living of the honours that their comrades should rightly bestow.

Cleitus had long made it clear that he was upset at Alexander's shift to more barbaric habits and at his flattery by others. Now, spurred on by wine, Cleitus refused to allow these men to abuse divinity and trivialize the deeds of ancient heroes in their effort to offer Alexander an empty favour. Furthermore, he said, Alexander's deeds were hardly as great and marvellous as they made them out to be. Alexander did not accomplish them on his own; the greater part belonged to the Macedonians. This speech of his upset Alexander, and I do not approve of it; it is enough, I think, to hold one's peace and not to make the mistake of joining others in their flattery. But some of these men recalled without warrant even the **deeds of Philip** and said that Philip's accomplishments were neither great

---

Dioscuri Castor and Polydeuces (Pollux), regularly termed the Dioscuri (literally 'Youths of Zeus'), were the patron cult-heroes of seafarers. Their mother was Leda, and Tyndareus was Leda's mortal husband, but the Dioscuri's parentage was traditionally ascribed to Zeus, who was said to have appeared to Leda in the form of a swan. Such dual parentage was a common feature of Greek heroes; Heracles himself had a mortal father in Amphitryon and a divine one in Zeus. Why does the geographical location of Maracanda make a sacrifice to the Dioscuri surprising?

new drinking habits Arrian suggests that Alexander's excessive drinking was a move towards orientalism, akin to his change of dress. But we have already seen Macedonians drunk (p. 20); they traditionally drank wine in great quantity and did not practise the common Greek custom of diluting it with water.

Cleitus it may be because Cleitus had been so vocal in his criticism already that Alexander had recently appointed him satrap of Bactria and Sogdiana. The nomination was an honour certainly, but would also remove Cleitus from the campaign proper, and keep him busy governing a region particularly difficult to control. Recall that Parmenion was removed by leaving him to handle affairs in Media.

deeds of Philip Curtius (8.1) records that Alexander himself belittled his father's accomplishments.

---

nor marvellous, and this, too, delighted Alexander. Cleitus was now no longer in control of himself, and so he spoke out, exalting the deeds of Philip and belittling Alexander and his achievements. So Cleitus continued, drunkenly reproaching Alexander in all sorts of ways, and even recalled that he himself actually saved Alexander's life during the cavalry battle with the Persians at the Granicus. In saying this, he went so far as to lift his right hand insolently and declare, 'This very hand, Alexander, saved you back then!' Alexander could no longer endure this drunken abuse. He sprang at Cleitus in a rage, and his fellow drinkers restrained him. But even then, Cleitus did not stop abusing him. Alexander began shouting, and even called out for his **Hypaspists**. When none of them obeyed, he declared that his own fate was that of Darius, whom Bessus and his men had arrested and carted off as nothing more than a king in name only. The Companions could no longer restrain him as he leapt forward. Some say he snatched a spear from a Bodyguard, struck Cleitus with it and killed him; others say it was a sarissa from one of the guards. Aristobulus does not say how the drunken situation began, but records that Cleitus alone was the cause of the mishap; when Alexander had grown angry and leapt up at him with intent to kill, the Bodyguard **Ptolemy son of Lagus** escorted Cleitus outside through the gates and over the wall and ditch of the citadel, where the event occurred. But Cleitus lacked self-control and turned back again. He came across Alexander shouting, 'Cleitus!' and answered, 'I am right here, Alexander, your Cleitus!' In that very moment he was struck by the sarissa and died.

4.9   I for my part especially blame Cleitus for his abuse towards his king. I pity Alexander for his misfortune, because in that event he showed that two vices had got the better of him: rage and drunkenness, both unseemly for a man of self-control to succumb to. But I approve of Alexander's subsequent behaviour, for he immediately recognized the wickedness of his act. Some say he pressed the sarissa against the wall and meant to fall on it, because it was not right that he should live after killing a friend while drinking. But most writers do not record this. They say that he withdrew to his bed and lay there lamenting, calling out to Cleitus by name and to Cleitus' sister, Dropides' daughter Lanice, who had been Alexander's wet-nurse: 'How splendidly have I, now that I am a man, repaid you for nursing me as a child! You saw your own sons fighting and dying for me, and now I myself have killed your brother with my own hand!' He would not stop branding himself a murderer of friends and stubbornly refused food or drink for three days. Nor did he care for his person in any other way. At this, the prophets

---

Hypaspists evidence that members of the Hypaspist corps functioned as a court guard, alongside the elite Bodyguards who protected Alexander's person. Alexander assumes that the Bodyguards have sided with Cleitus.

Ptolemy son of Lagus no other source refers to this action by Ptolemy. It may be that Aristobulus was attempting to win the favour of this king of Egypt when he wrote this.

began singing 'The Rage of Dionysus', because Alexander had neglected that god's sacrifice. Only at the encouragement of his Companions did Alexander reluctantly take food and care for his person, though still inadequately. And he also made the sacrifice to Dionysus, because he was not unwilling to have the misfortune attributed to the rage of a god rather than to his own wickedness. I praise Alexander wholeheartedly for neither boasting about his crime nor corrupting himself further by advocating and justifying the misdeed. Instead, he confessed to his error; after all, he was only human.

---

1 The cult of the Dioscuri (**4.8**) was not popular in Macedonia, and there is no reference to their worship elsewhere during the campaign. The Dioscuri's double parentage (divine and human) may well be the reason for their worship here. Why would Alexander be interested in calling attention to such a dual parentage?

2 What is the subtext of the flatterers' statements about the inferiority of Castor, Pollux and Heracles to Alexander (**4.8**)? In other words, what honours are these flatterers suggesting Alexander is deprived of?

3 Why do you suppose Arrian uses the passive voice ('he was struck by the sarissa'), in depicting the moment of Cleitus' death?

4 Plutarch (50.7) notably does not mention that this day was sacred to Dionysus. How would Arrian's inclusion of this detail, particularly at the opening of the episode, influence the way an ancient reader might interpret the event? How does it affect one's judgement of Alexander's character?

5 In this episode, one man verbally insults another, while the other commits murder. What assumptions or biases appear to influence Arrian's critique of their behaviour (**4.9**)? What biases of your own may affect your opinion of the event?

Callisthenes and Anaxarchus

Plutarch records below how two philosophers attempted by very different means to console Alexander in his grief after his murder of Cleitus.

Plutarch 52 **Callisthenes** the philosopher, a relative of Aristotle, and Anaxarchus of Abdera were brought to the side of the grief-stricken Alexander. Callisthenes began trying

---

'The Rage of Dionysus' a reference to the first line of the *Iliad*, which begins with an invocation to the Muse to sing the 'rage of Achilles'. The remark therefore suits well Arrian's desire to be a Homer for Alexander (see pp. 31–2). Arrian begins this episode by pointing out that Dionysus was overlooked in favour of sacrifice instead to the Dioscuri, just as Achilles was slighted by Agamemnon.

Callisthenes Alexander's official court historian, a position of great distinction; he was also supposed to have worked with Aristotle to create the edition of the *Iliad* treasured by Alexander.

gently to check his suffering in the usual way, by choosing his words carefully and adopting an indirect, painless approach. But Anaxarchus had followed from the start a unique path in philosophical thinking and had gained a reputation for disdain and contempt towards the usual methods. He entered and cried out, 'This is Alexander, on whom the civilized world fixes its eyes, and yet he has thrown himself upon the ground and weeps like a slave! He fears tradition and the people's criticism when he himself should rightly represent tradition and the standard of justice. Alexander, after all, has won the right to govern and to rule, not to be a slave ruled by meaningless concepts. Do you not know,' he said, 'that Zeus seated **Justice and Law** beside himself so that all he does as ruler is lawful and just?' By using such arguments Anaxarchus managed to assuage the king's suffering, but also rendered his behaviour in many ways more vain and lawless. And while Anaxarchus won Alexander's enthusiastic favour, he contributed to his displeasure at the company of Callisthenes, whose austerity never allowed him to be frivolously agreeable. They say that during dinner once, when the guests were talking about the climate and temperatures, Callisthenes agreed with those who held that the weather there was colder and wintrier than in Greece. When Anaxarchus countered vehemently, Callisthenes replied, 'But you must confess this weather is colder than that! You yourself would spend the winter in a **threadbare cloak** back in Greece, while here you recline at meals under three rugs!' Needless to say, this provoked Anaxarchus even further.

1	What is the reasoning behind Anaxarchus' argument?
2	What is the subtext of Callisthenes' remark about Anaxarchus?
3	What larger issues do Callisthenes and Anaxarchus represent in this episode?

The Rock and Roxane

Alexander was now in his third year of campaigning against the Bactrians and Sogdianians, who after being routed in battle would repeatedly gather again to ambush Macedonian soldiers and raid their outposts. The rugged landscape helped them in this, by providing them with many hidden and defensible places for retreat. In the following episode Alexander assaults one of the more notable places of refuge, the Rock of Sogdiana.

Justice and Law Anaxarchus sophistically cobbles together his own version of Zeus. Justice is an agent of Zeus in Hesiod's *Works and Days* (256–62) and Law attends Zeus in an ode by Pindar (*Olympian* 8.21–3). The reasons given for their adoption by Zeus appear to be Anaxarchus' own.

threadbare cloak the *tribōn*, a garment regularly worn by philosophers, who traditionally rejected materialism and luxury.

Arrian 4.18　At the first signs of spring Alexander began his advance against the **rock in Sogdiana**, where many of the Sogdianians had reportedly taken refuge. The wife and children of **Oxyartes** the Bactrian were said to have holed up at this rock as well. He mistakenly deemed it utterly impregnable, and so had tucked them safely away there while he led the revolt against Alexander. Alexander thought, therefore, that if he could take this rock, those Sogdianians who favoured revolution would have no hope left.

When he had drawn near the rock, he discovered that it was precipitous on all sides and resistant to attack, and that the barbarians had stockpiled food enough to weather a lengthy siege. Furthermore, the heavy **snowfall** made the assault more difficult for the Macedonians and at the same time supplied the barbarians with plenty of water. Nevertheless, Alexander determined to attack the place. In fact, a certain boast by the barbarians had provoked Alexander to anger and the pursuit of glory. The barbarians had been summoned to discuss a treaty offering them safe passage to their homes upon their surrendering the rock. They, however, responded with jeers in their native tongue, inviting Alexander to look for winged soldiers who could take the rock for him, since no others would be able to. At that, Alexander announced a prize of 12 talents for the first man to the top, a second prize for the second, a third for the third, and so on, down to 300 darics for the last man up. This announcement incited the already eager Macedonians still further.

4.19　All those who had experience in scaling rocks during earlier sieges – about 300 in number – were marshalled together. They had fashioned the small iron pegs used to stake down their tents into spikes for driving into the ice where it appeared solid and into any earth that looked free of snow. To these they bound strong cords of linen and began advancing during the night towards the base of the steepest part of the rock, which was also the least guarded. They drove the spikes into the rock face wherever it showed through and into patches of ice that would not break apart, and so dragged themselves gradually upward, each at a different point along the rock. As many as 30 died in the ascent, and their bodies were never recovered for burial, since they had fallen into the snowdrifts at many different points. The survivors reached the top at dawn, and once they took the peak of the hill, they began waving flags to the Macedonian camp, just as Alexander had commanded. He then sent a herald to tell the barbarians' advance guard to stop wasting their

---

rock in Sogdiana　called the 'Rock of Ariamazes' by Curtius (7.11), who locates Alexander's use of the 'winged men' there in the summer of 328 BC. Arrian, however, mistakenly dates this episode to the beginning of spring in 327. The present extract has accordingly been placed earlier in this text.

Oxyartes　a Bactrian noble and influential leader in the revolts by the Bactrian and Sogdian peoples.

snowfall　the snow described in this episode, which must have occurred in the summer of 328 BC, is not historical. Arrian has probably conflated Ptolemy's account of this siege with a winter siege of another rock.

time and surrender themselves, for the winged men had in fact been found and were currently holding the top of the rock. And as the herald spoke he pointed to the soldiers upon the crest.

The barbarians were totally shocked by this improbable sight, and, thinking that those who held the summit were greater in number and well armed, they **gave themselves up**. They were that stricken with fear at the sight of those few Macedonians. The wives and children of many were taken, including the wife and children of Oxyartes. He had a daughter of marrying age named Roxane who was, according to those on Alexander's campaign, the most beautiful of Asian women after the wife of Darius. They say, too, that when Alexander saw her he fell in love with her, and that because of his love he was unwilling to violate her as a war-captive. Instead, he thought it appropriate to marry her. I approve rather than criticize this act of Alexander's. As for Darius' wife, who was said truly to be the most beautiful woman in Asia, Alexander either felt no desire for her or he was in command of himself, although young and at the very pinnacle of success, when people tend to commit abuses. Instead, he felt respect towards her and spared her, possessed as he was of great self-control and a desire for noble glory that suited the situation.

4.20   There is in fact a **common story** that soon after the battle between Darius and Alexander near Issus, the eunuch who guarded Darius' wife ran away and went to him. When Darius saw him, he first asked whether his children, mother and wife were alive. He was told that not only were they still alive, they also held their royal titles and received the care and attention that they had enjoyed while with Darius. At that, Darius next asked whether his wife was still faithful to him. When he learned that she was, he asked whether Alexander had violated her by force. The eunuch then swore an oath, saying, 'King, your wife is just as you left her, and Alexander is the most noble and restrained of men.' At these words Darius extended his hands towards the sky and prayed: '**Zeus Basileus**, whose domain is the direction of kingly affairs among mortals, may you now preserve for me my rule over the Persians and Medians, even as you have bestowed it upon me. But if

---

gave themselves up   according to Curtius (7.5), Alexander whipped and crucified the nobles who had held the rock, and turned over many of those who surrendered as slaves to the inhabitants of newly founded cities. If true, either Arrian or his sources notably omitted these details.

common story   versions of this story are recounted by Plutarch (*Life of Alexander* 30; *Moralia* 338 E–F) and Curtius (4.10). In those versions, the interview between Darius and the eunuch occurs later, prior to the battle at Gaugamela, after Statira had already died during childbirth.

Zeus Basileus   Arrian follows Greek tradition in identifying the Persian god Ahura Mazda with Zeus, as king (*basileus*) of the pantheon.

you think I should no longer be king of Asia, hand my rule over to no one else but Alexander!' So it is that not even enemies overlook acts of self-restraint.

Once Oxyartes heard that his children were captives and learned also about his daughter Roxane, specifically what Alexander intended for her, he plucked up courage to approach Alexander and was **held in honour** by him, as suited such a happy occasion.

> 1 What narrative elements in Arrian's account of this siege contribute to the tone of suspense? How would this tone be affected if the detail of snowfall were left out?
>
> 2 Why do you suppose some would have disapproved of this marriage?
>
> 3 Why does Arrian choose to relate the tale of Alexander's behaviour towards Statira in this context?
>
> 4 Observe Arrian's remark at that story's conclusion. What is the moral, and how does it pertain to Alexander at this point in the narrative?

Customs mixed

> In the passage below, Plutarch briefly discusses Alexander's marriage to Roxane, notably as an effort to forge a connection between the Macedonian and native peoples.

Plutarch 47   Alexander continued to model his own way of life increasingly on the native customs and to link them with the Macedonian traditions, for he thought that mixed customs and common feeling would establish behaviour founded on goodwill better than force would, once he had moved on. For this reason he also selected **30,000 boys**, and assigned many men to oversee their learning the Greek language and training in Macedonian arms. The matter of Roxane was the result of passion after he had laid eyes on the young and beautiful woman during a dance at a drinking party. But he also thought that this marriage suited the current circumstances well. The union heartened the barbarians, and they felt

---

held in honour   Oxyartes probably joined Alexander's court before Alexander married Roxane. According to Curtius (8.4), Alexander fell in love when seeing her dance in the early spring of 327 BC, months after her capture in the summer of 328.

30,000 boys   the Epigoni (literally 'the Successors'). They were to be trained as soldiers in the Macedonian tradition, a proposal that irked many of the older Macedonian soldiers, who wished to maintain a clear distinction between Macedonians and barbarians. Curtius (8.5) records that immediately after Alexander's marriage to Roxane, he ordered that these boys be gathered from all the various satrapies to serve simultaneously as hostages and soldiers. What Macedonian royal tradition does Alexander's policy recall (see p. 2)?

intense adoration for Alexander because he had shown supreme self-restraint in this situation. She was the only woman ever to conquer him with desire, and yet he would not allow himself to touch her without a legal marriage.

> • Plutarch is the only extant ancient source that proposes a reason for Alexander's marriage other than love. How does his pairing of the marriage with the creation of the Epigoni support this motive?

Hephaestion versus Craterus

Plutarch 47   Alexander observed that, of his favourite Friends, Hephaestion approved of his change of ways and joined him in it while **Craterus** stayed true to the ancestral customs. Alexander therefore began to deal with the barbarians through the former and the Greeks and Macedonians through the latter. The truth of the matter was that he liked the one better but respected the other more; he would always say that he considered Hephaestion dear to Alexander and Craterus dear to the King. For this reason, the two privately harboured considerable rancour towards one another and would often clash. Once, during the invasion of India, they even drew their swords and faced off. As friends rallied to the side of each man, Alexander rode up and started to revile Hephaestion publicly, calling him deranged and insane for failing to see that he was nothing without Alexander. He bitterly upbraided Craterus too, but in private. He then brought the two together, reconciled them, and swore an oath to Ammon and the rest of the gods that, while he truly loved these two best of all men, if he ever found them quarrelling again he would kill them both. They say that after that no harsh words were exchanged between the two – even in fun – nor any action directed by one against the other.

> 1   What does it mean that one man was dear to Alexander and the other to the King? How does this distinction contribute to Plutarch's purpose in illustrating Alexander's character?
>
> 2   Why do you suppose Alexander upbraided Hephaestion publicly, but Craterus in private?

Callisthenes, *proskynesis* and the Pages' conspiracy

> In addition to his change in attire, his marriage to Roxane and his creation of the Epigoni, Alexander also attempted to introduce the Persian tradition of performing *proskynesis* to the king, shortly before the advance into India in 327 BC.

Craterus   as we have seen, he was commander of the entire infantry on the left wing at Issus and Gaugamela (see pp. 47, 79), and actively involved in Philotas' undoing (pp. 101 and 102 note). Hephaestion has not yet played a major military role, but certainly enjoyed a close relationship with Alexander (see p. 31).

Arrian 4.10 They say that Callisthenes the Olynthian, a student of Aristotle's teachings known for his rather tactless behaviour, did not approve of this [Alexander's desire to introduce the practice of *proskynesis*]. And even I agree with Callisthenes about this. But I think those other things Callisthenes said, if true, are unreasonable: that Alexander and his deeds depended on Callisthenes and the history he was writing; that he had not come seeking glory from Alexander, but rather to glorify Alexander throughout the world; and, further still, that Alexander's share in divinity hinged not on the tales Olympias fabricated about his parentage, but on what he himself should write and publish for all humanity. And there are some who have written the following, too. When Philotas once asked Callisthenes which of the Athenians he thought most deserved honour, he responded that **Harmodius and Aristogiton** did, because they slew one of the two tyrants and dissolved the tyranny. Philotas then asked him whether a fugitive tyrannicide could find shelter anywhere in Greece, and Callisthenes replied that the fugitive would receive asylum among the Athenians at least, if nowhere else, since they had waged war for Heracles' children against **Eurystheus**, the tyrant of Greece.

There is a common story also along the following lines about how Callisthenes opposed Alexander on the matter of *proskynesis*. Alexander had arranged that the sophists and the most highly esteemed of the Persians and Medians would bring up the issue at a drinking party. Anaxarchus broached the subject by saying that

proskynesis performed most simply by lifting the right hand turned inward up to the mouth to blow a kiss, but the act could be more elaborate, including a bow or even prostration on the ground (see pp. 55, 114). Greeks employed such gestures only in worshipping deities, but people of the Near East performed the act before social superiors, most notably their rulers. Alexander, as the Great King of Persia, may have felt a need to require this gesture of all his subjects in order to maintain his right to rule in the eyes of the conquered. Many Greeks and Macedonians, however, would naturally have felt uncomfortable performing the sacred act before a mortal, and would readily suppose that Alexander – himself a Macedonian – also viewed *proskynesis* as an act of worship. All the ancient sources do in fact find divine aspirations in Alexander's request that Greeks perform this act.

Harmodius and Aristogiton they attempted to assassinate Hippias, a tyrant of Athens, in 514 BC. They managed to kill only Hipparchus, Hippias' brother, and were executed. But after Hippias was expelled four years later, the Athenians erected bronze statues of Harmodius and Aristogiton, set up an annual civic sacrifice at their tomb and provided free meals for all their descendants. The pair became a convenient symbol for the defeat of tyranny, and later popular tradition, which held that Hipparchus had been tyrant at the time, credited them with ending the tyranny themselves.

Eurystheus the Delphic oracle required Heracles' enslavement to Eurystheus for killing his family in a fit of madness, and Eurystheus continued to persecute Heracles' sons after his death. They eventually overthrew him with the support of Athens. The Athenians saw themselves as champions of democracy and, in Athenian drama, Athens is a place where asylum can be found and conflict resolved.

In the limestone relief (top), from the Treasury at Persepolis (c. 515 BC), a Median official kisses his fingertips before the Achaemenid king Darius I. The other, much older relief from the Black Obelisk found at Nimrud in northern Iraq depicts Jehu, the ruler of Israel, prostrating himself before the Assyrian king Shalmaneser III (ruled 859–824 BC). Greeks of Alexander's day termed both displays of respect proskynesis, *and customarily reserved them for the worship of deities only.*

it was far more appropriate to consider Alexander a god than either Dionysus or Heracles – not because of Alexander's great and numerous deeds, but because Dionysus was Theban and had nothing to do with Macedonians, while Heracles, an Argive, was connected to Macedonia only through Alexander's line. It would be most just, then, he argued, for the Macedonians to give their king **divine honours**, because there was absolutely no question that on his departure from humankind they would honour him as a god. How much more just, then, to reward him now while he lived rather than once he had died and could no longer profit from the honour.

4.11   After Anaxarchus spoke these and similar words, those privy to the plan approved the speech and were even ready to initiate *proskynesis*. But most of the **Macedonians** were bothered by his argument and held their silence. Callisthenes then spoke in reply: '**Anaxarchus**, I declare Alexander to be worthy of any honour befitting a mortal. But people have distinguished between **honours mortal and divine** in many different ways. We build temples, for example, erect statues and reserve sacred precincts for gods. We sacrifice to them and pour them libations; hymns, too, are composed for gods, while eulogies are intended for people. But the most important of these markers is our custom of *proskynesis*. Mortals **kiss** one another when they meet, but they practise *proskynesis* towards what is divine because, I think, the divine is set on high and may not be touched. Dances, likewise, are held for gods, and paeans are sung to them. And all these distinctions are not at all surprising, because even among the gods themselves different honours

---

divine honours they had been conferred on Greek kings prior to Alexander, but this practice was very rare and always controversial. Even kings of the later Hellenistic period received a mixture of sacred and secular honours, which at most only blurred the distinction between god and mortal.

Macedonians judging from Anaxarchus' line of argument, his audience appears to have been the Macedonians, whose pride he was appealing to in celebrating Alexander's Macedonian roots. Alexander may have had reason to hope that younger soldiers would support the practice of *proskynesis*, but his older Companions, many of whom had fought for Philip and known Alexander as a boy, would probably have been most offended.

Anaxarchus Callisthenes explicitly addresses Anaxarchus, but the speech itself is a fiction. Arrian has adapted an argument invented by one of his Hellenistic sources. The debate about the deification of mortals continued through the Hellenistic period, and this speech is packed with the sort of arguments made at that time.

honours mortal and divine the distinctions between human and divine honours are not as sharp as Callisthenes suggests. Men could be sculpted, for example, and dead heroes as well as gods had sacred precincts set aside for them. Even paeans, songs originally sung only to gods, had by Alexander's time been used to celebrate Lysander.

kiss Callisthenes is drawing a distinction between the practice of kissing the cheek of an acquaintance and the mimed kiss (*proskynesis*) offered to a divinity.

belong to each, and yes, by Zeus, the honours paid to heroes are different too, and serve to distinguish heroes from true divinity. It is unreasonable, then, to throw all this into disarray by granting mortals an immoderate status through excessive honours, and to lower the gods – insofar as mortals can, at any rate – to a disgraceful and unfitting level by honouring them in the same way as people.

'Alexander certainly would not allow some common person to adopt for himself regal honours through a show of hands or an unjust vote. Just so, the gods would all the more be right to frown on any mortals who adopted divine honours for themselves or even allowed others to grant them. Alexander is beyond measure – by reputation and in very truth – the most noble of all noble men, the most kingly of kings, and the most worthy of all generals. But **you of all people**, Anaxarchus, ought to have delivered these arguments and countered any against them, since you accompany Alexander in order to offer him wisdom and learning. It was inappropriate for you to introduce this subject in the first place. Instead you ought to have remembered that you attend and offer counsel to neither a Cambyses nor a Xerxes, but a son of Philip and descendant of Heracles. His forefathers came from Argos to Macedonia and have ruled the Macedonians not by force, but by tradition. Not even Heracles received divine honours from the Greeks while he lived, nor even after death, until the divine oracle at Delphi commanded them to honour him as a god.

'Now, if we are leaning towards barbaric opinions because this discussion is taking place in a barbarian land, I for one think you would do well to remember Greece, Alexander. You began this campaign to add Asia to Greece, and for Greece's sake. Consider, then, your return. Will you really force the Greeks, a most free people, into *proskynesis*? Or do you plan to let the Greeks be and to impose this dishonour on the Macedonians alone? Or will you yourself put this issue to rest once and for all, by receiving mortal honours in the Greek way from Greeks and Macedonians, and in the barbaric way from barbarians? They say that Cyrus son of Cambyses was the first mortal to receive *proskynesis*, and that afterwards the base practice persisted among Persians and Medians. If that is true, you should remember also that it was the **Scythians**, poor men but men in charge of themselves, who punished that Cyrus. Other Scythians in turn chastened Darius. Athenians and

---

you of all people Callisthenes names Anaxarchus again here. While Alexander clearly supported the adoption of *proskynesis* and arranged for its discussion here among the Macedonian generals, Callisthenes stresses Anaxarchus' moral obligation as a philosopher attending the king to check this excess.

Scythians Cyrus the Great, founder of the Persian Empire, was killed in battle in a defeat by the Scythians in 530 BC. Darius I led a failed campaign against the Scythians in 314–313.

Lacedaemonians humbled Xerxes. **Artaxerxes** was humbled by the Ten Thousand of Clearchus and Xenophon. And today's Darius has been brought low by an Alexander who himself – like those other victors – received no *proskynesis*.'

---

1 What does Arrian imply by having Philotas in particular ask such questions of Callisthenes (**4.10**)?

2 Carefully consider Anaxarchus' argument for Alexander's divinity. According to his reasoning, from what source is divinity derived?

3 Who is Callisthenes' real audience (**4.11**)? Why does he name Anaxarchus as his addressee instead?

4 Callisthenes names Alexander's ancestor Heracles and traces the hero's line from Argos to Macedonia. What specific part of Anaxarchus' argument is Callisthenes attempting to counter by pointing to this ancestry?

5 Callisthenes presents three alternatives from which Alexander must choose on his return from Asia. Which of the three would most offend the guests at this drinking party?

6 What does Callisthenes imply is the cause of the Persian defeats he cites? Does the argument convince you?

Arrian 4.12

Callisthenes upset Alexander greatly by such arguments, but Callisthenes had voiced the sentiments of the Macedonians, and Alexander knew it. He therefore sent word that from then on the Macedonians should forget about *proskynesis*.

But when silence followed this debate, the **eldest of the Persians** rose and performed *proskynesis*, one after the other, and when **Leonnatus**, a Companion, thought one of the Persians had performed it poorly, he ridiculed the man for his base demeanour. Alexander grew angry with him then, though they were later once again on good terms. There is another story, recorded as follows. Alexander passed around a golden drinking bowl that went first to those who had agreed with him on the issue of *proskynesis*. The first to drink from the bowl stood up, performed *proskynesis*, and received a **kiss** from Alexander, and everyone in turn

---

Artaxerxes in 401 BC Cyrus the Younger launched his campaign to dethrone Artaxerxes. Cyrus' allied force of Greek mercenaries (the Ten Thousand) was victorious in the battle, but Cyrus himself was killed and the campaign ended in failure. When Clearchus and the other Greek officers were captured and executed, Xenophon and the other newly elected commanders escaped through hostile territory to the Black Sea.

eldest of the Persians Alexander's original plan may have been to have the discussion of *proskynesis* followed by its performance by the Persians and then the Greeks and Macedonians. If this is true, the Persians now follow through with the plan even though the discussion did not go as Alexander had hoped.

Leonnatus not only a Companion, but also one of Alexander's Bodyguards.

kiss a kiss was given by Persian kings as a reward for outstanding service, and indicated status as a Kinsman. Not to receive the kiss when sought or expected was a dishonour in the eyes of the Persians.

began following suit. But when the toast came to Callisthenes, he stood up, drank from the bowl, and then – without performing *proskynesis* – stepped forward ready to kiss Alexander. Alexander happened to be talking with Hephaestion at the moment, and so did not notice whether Callisthenes had actually performed *proskynesis*. But then the Companion Demetrius, son of Pythonax, pointed out that Callisthenes was trying to kiss Alexander without performing *proskynesis*. As a result, Alexander refused to let Callisthenes kiss him, to which Callisthenes replied, 'And so I go away with one kiss fewer.'

In these cases, I do not at all condone Alexander's **momentary offences**, nor Callisthenes' churlishness. I believe that everyone should be happy to behave appropriately before a king and to magnify the king's affairs as much as possible, especially those who have determined it worth while to attend the king in the first place. I therefore think it was reasonable for Alexander to feel hatred towards Callisthenes, for his indiscretion and senseless lack of restraint. These traits, I think, made Callisthenes' slanderers so readily believed when they claimed that Callisthenes was complicit in that plot the Pages hatched against Alexander, and, as some alleged, that Callisthenes even incited them to the conspiracy. The events surrounding this conspiracy occurred as follows.

---

1   What does Alexander hope to achieve by rewarding *proskynesis* with the kiss, a distinctly Persian reward?

2   The performance of *proskynesis* does not appear to have been compulsory. It was required only for the reward of a kiss. Why would Callisthenes, who surely knew this, have sought a kiss anyway?

3   What does the behaviour of Demetrius reveal about tensions in Alexander's court?

Arrian 4.13   There was the tradition already in Philip's day that once the sons of Macedonian nobles reached adolescence, they were **enrolled** in the service of the king, and it was their responsibility to minister to the daily needs of his person and to guard him as he slept. Whenever the king rode out, they would take the horses from the

---

momentary offences Arrian here criticizes Alexander's acts, but focuses most of his attention upon Callisthenes' character. Arrian himself was in the service of the Roman Empire (see p. 5), so that his opinion must reflect his own notions about proper behaviour before the Roman *princeps*. Roman emperors such as Hadrian permitted different subject peoples to behave in different ways, e.g. to perform sacrifices in his honour and to regard him as a divinity even during his lifetime. Alexander's quest for divinity would not have offended Arrian as much as the Greeks contemporary with Alexander.

enrolled formal (and mandatory) enrolment as Pages of sons of important noblemen was probably an innovation of Philip's. Pages may have served the Macedonian kings on a voluntary basis for a long time. They enrolled at 14 and served until manhood, perhaps 18 to 20 years of age. This batch of Pages would have arrived from Macedonia in 331 BC.

grooms, lead them out, and put the king on his mount in the **Persian style**. They also enjoyed the honour of being the king's comrades in the hunt. Hermolaus son of Sopolis was one of these Pages. He was known for his philosophical disposition and for accompanying Callisthenes for this reason. The following story about Hermolaus is well known. When Alexander was charged by a wild boar during a hunt, Hermolaus struck it before Alexander could, and the boar died from the blow. Alexander was livid at Hermolaus for stealing this opportunity from him, and in his rage ordered that he be **whipped** while the rest of the Pages looked on. And he stripped Hermolaus of his horse as well.

Hermolaus was deeply distressed at this abuse and told his lover Sostratus son of Amyntus, a fellow Page of his own age, that life would mean nothing to him if he failed to take vengeance on Alexander for the abuse. Sostratus, who loved him, was easily persuaded to help with the deed, and they in turn persuaded Antipater, son of the Asclepiodorus who had been satrap of Syria, Epimenes son of Arseus, Anticles son of Theocritus and Philotas son of Carsis the Thracian. They decided that the next time it was Antipater's turn for the nightly guard duty, they would attack Alexander as he slept and kill him.

As it turned out, however, Alexander continued drinking that night until dawn. Some say this was by chance, but Aristobulus wrote the following. A Syrian woman used to follow Alexander around and enter into a state of divine possession. At first Alexander and his men would ridicule her, but when she appeared to speak only the truth during her ravings, Alexander stopped ignoring her. He granted her access to his presence both day and night, and by this time she often stood by him as he slept. She was now in a state of divine possession when Alexander happened on her after his night's drinking. She begged him to go back and keep on drinking the whole night through, and because Alexander considered this utterance divine, he did so. In this way the Pages' plan was foiled.

On the following day, one of the conspirators, Epimenes son of Arseus, revealed the plot to his lover Charicles son of Menander. Charicles told Eurylochus brother of Epimenes, and he went to Alexander's tent and reported the whole affair to the Bodyguard **Ptolemy** son of Lagus. Ptolemy told Alexander, and Alexander called

---

Persian style   the term 'Persian' here is not pejorative. The phrase was commonly used in the fourth century BC for this aided manner of mounting, and the assistance was an honour paid to the Macedonian kings.

whipped   according to Curtius (8.6), only the Macedonian king could order such corporal punishment.

Ptolemy   he and Leonnatus both learned of the conspiracy together, according to Curtius (8.6). If Arrian's source here is Ptolemy, then Ptolemy may have intentionally appropriated for himself the credit for reporting the conspiracy.

for the arrest of all whom Eurylochus had named. These, when **tortured**, gave up details of the plot and named others of the conspirators also.

4.14 Aristobulus records that **Callisthenes** actually incited the Pages towards the rash act, and Ptolemy says the same, but most report that because of Alexander's deep-seated hate for Callisthenes and because Hermolaus was especially close to the philosopher, it was easy for Alexander to believe the worst about Callisthenes. Some have written also that when Hermolaus was brought before the Macedonians he confessed to the conspiracy, because, as he said, it was no longer possible for a free man to endure Alexander's offences. Hermolaus even proceeded to list them all: the unjust death of Philotas, the illegal execution of his father Parmenion and of the others killed then, how Cleitus met his end amid drunkenness, the Median clothes Alexander wore, the plans to introduce *proskynesis* which he had not yet given up, and the way he drank and slept. Hermolaus declared that he would no longer endure these things and that he wished to liberate both himself and the rest of the Macedonians.

He and the others arrested with him were **stoned to death** by those Macedonians present. According to Aristobulus, Callisthenes was bound with fetters, continually dragged around with the army, and ultimately died from illness. But Ptolemy son of Lagus records that he was tortured and then crucified. So even those who offer a completely faithful narrative and who were actually with Alexander at the time have disagreed about events that were notorious and no secret to them. Others have written many other sorts of things about this affair, but let what is written here be enough for me.

---

tortured the torture of noble youths would have occurred after conviction. There must have been an initial trial within the court to confirm guilt, after which torture was used to obtain more evidence and the names of others involved. Lastly, there was a formal, public accusation by the king and the final response of the guilty before the assembled Macedonian army.

Callisthenes according to Arrian here, both Ptolemy and Aristobulus held Callisthenes responsible for encouraging the conspiracy. Arrian himself disagrees, however, and none of the extant sources believes in Callisthenes' involvement. Plutarch (55) in fact records that even under torture the Pages refused to name Callisthenes, and describes a letter written by Alexander that supports Callisthenes' innocence.

stoned to death a regular form of execution among the Macedonians. Those who took part in the stoning were those present at the public announcement of the conspirators' guilt. Note the very different fate of Callisthenes, strong evidence that he could not be implicated directly in the conspiracy. The version recorded by Alexander's chamberlain Chares (Plutarch 55) agrees with Aristobulus' version of Callisthenes' death, specifically that he was being held for trial back in Greece by the Corinthian League.

1 Arrian uses his previous discussion of Callisthenes' character (**4.12**) to introduce his account of the Pages' conspiracy, even though he does not appear to believe that Callisthenes was involved. How does introducing the conspiracy in this way affect the reader's perception of Callisthenes?

2 Given what you have learned about the Macedonian army and Alexander's own young life, how serious a punishment is the taking of a Page's horse (**4.13**)?

3 What kinds of surprises would this fresh batch of Macedonian Pages have found on joining the campaign after growing up in Macedonia?

4 Arrian presents Alexander's punishment of Hermolaus as the reason for the assassination plot. Do you think this alone was sufficient motivation for all six Pages?

5 The crucifixion reported by Ptolemy (**4.14**) is particularly remarkable. To this point no Greek had suffered this cruel manner of execution, normally reserved for enemies. Which of the two versions, Ptolemy's or Aristobulus', appears to defend Alexander's actions more? To what extent does the defence of Alexander qualify that source's dependability?

The Rock of Aornus

With some level of control finally established in Sogdiana and Bactria, Alexander advanced east towards India (modern Pakistan) in 327–326 BC. Along the way local populations found refuge on the nearby Mount Aornus. Alexander was by now used to such practices, as at the Rock of Sogdiana, but this mountain offered him an opportunity to surpass his ancestor Heracles.

Arrian 4.28   All the barbarians abandoned their cities *en masse* and fled to a place in that region called the Rock of Aornus. This rock is massive, and there is a common story that **Heracles** son of Zeus failed to capture it. Now, I am not able to believe without question that Heracles – the Theban one, the Tyrian one or the Egyptian one – ever reached the Indians. I tend to think he did not, since people will magnify the difficulty of all that is arduous to the point of claiming that things would have

---

Heracles   no Mediterranean deity previously identified with Heracles was supposed to have reached the Indians. Heracles does make appearances in myths treating Spain and the foundation of Rome, and these reflect his association with the spread of Greek culture as a civilizing force. Greeks were already accustomed to calling other foreign deities by the name of their familiar Theban Heracles, as Arrian mentions here; the 'Tyrian' or 'Phoenician' Heracles was the god Melcarth at Tyre (see p. 60), while the 'Egyptian' Heracles was the god Shu. In the present case, the identification of a figure from local legend with Heracles provides Alexander the opportunity symbolically to surpass his heroic ancestor.

The Rock of Aornus is generally identified with this mountain, Pir-Sar, next to the Indus River in modern Pakistan. It towers 1,500 metres (5,000 feet) above the river below it.

been impossible even for Heracles. I believe that is the case with this rock, that Heracles is included as a boast for the tale. They say the rock's circumference is as many as 200 stades [37 km/23 miles], its height where it is flattest is 11 stades [2,000 metres/6,600 feet], and the only way up is hand-hewn and difficult. They say too that on the rock's peak water flows abundant and pure from a perennial spring, and that there is wood and good arable land, enough even for 1,000 men to work. When Alexander heard that, a longing seized him to take this mountain, too, especially because of the story told of Heracles …

After arriving at the city of Embolima, founded near the rock of Aornus, Alexander left Craterus and part of the army behind with orders to gather as much food as possible into the city and anything else necessary for a long stay. Alexander hoped that the Macedonians could use Embolima as a base of operations and by a lengthy siege wear down those holding the rock, if it could not be taken by direct assault. Alexander took the archers, the Agrianians and the battalion of Coenus, as well as the most nimble and best-armed men from the rest of the phalanx, as many as 200 of the Companion Cavalry and 100 mounted archers. He then advanced towards the rock. On the first day he made camp where he thought fit, and on the next he advanced a little closer to the rock and made camp again.

4.29   At that time, some men from the surrounding area came to Alexander. They turned themselves over and said they would lead him to that part of the rock most suited for assault, from where it would be easy to take the place. Alexander sent **Ptolemy son of Lagus**, who was a Bodyguard and leader of the Agrianians, along with all the light troops, including those selected from the Hypaspists. He ordered Ptolemy to seize the position, to hold it with a strong garrison, and then to signal to him once it was in his possession. Ptolemy made the rugged and difficult journey and gained possession of the place by surprise. He fortified it with an encircling palisade and trench, and sent a signal-fire up from the mountain where Alexander could see it. The blaze was spotted immediately, and Alexander led his army forward the next day; but when the barbarians began resisting he got no farther, thanks to the rough terrain. When the barbarians recognized that Alexander's assault was futile, they turned and attacked Ptolemy's men. The fighting between the barbarians and the Macedonians was ferocious; the Indians strove eagerly to tear apart the palisade, while Ptolemy struggled to protect the position. The barbarians sustained the worst damage in the skirmish and withdrew as night was coming on.

Alexander chose one of the Indian deserters who was both trustworthy and knew the area, and sent him to Ptolemy by night, carrying a **letter** with orders that, when Alexander himself attacked the rock, Ptolemy should attack the barbarians below the mountain and not be satisfied with holding his position under garrison. That way, the Indians would be assaulted from both directions and fighting on two fronts. At first light Alexander set out from the camp and led the army towards that approach which Ptolemy had taken by surprise. He judged that if he could force his way in there and combine his men with Ptolemy's his task would no longer be difficult, and that is precisely what happened. Up until midday the fighting was ferocious between the Indians and the Macedonians; the latter tried to force their way up, while the former shot missiles at those ascending. But when the Macedonians did not immediately make it up, more and more of them kept coming, and those who had previously been fighting rested. This went on until the afternoon, when they managed with difficulty to take the approach and combine forces with Ptolemy. From there the army, now together and whole, once again advanced against the rock. This assault, however, was still unsuccessful at the end of the day.

At dawn Alexander ordered his soldiers to cut 100 stakes each. Once these had been cut, he himself began piling them up, starting from the crest of the hill where

---

Ptolemy son of Lagus   one of Arrian's primary sources. Arrian is here relying on Ptolemy's self-promoting history for this account. The other extant sources do not mention Ptolemy by name in their accounts of this episode.

letter   this letter suggests that Alexander originally did not intend Ptolemy to attack from his position. Why do you suppose Alexander wanted the position held?

they had made camp, and building towards the rock in a great mound. He thought that arrows, as well as missiles shot from the **war engines**, could reach the front lines of the enemy from this mound. And so they continued to build it, each and every man contributing to the job, while Alexander himself stood at hand with a watchful eye, praising those who made spirited progress, but reprimanding anyone slow to get the work started.

4.30   During the very first day the army built a mound about 1 stade [185 metres/600 feet] long. On the next the slingers began shooting at the Indians from this structure, while missiles shot from the war engines repulsed the Indian charges against the men constructing the mound. This construction continued for three days without cease, and on the fourth a few of the Macedonians forcibly occupied a small hillock the same height as the rock itself. Alexander, far from idle, then extended the mound forward, hoping to join that construction to the hillock those few men were holding for him.

The Indians had already been shocked by the unspeakable bravery of those Macedonians who had forced their way onto the hillock, and when they could now see the connecting mound, they ceased fighting and sent heralds saying that they wished to turn the rock over to Alexander, if terms could be agreed upon. Their plan was, however, to spend the day discussing the terms, only in fact to scatter one and all to their respective homes during the night. When Alexander learned this he permitted them time to withdraw and to remove the garrison that ringed the whole area, but in fact waited only till they had begun their withdrawal. At that moment he took nearly 700 of the Bodyguards and Hypaspists below the abandoned portion of the rock and scaled it. Alexander went first, and the Macedonians made the ascent in succession, pulling one another up as they climbed. When the signal was given, these men turned against the retreating barbarians and slaughtered many of them as they fled. Others threw themselves down from the cliffs in a panicked retreat and died.

The rock that had been unattainable for Heracles now belonged to Alexander. He made sacrifice on it and garrisoned it, appointing **Sisicottus** to oversee this

---

war engines   because missiles could be shot well over 300 metres (980 feet) by torsion catapults at this time, Alexander's men must have been filling a ravine significantly wider than that. The stakes were perhaps used in the framework for the mound. The army probably spent several days cutting timber and gathering other materials before beginning the actual construction. The length of time taken seems to be confirmed by a fragment of Alexander's chamberlain Chares (preserved in Athenaeus, *The Learned Banquet* 3.97), who recorded in his *Histories of Alexander* that with spring coming on, snow was preserved in pits and covered with branches so that there would be drinking water for the men labouring to build the mound.

Sisicottus   according to Curtius (8.11), he was given control over the region around the Rock of Aornus too.

garrison. Sisicottus had long ago deserted the Indians for Bessus at Bactra, but once Alexander controlled the Bactrian region, Sisicottus joined him and proved particularly faithful.

---

1   In what other instances has Alexander been spurred to some action by local legend?

2   What does the phrase 'best-armed men' (**4.28**) indicate about the state of Alexander's phalanx?

3   How dependent do you imagine Alexander's success was on native informants such as this letter-bearer?

4   Arrian was probably drawing on Ptolemy's account as a source for the beginning of this assault (**4.29**). At what point in the narrative might he have switched to Aristobulus? Explain your reasoning.

5   How does Arrian justify the deception and slaughter by Alexander here?

Rivalling Dionysus

After relating the proceding account of Alexander's rivalry with the hero Heracles, Arrian next shares a tale that features Alexander's emulation of a god.

Arrian 5.1   They say that there was a city called **Nysa** in the land Alexander reached between the Cophen and Indus rivers, and that **Dionysus** founded it when he subdued the Indians – whoever this Dionysus was, and whenever and from wherever he led his invasion against them. I myself cannot determine whether it was from Thebes or from Lydian Tmolus that Dionysus set out with his army against the Indians because, while he attacked so many warlike peoples then unknown to the Greeks, he subdued none of them by force except the Indians. But it is best not to examine

---

Nysa   Arrian remarkably breaks his historical narrative to introduce his fifth book with a focus on this city, immediately before Alexander's crossing of the Indus River. India was famous in the Mediterranean for its exotica, and the focus on the fantastical here may be meant to introduce a fanciful element immediately prior to Alexander's entrance into a more exotic realm. Before Alexander's day, any trade between Greeks and Indians was managed by intermediaries. India was certainly a passion for Arrian, who also wrote the *Indica*, a description of the region based primarily on the writings of Alexander's admiral Nearchus. According to Plutarch (58) and Curtius (8.10) the Nysaeans resisted for a time before surrendering to Alexander.

Dionysus   Alexander may have viewed Dionysus as another of his ancestors. Some legends held that Dionysus was the father of Deianira, the mother of Heracles' son Hyllus. The Macedonian kings traced their lineage through Hyllus to Heracles. While according to legend Dionysus did set out from Lydia and conquered the eastern lands, even as far as Bactria (cf. Euripides, *Bacchae* 15), no extant source connects the god with India before the time of Alexander. This detail was probably developed during the campaign.

too strictly those age-old tales about the divine, since what seems unbelievable can appear almost credible once a divine element is added to the tale.

When Alexander came to Nysa, the Nysaeans sent him their most powerful citizen, Acuphis by name, and 30 of their most respected elders to ask Alexander to leave the city to the god. These men entered Alexander's tent and found him sitting down, still covered in dust from the march and in full armour, with helmet on and spear in hand. Astounded at the sight, they fell to the ground and remained there in silence for a long time. But when Alexander raised them up and ordered them to take courage, Acuphis began to speak: 'King, the Nysaeans ask that you leave them free to rule themselves, out of respect for Dionysus; for when Dionysus subdued the race of Indians and was returning to the Greek sea, he took his soldiers who were no longer fit for service – his own **bacchants**, in fact – and founded this city with them as a memorial of his wandering and his victory for future generations, just as you yourself founded one Alexandria at Mount Caucasus, another in the land of the Egyptians, and the **many others** you have already founded and will found in the future, evidence of deeds more numerous than Dionysus' own. Dionysus named this city after his nurse Nysa, and he named the land Nysaea. Dionysus named the mountain standing near the city **Merus**, because according to the myth he grew within the thigh (*mēros*) of Zeus. Ever since then, we have lived free in Nysa, ruled ourselves, and governed it in good order. And let this be proof to you that Dionysus founded this city: while ivy grows nowhere else in the land of the Indians, it grows here with us.'

5.2 Alexander was pleased indeed to hear all these things. He wanted the tales about Dionysus' wanderings and the founding of Nysa to be true, because that would mean he himself had already come as far as Dionysus and would surely go farther than he had. Furthermore, Alexander thought the Macedonians would consider rivalry with the exploits of Dionysus a most attractive reason for labouring onward.

---

bacchants   the male attendants of Dionysus, also named Bacchus.

many others   there is no sure count of the number of cities founded by Alexander, though there were indeed many. Alexander founded (or renamed) a great many cities, at least 11, as Alexandria, after himself. Two of these – Al-Iskandariya, Egypt (familiar still to Westerners as Alexandria) and Kandahar, Afghanistan – still bear the traces of their original names.

Merus   Dionysus was the son of Zeus and the mortal Semele. Her family doubted that she carried Zeus' child, and so she demanded to see Zeus in his true form. The request was granted and the experience incinerated her, but Zeus rescued the baby Dionysus and sewed him into his own thigh until he reached term. When Dionysus later returned to Thebes, he punished the populace for doubting his divinity, as described in Euripides' tragedy *Bacchae*. Deriving names in this way is a common Greek habit, indulged in also by Greek historians and ethnographers.

Alexander granted freedom and autonomy to the inhabitants of Nysa, and when he learned about their laws and that their government was composed of the best people, he praised these practices. He also demanded that they send 300 of their cavalry to join him, along with the 100 best from the 300 outstanding members of their governing body. He ordered Acuphis to choose these, and appointed him as hyparch over the Nysaean region. It is said that when Acuphis heard the orders he smiled; when Alexander asked why, Acuphis replied, 'Just how, King, could a single city stripped of 100 good men still be governed well? If you care about the Nysaeans, take the 300 cavalry, and even more if you wish, but instead of the 100 best men, take twice as many worthless ones. That way, when you return here again you will see the city in the same fine condition.' Alexander thought these words wise and was persuaded. He ordered the cavalry sent to him, but not the 100 chosen men, nor even any others in their place. He did demand, however, that Acuphis send his son and his daughter's son to join him.

A longing gripped Alexander to see the spot where the Nysaeans boasted there was evidence of Dionysus' presence. According to the story, Alexander went to Mount Merus with the Companion Cavalry and the infantry division, and found the mountain abounding in ivy and laurel. He found groves of every sort, and saw that it was shady and good for hunting all types of game. The Macedonians enjoyed seeing ivy after so long (there is no ivy in the land of the Indians, not even where they have vines), and they lost no time making crowns, which they wore as they sang hymns to Dionysus and invoked the names of the god. Alexander sacrificed to Dionysus here and feasted in the company of his Companions. Some even record (if anyone actually finds these things credible) that many of those present and crowned with ivy – Macedonians of no small reputation – were possessed by Dionysus amid invocations to the god, honoured him with ritual cries and even entered a **Bacchic frenzy**.

Bacchic frenzy we have already read about descriptions of Olympias' participation in such rites (see p. 10), and you will recall that events at Maracanda were attributed by some to Dionysus' ability to induce madness (see pp. 105–7). Arrian here betrays his discomfort at the manner of worship by these 'Macedonians of no small reputation', but in this context, Alexander's march east is being implicitly compared to Dionysus' mythical westward march of cultural and religious conquest from Asia to Greece.

1   Based on your reading of this episode, why might the people of Nysa and Alexander both have wished to establish Nysa as the end-point for Dionysus' eastern conquest?

2   Who are the various figures to whom Alexander has been compared (by himself or by others) thus far? Do you think that this practice of offering comparisons puts Alexander in a good light, or does it suggest that he is overreaching himself?

3   How does Acuphis' behaviour towards Alexander contribute to his depiction of the relationship between Alexander and Dionysus (5.1)?

4   How do the rights given to Nysa by Alexander coincide with Acuphis' original request of him?

5   Why would Alexander have required Acuphis' son and grandson to join the expedition?

6   What are Alexander's concerns about the Macedonians in this episode? How might the revelry permitted on Mount Merus have helped to address these concerns?

Battle with Porus

Alexander continued east and crossed the Indus River. When he reached the Hydaspes, the army of the Indian king Porus was waiting for him on the other side. 'Porus' was not strictly a name, but the title of the King of Paurava, the region between the rivers Hydaspes and Acesines. This king had not been subject to Darius; Alexander is by this point invading territory beyond the former Persian Empire. The coming battle with Porus would be the last of Alexander's major battles in his campaign eastward.

Arrian 5.9   Alexander made camp on the bank of the **Hydaspes**. Porus was spotted along the opposite bank with all his army and his troop of elephants; he was holding this position across from Alexander's camp intentionally, to guard against his crossing, but he sent garrisons, each with a commander, to other parts of the river that were fairly easy to cross, to deny the Macedonians the opportunity to cross at those points as well. When Alexander saw this, he decided to move his army to multiple locations. His intent was to keep Porus in a state of uncertainty, and he actually separated his army into many divisions for this purpose. Some he himself led off here and there through the countryside, pillaging enemy lands and noting where the river seemed easiest to cross. Others he assigned to other commanders, and he kept them moving to different locations as well. Grain was brought into the camp from everywhere in the territory on Alexander's side of the Hydaspes so

---

Hydaspes   while Arrian offers such geographical features as a bend in the river and a pair of islands (see plan on p. 134), annual flooding regularly causes islands to disappear and re-emerge. Furthermore, the Hydaspes itself (modern Jhelum) has shifted west since antiquity, so that the precise location of the conflict is unknown.

that it would be clear to Porus that Alexander intended to continue to occupy the bank until the river's water receded during the winter and offered a crossing then.

Alexander's boats kept sailing up and down the river; skins were filled with hay; and the bank appeared to be swarming, crowded everywhere with cavalry and infantry. All this gave Porus no rest. He could not even decide what spot was most important to protect so that he could then prepare to defend that place above all others. This was also because all the Indian rivers were then flowing with deep, turbulent waters and a swift current, for it was **that time of year** when the sun begins to lower its arc, just after the summer solstice. During that season, water falls on India in great quantity from the sky, and the snows from the Caucasus, where most of the rivers' sources are, have melted and raised the rivers to a high level. During the winter, however, the rivers recede, turning small and clear and crossable at some points, except for the Indus and Ganges, and perhaps also some other. But the Hydaspes, at least, does become fordable then.

5.10　　Alexander therefore declared publicly that he would remain on the bank throughout the summer if he was prevented from fording the river at that time. As he waited, however, he was no less watchful, for he still hoped to seize his crossing swiftly and unnoticed. Now, Alexander knew he could not cross where Porus was camped on the bank of the Hydaspes, since that spot was packed with elephants and because there was a great army there – well deployed and well armed – intent on attacking them as they emerged from the river. Alexander believed that his horses would refuse to cross to that point on the opposite bank. The elephants there would attack first and terrify them with their unfamiliar aspect and their noisy trumpeting, so that the horses would not even stay put on the **stuffed skins** during the crossing, but lose their wits and jump into the water at the sight of the elephants ahead. And so Alexander meant to steal his crossing by doing the following.

He began leading most of his cavalry up and down the bank during the night. In doing so, he kept raising shouts and war cries to **Enyalius**, and making every other kind of clamour characteristic of soldiers preparing to make a crossing. In response Porus kept deploying his elephants in counter-movements in the direction of the shouting. Alexander therefore began making such movements and counter-movements regular practice each night, and after a long time had passed with nightly shouts and war cries but nothing else, Porus stopped changing his

---

that time of year　the battle probably took place in May, despite Arrian's reference to the solstice here. The solstice marks the peak of the monsoon, which lasts until October, but the spring rains would already have raised the river's waters by late spring. They would not recede again until winter.

stuffed skins　skins stuffed with hay served as makeshift flotation devices for transport over water. Alexander had previously filled leather with hay for the same purpose when crossing the Danube (Arrian 1.3).

Enyalius　the war god.

position in response to Alexander's cavalry movements. Because he saw that his fears of attack were unrealized, he instead began to remain at his encampment, and to station scouts at many points along the bank. Once Alexander had managed to persuade Porus to ignore his nightly operations, he came up with a plan along the following lines.

5.11   A stretch of land densely packed with trees of every sort extended from the bank of the Hydaspes where the river turned abruptly. Across from this was a wooded island that was deserted and without trails. Alexander recognized that both the headland and the island were wooded places capable of concealing an attempt to cross, and so he decided to lead his army over at that point. This was about **150 stades** [28 km/17.5 miles] from his main camp, and he stationed garrisons all along the bank, close enough together for them to see one another and to hear easily any order passed on from either direction. For many nights, then, the army continued shouting and burning fires at all points.

Once Alexander had decided to try this approach, he openly began preparing for the crossing in the camp itself. He left Craterus in charge there with his **hipparchy**, the cavalries of Arachotia and Parapamisadae, the battalions of Alcetus and Polyperchon from the phalanx of the Macedonians, the district chiefs of the region's Indians, and the 5,000 men with them. Craterus had orders not to cross the river until he either received report that Porus was leading his entire force against Alexander or until he learned that Porus was fleeing and that the Macedonians were victorious. 'If Porus marches only a portion of his army against me, leaving another portion behind at his camp with some elephants, you must remain in place. If, however, Porus marches against me with all his elephants, but leaves behind at camp any portion of the rest of his army, you must cross on the double, since only his elephants,' he said, 'prevent our horses from landing; the rest of the army poses no problem.'

5.12   These were Alexander's orders to Craterus. Between the island and the main camp where Craterus had been left in charge, **Meleager, Attalus and Gorgias** were stationed with the mercenary cavalry and infantry. They were commanded to divide their men and cross over in separate units as soon as they saw the Indians in the thick of battle.

---

150 stades   it is not clear from Arrian in what direction from the camp this crossing lay, but Curtius (8.13) suggests that it may have been upstream.

hipparchy   any of several Companion Cavalry divisions created after the execution of the prominent commander Philotas (and his father Parmenion) in 330.

Meleager, Attalus and Gorgias   this assignment is a notable change. These three commanders were normally in charge of battalions in the Macedonian infantry phalanx. Although they probably followed Alexander's orders to cross, Arrian does not mention their crossing in his account of the battle.

Alexander took with him the Companion *Agēma*, the hipparchies of Hephaestion, of Perdiccas and of Demetrius, the cavalries of the Bactrians and the Sogdianians, the Scythian horse, the Dahae's mounted archers, the phalanx's Hypaspists and its battalions under **Cleitus** and Coenus, the archers and the Agrianians. These he led unobserved, a good distance back from the bank, so that he might take them unseen towards the island and headland where he had decided to make the crossing. The skins, which had already been brought there long before, were stuffed by night with hay and sewn shut with care. A torrential rain fell that night, so that Alexander's preparations and his attempt to cross were obscured; the thunder and rain drowned out both the clanging of armour and the shouting of commands. Most of the boats had been carried in pieces to the crossing-point, then surreptitiously reassembled and stashed in the wood. The 30-oared ships, too, were among these. By dawn the wind and rain had ceased, and the whole cavalry boarded the skins, with all the infantry the boats could hold. These were crossing along the island so that Porus' scouts would not see them until they had passed the island and were only a short distance from the shore.

---

1   What are the differences between this situation and those of the battles at the Granicus and Issus, where Alexander did charge directly across rivers to attack the enemy (pp. 37 and 50)?

2   Before the battle of Gaugamela Alexander rejected the idea of a night attack and insisted that he would not steal his victory. Do his deceptive manoeuvres against Porus count as stealing a victory? Why or why not?

Arrian 5.13 Alexander boarded a 30-oared ship and began crossing. He was accompanied by the Bodyguards Ptolemy, Perdiccas and Lysimachus, by the Companion Seleucus, who later became king, and by half the Hypaspists. Further 30-oared ships carried the other Hypaspists. Once the army passed the island, their assault on the bank was visible to the scouts, who spotted them and rode to Porus as swiftly as their horses could gallop.

Alexander was the first to step from his boat onto the bank. He took the men from the other 30-oared ships and began deploying the members of the cavalry, which he had ordered to disembark first. He then advanced with them in formation, but in his ignorance of the area he had unwittingly disembarked not onto firm ground, but onto another island. It too was large, and its size was primarily what had deceived him, that and the fact that it was cut off from the mainland by only

---

Agēma   generally, a division or corps of an army, but in the Macedonian army it often refers, as here, to a special unit of the Companion Cavalry.

Cleitus   Macedonian commander called 'Cleitus the White', to distinguish him from 'Cleitus the Black', who saved Alexander's life at the Granicus and was later killed by the king.

a little stream from the river. But the torrential rain that had lasted most of the night had raised the water level, and Alexander's cavalry were not able to locate the **way across**. There was fear that Alexander would have to prepare for this next crossing as elaborately as for the first, and even when they eventually found the ford, Alexander could scarcely lead them over. Where it was deepest, the water was above the infantry's chests, and the horses could keep only their heads above the river as they crossed. But once this stream, too, had been forded, Alexander marshalled the Companion *Agema* and the best soldiers of the other hipparchies to the right **wing** [. . .] and positioned the mounted archers in front of the whole cavalry. Behind the cavalry he placed the first of the infantry, the Royal Hypaspists that Seleucus commanded. Next to them he located the **Royal** *Agema*, and to their left the rest of the Hypaspists according to the individual commands that fell to each at that time. He positioned the archers, the Agrianians and the javelin-men on either wing of the phalanx.

5.14   After deploying the army in this formation, Alexander ordered the infantry – just short of 6,000 – to follow him at a walk and in good order. But since he thought his side was strongest in horse, he himself led the cavalry – around 5,000 – ahead at full speed. He ordered the commander Tauron to lead his archers forward at full speed as well, for he had decided that if Porus met him with his whole force, he would either subdue them with little trouble by a cavalry charge or hold them off until the infantry joined him in the fighting. Furthermore, if the Indians panicked and fled in the face of his crossing's uncommon daring, Alexander would not be far behind them in their flight, and more slaughter during that retreat would mean less fighting later.

According to Aristobulus, **Porus' son** reached Alexander with 60 **chariots** before he had managed the second crossing from the small island. He could have thwarted Alexander's crossing, in fact, which was difficult even without opposition, if only the Indians had leapt down from their chariots and attacked the first of the men

---

way across   Curtius does not mention this second crossing at all. Plutarch (60), on the other hand, refers to a letter that represents Arrian's stream as the major channel of the river. Plutarch's account of this episode is highly sensational, however, including the deaths of crossing Macedonians by bolts of lightning in the storm, which Plutarch records only began during the crossing.

wing [. . .]   there appears to be a lacuna (gap in the manuscript) here in Arrian's text, where he would have described the left of the cavalry.

Royal *Agema*   apparently a group of the Hypaspists distinct from the Royal Hypaspist Guard and the Hypaspists proper.

Porus' son   according to Curtius (8.14), the leader of this force was Hages, a brother of Porus.

chariots   Curtius (8.14) describes the Indian war chariots in some detail. Each of these chariots typically held six soldiers, making them impractical to fight from.

to disembark. Instead, Porus' son drove his chariots past them and so rendered Alexander's crossing free of risk. Alexander then sent the mounted archers against the chariots, and these routed the Indians without difficulty, inflicting wounds as they went. **Some say** that a battle did in fact occur during the landing, between those Indians who had arrived with Porus' son and Alexander's cavalry. They say that Porus' son actually arrived with a greater force, and that he wounded Alexander himself and slew Bucephalas, the horse that was dearest to Alexander.

But Ptolemy son of Lagus, with whom I myself agree, records otherwise, that Porus did send his son, but not with 60 chariots only. Rightly so, for it would have been unreasonable for Porus, after hearing from his scouts that Alexander himself or a part of his army had actually crossed the Hydaspes, to send out his own son with a mere 60 chariots. These would have been too numerous and cumbersome for reconnaissance, and yet utterly insufficient either to thwart those who had not yet crossed or to attack those already on land. Ptolemy records instead that Porus' son arrived with 2,000 cavalry and 120 chariots, but that Alexander had already made it all the way across, even from the island on which he had disembarked.

5.15 Alexander deployed the archers first, according to Ptolemy, while he himself led the cavalry. He was convinced that Porus was marching towards him with his entire force, and that the cavalry he saw was advancing at the head of the rest of Porus' army. But when he obtained an accurate count of the Indian troops, he swiftly attacked them with his cavalry. The Indians yielded when they saw that Alexander himself and his column of cavalry were attacking not as a front, but **squadron by squadron**. About 400 of the Indian cavalry fell, and the son of Porus with them. The chariots were seized along with their horses; they had hampered the Indians' retreat and had proven useless during the fighting because of the mud.

The cavalry that had escaped the rout informed Porus that Alexander and his army had crossed in great force and that Porus' son had died in the battle. But Porus was unsure how to proceed, since the soldiers from Alexander's main camp across the river – those who had been left behind with Craterus – appeared to be attempting a crossing, too. He ultimately chose to ride with his whole army against Alexander himself and to take on the stronger force of the Macedonians and their king, though he did leave behind a few of the elephants and a small portion of his army at the camp to frighten Craterus and his cavalry away from the near bank. Porus led his whole cavalry (up to 4,000 horse), all his 300 chariots, 200 of the elephants and all his infantry fit for action – as many as 30,000 – against Alexander. He deployed his army when he came to ground that did not seem muddy, but looked sufficiently

---

Some say Arrian's typical wording when introducing material he deems dubious.

squadron by squadron Arrian means that the cavalry were approaching as a column rather than a front. Because of the short width of a column, the Indians probably assumed at first that Alexander had far fewer numbers. They realized the truth and decided on flight, only too late.

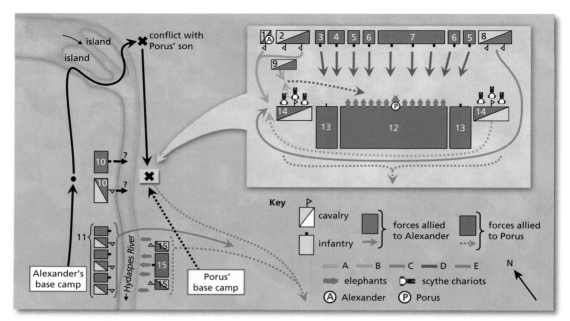

Forces allied to Alexander
1 Alexander and Companion *Agēma*
2 Companion Cavalry
3 Royal Hypaspists
4 Hypaspists
5 archers
6 Agrianians and javelin-men
7 Macedonian phalanx
8 cavalry under Coenus
9 mounted archers
10 mercenary infantry and cavalry under Meleager, Attalus and Gorgias
11 mixed infantry and cavalry under Craterus

Forces allied to Porus
12 Indian infantry and elephants
13 Indian infantry
14 Indian cavalry
15 Indian infantry and cavalry

The battle of the Hydaspes, May 326 BC, according to Arrian.
Alexander leaves troops behind at two points along the west bank of the Hydaspes River before crossing farther north with more troops of his own. He has a brief engagement with Porus' son on the other side of the river and then marches downriver to face Porus and the rest of the Indian forces. A) When Alexander's army meets Porus', the Macedonian mounted archers attack first. Porus recognizes that his left cavalry needs reinforcement and transfers his right cavalry there. B) Alexander and his whole Companion Cavalry attempt to flank the advancing Indian cavalry, but meet the reinforcements brought round from the Indian right. C) Coenus follows the orders issued to him prior to the action. He pursues the cavalry that left the Indian right and attacks them from behind. D) The combined attack of Alexander and Coenus deals a severe blow to the organization and the morale of the Indian cavalry, who fall back onto their infantry and elephants – with catastrophic results. The Macedonian infantry now advance with vigour, and the whole disorganized Indian force is eventually encircled. E) In the end, many of the Indians break free and flee, and Craterus' forces, which have now crossed the river, help take up the chase.

level and firm because of the sand – ideal for the advances and withdrawals of his cavalry. First came the elephants, arranged in a front, each separated from the next by about **30 metres** [100 feet], so that they would form a front before his whole phalanx of infantry and would terrify Alexander's cavalry at every point.

---

30 metres this much space between 200 elephants amounts to a front line of over 6 kilometres (nearly 4 miles), excluding the flanking infantry and cavalry.

Porus did not think any of the enemy would dare to push their way into the spaces between the elephants; the horses' terror would prevent the cavalry from doing so, and the infantry would be even more reluctant, since Porus' advancing hoplites would block them along the front and the elephants would turn towards them and trample them down. Porus' infantry were positioned along with the elephants, not on an even front line with the beasts, but in a second line behind them, so that the companies were embedded slightly into the spaces between. Porus stationed other infantry on the wings as well, even beyond the elephants. Then, on either side of the infantry the cavalry had been deployed, and in front of these were chariots on both wings.

5.16   This was Porus' formation. But Alexander, as soon as he saw the Indians being deployed, halted his own cavalry's advance to wait for members of his infantry, who were continually arriving from behind. After the phalanx had marched quickly to join him and they were now together, Alexander did not hand his worn-out and gasping soldiers over to well-rested barbarians by deploying them and advancing immediately. Instead, he rested his infantry and rode around beside them until their enthusiasm returned. After seeing the Indians' formation, Alexander decided not to advance against their centre, where the elephants were set forward and the infantry had been deployed in tight formation behind the spaces between the beasts. He shied away for the very reasons that Porus had deployed his forces in this way. Instead, since he was stronger in cavalry Alexander took most of his horse and rode them over against the enemies' left wing to attack them there. He sent Coenus to the [enemy] right, with his own **hipparchy** and Demetrius', and ordered that, when the barbarians saw the column of cavalry opposite them and rode over to meet it, Coenus and these forces should follow **on their rear**. He assigned Seleucus, Antigenes and Tauron command of the infantry phalanx, and ordered them not to join the fight until they saw that Alexander's own cavalry had thrown the enemy infantry phalanx and their horse into confusion.

The armies were soon within shooting range, and Alexander sent his archers, as many as 1,000, against the Indians' left, to upset them by their dense barrage of arrows and the onslaught of their horses. Then Alexander and his Companions led the cavalry swiftly against the enemy left, intent on attacking as quickly as

---

hipparchy   Arrian made no reference to this in his previous list of Alexander's units. It should perhaps be identified as the Sogdianian and Bactrian cavalry, which are listed but go without mention in the battle narrative. Coenus had commanded Bactrian and Sogdianian cavalry while campaigning in Sogdiana in 328–327 BC. Here he also likely commands the hipparchy of Demetrius.

on their rear   Alexander imagines the cavalry on Porus' right moving left behind the Indian infantry to the other wing to reinforce those cavalry under aggressive attack by the Macedonian right.

possible the now disorganized barbarians **at their flank**, before their cavalry could be spread out into an opposing front.

5.17   In the meantime, the Indians brought all their cavalry together from every other part and these were riding parallel to Alexander, extending the line to counter any forward movement by him. Then Coenus and his men, as ordered, appeared on the cavalry's rear. When the Indians saw this, they were forced to arrange their cavalry formation into **two fronts**. One group, the largest and strongest, faced Alexander, while the others turned against Coenus' men. This upset not only the Indians' organization but also their resolve. Alexander saw his chance when the enemy cavalry turned in the other direction, and he attacked those facing him. When he did, the Indians did not even stand against the onrush of Alexander's cavalry. Instead, they were broken apart and driven back to their elephants as if to a protective wall. At the same time, the drivers of the elephants were bringing their beasts forward against the cavalry, but then the Macedonian infantry phalanx itself advanced against the elephants. They threw **javelins** at the drivers and stood around the beasts themselves, hitting them with missiles from all sides. This fighting was like none of their previous contests. The beasts kept running forward against the infantry battalions and ravaging the Macedonian phalanx wherever they turned, despite the infantry's tight formation. When the Indian cavalry saw the fighting that occupied the Macedonian infantry, they turned around and rode against the Macedonian cavalry on their own. But when Alexander's horsemen, far superior in might and experience, dominated them once more, they were pushed back again towards the elephants. In this action all Alexander's cavalry had formed a single squadron, a result of the fighting itself and not of an order. And wherever this squadron attacked the Indian ranks, they came out of it with heavy casualties. Meanwhile, because the elephants had been forced into a narrow space, they inflicted injuries on their own soldiers as much as on the enemy, trampling them down as they turned around and stumbled about.

---

at their flank   Alexander's cavalry was attempting to ride *around* the left flank of the cavalry on Porus' left. The hope was that the Indians would be unable to retaliate under a hail of missiles from the archers' initial attack. The Indian cavalry that came to help the left enabled them to extend the line and fill in any gaps in it, thereby countering Alexander's flanking movement. But among these reinforcements were the cavalry of the right, which Coenus had been ordered to pursue.

two fronts   this suggests that much of the Indian cavalry had moved from the right behind the lines to support the left cavalry, and had done so carefully, to keep Coenus from seeing that the force there was diminishing. These would have merged with the left cavalry by the time Coenus had recognized their movement from the right. The newly increased body of cavalry on the left would later have had to divide again so that part could face Coenus as he approached from behind.

javelins   the members of the infantry must have had these weapons in reserve, in addition to the sarissae. According to Curtius (8.14), they carried sickles as well, and used these to hack at the elephants' trunks.

The slaughter of the Indian cavalry, too, was tremendous, since they were hemmed in tightly around the elephants, many of whose drivers had been hit by javelins. The elephants themselves were wounded also, and because of their exhaustion and the loss of their drivers, they were no longer spread out evenly in their fighting. Instead, their pain actually drove them mad, so that they attacked friendly and enemy forces alike, heaving, trampling and slaughtering in every direction. But the Macedonians, who were attacking the beasts in open space and with their wits about them, would yield whenever the elephants attacked, and then close in and hurl javelins at them once they turned away. The Indians, therefore, since they were falling back among the elephants, in fact sustained the majority of the injuries delivered by the beasts. When the elephants were tired out and their charges were no longer vigorous, they merely trumpeted and began to recede like backing ships. Alexander then **encircled** the entire division with his cavalry and signalled the infantry to march their phalanx forward, with their shields drawn together in the densest possible formation. In this way all but a few of the Indian cavalry were cut down in the fighting and the infantry, too, were being slaughtered as the Macedonians attacked from every side. At this point all the Indians turned and fled through a gap where Alexander's cavalry had parted.

---

1   Given what you now know of ancient warfare, why do you suppose Alexander landed his cavalry (rather than his infantry) first (**5.13**)?

2   How is Alexander's battle formation here (**5.13**) strikingly different from those of other battles? What is the reason for this new organization of troops?

3   How many times larger, according to Arrian, is Porus' army than Alexander's? Given Arrian's numbers for the enemy in past battles, what would you assume about them here?

4   Estimate the length of Alexander's infantry front, assuming that the 6,000 men were standing a generous metre (3 feet) apart in a formation eight men deep. According to Arian's numbers, how does the length of Alexander's infantry line compare with that of Porus (see p. 134 and note)?

5   What factors do you suppose might have compromised the mobility of Porus' infantry?

6   What does Alexander's ability to surround the Indian forces (**5.17**) suggest about the relative numbers of the two armies?

---

encircled   according to this description, Alexander's infantry faced the Indians in an even line, while his cavalry formed an arc behind them and to their sides.

Arrian 5.18   At the same time, Craterus and the **other commanders** who had been left behind on the far bank of the Hydaspes, when they saw that Alexander had won a splendid victory, made their own crossing, and achieved no less slaughter as the Indians retreated, for they were well rested and replaced Alexander's exhausted men in the pursuit.

Just under 20,000 Indian infantry were slain, and around 3,000 cavalry; all the chariots were completely demolished. Two sons of Porus fell, as did Spitaces, the governor of that area's Indians, together with all the drivers of the elephants and chariots, and all the cavalry and infantry generals of Porus' army. All the elephants that had not been killed were seized. On Alexander's side, no more than a mere 80 out of 6,000 infantry were slain in the **first attack**. Ten of the mounted archers, those who were in fact the first to join in combat, died, as did about twenty of the Companion Cavalry and some 200 of the other horse.

Porus had displayed great valour in the fighting, not only as a general but also as a noble soldier. He witnessed the slaughter of his cavalry, beheld his elephants – some fallen on the spot, others bereft of their riders and wandering astray in their distress – and observed that most of his infantry were slain. Yet, as long as some portion of the Indians remained steadfast in the battle and struggled on, Porus did not initiate the flight of his men by his own retreat, as Darius had done. But once he had been **wounded** in the right shoulder, the only place he kept bare as he ranged in battle (his cuirass was remarkably strong and well joined, and kept the missiles off the rest of his body, as those who saw him later learned), only then did he turn his elephant about and begin to retreat. Alexander had seen this great and noble man during the battle and was eager to keep him alive. He therefore sent **Taxiles** the Indian to him first. He rode up as close as he thought safe to the elephant that bore Porus, and ordered him to halt the beast, since flight was now futile, and listen to Alexander's message. But when Porus saw Taxiles, an old personal enemy, he turned the elephant towards him and came at him to strike him with a javelin. (He might have killed Taxiles, had he not backed his horse away from Porus in time.) After that, instead of growing angry with Porus, Alexander kept sending other men in turn, including one Meroes, an Indian who Alexander learned was an old friend of Porus. When Porus heard Meroes' words and was at the same time overcome by thirst, he halted his elephant and

---

other commanders   probably Meleager, Attalus and Gorgias.

first attack   this phrase is probably meant to contrast the main battle with the attack of Craterus and the others who crossed the river later.

wounded   according to Curtius (8.14), Porus had received nine wounds in his back and chest, impossible if Arrian's description of his armour is correct.

Taxiles   his real name was Omphis (Curtius 8.12), Taxiles being a title for any ruler of the region around Taxila, the largest city between the Indus and Hydaspes rivers.

This silver coin was perhaps issued as early as 324 BC, by Alexander himself. Obverse: Alexander charges Porus, who hurls a javelin from atop his elephant. Reverse: Alexander is crowned by Nike, goddess of victory, as he himself holds a spear and thunderbolt. If such coins were in fact issued by Alexander, then this thunderbolt offers indisputable proof of his claim to divinity.

dismounted. Then, once he had drunk and refreshed himself, he demanded to be brought to Alexander immediately.

5.19 This was done, and when Alexander learned of Porus' approach, he rode ahead of the battle-line with a few of his Companions to meet him. Alexander stayed his horse and marvelled at Porus' height, easily over 2.3 metres (7.5 feet), and his beauty. He plainly had not been defeated in mind, but stood as one noble man before another after struggling valiantly against a fellow king for the sake of his own kingdom. Alexander first addressed him, commanding him to tell him what he wished to happen to him. The story goes that Porus replied, 'Treat me **in kingly fashion**, Alexander.' Alexander was delighted at this reply and said, 'That will be granted for my part, Porus, but for your own sake, now, demand whatever it is you hold dear.' Porus said that everything was included in that one request, and this response delighted Alexander further still. He granted Porus sovereignty

---

dismounted   other accounts of Porus' dismounting are highly romantic. Plutarch (60) has Porus' devoted elephant lower his wounded rider to the ground with his trunk and remove the javelins from his body.

in kingly fashion   as in English, the Greek wording permits the senses 'treat me as a king should' and 'treat me as a king'. Alexander's response suggests that he understands the first meaning, but Porus' reiteration challenges Alexander to recognize the second meaning. The riddling statement implies that the two requests are in fact one and the same, assuming that being generous is an important component of good kingship. To treat Porus as a king would itself be a kingly act.

over the same Indians as before and added still **more territory** – even more than he had ruled previously – to Porus' former domain. In this way Alexander treated a noble man in kingly fashion and from that time forward he enjoyed Porus' loyalty. So ended Alexander's battle against Porus and the Indians on the far side of the Hydaspes River, during the archonship of Hegemon in Athens, in the month of **Munychion**.

---

1 How well does the number of infantry dead on Alexander's side (**5.18**) fit with Arrian's actual description of the battle?

2 It is plausible that Porus' 300 chariots (all demolished) are not mentioned during the battle narrative because they were relatively ineffective. What evidence is there that the chariots would not have been effective?

3 In all other accounts, Porus does not willingly surrender, but is overcome by his injuries and captured. Which do you believe more likely to be true? Why?

4 Who else have we seen previously impress Alexander through their speech to him? What do these figures have in common?

Bucephalas' obituary

Arrian 5.19   Alexander founded cities both at the site of the battle and at the point where he had set out across the Hydaspes River. The first he called **Nicaea**, after the victory against the Indians, and the other Bucephala, to commemorate his horse Bucephalas who died there. The horse was **not wounded** by anyone, but exhausted by fever and old age, for he was about 30 at the time. Bucephalas had endured hardship and risk with Alexander often before, and only Alexander would mount him, because Bucephalas thought all other riders unworthy. He was a horse great in size and noble in spirit. He had been branded with the sign of an **ox's head**, and some say that this was the reason for the name he bore. Others record that there was a white marking on the head of this otherwise dark horse, and that it closely resembled the head of an ox. When Bucephalas went missing once in the land of the Uxians, Alexander announced throughout the region that he would slaughter them all if they did not return his horse. Bucephalas was returned immediately

---

more territory   the addition to Porus' territory was in fact gradual, as Alexander later granted him increasingly more land.

Munychion   Attic month that fell between mid-April and mid-May. The year was 326 BC.

Nicaea   the city is literally named for *Nike*, the Greek goddess 'Victory'.

not wounded   according to Plutarch (61), the majority of the sources relate that Bucephalas did die from wounds after the battle. Arrian is using the version of Bucephalas' death recorded by Onesicritus, who is alone in giving Bucephalas' age.

ox's head   the name Bucephalas means 'ox-head' in Greek (see p. 14).

On this silver coin issued by Ptolemy I, ruler of Egypt (323–285 BC), Alexander wears an elephant headdress, which recalls his conquest of India. The image is modelled on representations of Alexander's ancestor Heracles, who regularly wore the impenetrable skin of the Nemean lion.

after the announcement was made – so great was Alexander's passion for Bucephalas and so great was the barbarians' fear of Alexander. May Bucephalas be permitted here this much honour by me, for Alexander's sake.

> • Onesicritus' account of the expedition was rather romantic; 30 years is too old for any horse to have participated in the battle, and it is probably no coincidence that Alexander himself was 30 years old at this time. By giving them a common age, Onesicritus is intentionally representing the two as somehow inextricably connected. In what other ways does Arrian here emphasize the close connection between Alexander and Bucephalas?

Mutiny

After defeating Porus, Alexander continued east, crossing the Acesines and Hydraotes rivers and securing the surrounding territories. When he reached the Hyphasis River, however, the following incident occurred.

Plutarch 62   The struggle against Porus dampened the Macedonians' enthusiasm and put a stop to any further progress into India. Although Porus had **deployed** only 20,000 infantry and 2,000 cavalry, the Macedonians had only barely repelled him. And so the Macedonians took a firm stand against Alexander afterwards, when

---

deployed   you will recall that Arrian's numbers for Porus' troops are significantly higher (see pp. 133–4).

he tried to force them to cross the **Ganges**, too. They had heard that this river was 32 stades [6 km/3¾ miles] wide and 100 fathoms deep, and that its opposite bank was blotted out by hordes of armed men, cavalry and elephants. It was said that 80,000 horse, plus 200,000 infantry, 8,000 chariots and 6,000 war elephants were waiting under the command of the kings of the **Gandarites** and **Praesii**. This was, in fact, no exaggeration, for **Androcottus**, on becoming king a little later, made a present of 500 elephants to Seleucus and went around subduing the whole of India with an army of 600,000 men.

In an ill-tempered rage, Alexander at first shut himself up in his tent and stayed there; he could find no delight in past achievements without also crossing the Ganges, and to him retreat meant admission of defeat. But his Friends **consoled** him appropriately, and the soldiers stood pleading with shouts and wailing outside his doors. When Alexander was moved to pity and began breaking camp, he devised many clever and deceitful **schemes** to increase his reputation. He had oversized arms and horse mangers made, as well as bits that were heavier than normal. These he scattered around and left behind. He also erected **altars** to the gods, and the kings of the Praesii to this day honour them by sacrificing in the Greek style on crossing the river. As a boy, Androcottus saw Alexander himself, and he is reported to have said often later that Alexander came just short of taking over his country, because the Indian king at that time was loathed and despised for his depravity and ignoble birth.

Ganges the Upper Ganges was only 250 miles away from the point of the mutiny on the Hyphasis.

Gandarites, Praesii the Gandarites may have been a people just east of the Hyphasis. The Praesii inhabited the region east of the Upper Ganges.

Androcottus the Greek spelling of the name Chandragupta. It offers fascinating insight into how the Greek ear heard these foreign sounds and turned them into more familiar-sounding names. Chandragupta founded the Mauryan dynasty in 322 or 312 BC. Arrian would have had access to the writings of Megasthenes, who served King Seleucus as envoy and frequently visited Chandragupta's court. The 500 elephants were probably far fewer, 'five hundred' being an Indian expression to denote any significant number.

consoled according to Arrian (5.25–7) and Curtius (9.2–3), Coenus spoke on the soldiers' behalf after Alexander addressed the troops. Alexander then remained in his tent, perhaps as a ploy to get the soldiers to change their minds. He finally relented, they record, when he sacrificed prior to continuing eastward and the omens proved unfavourable.

schemes according to Diodorus (17.95), Alexander also made his camp appear three times larger, and left behind soldiers' beds 2.3 metres (7.5 feet) long. His hope was that he would leave a lasting impression on the local peoples before moving on, and perhaps deter them from pursuing future rebellion and war.

altars 23 metres (75 feet) high, according to Diodorus (17.95). Arrian (5.29) probably correctly records that these altars were both testament to and thanks for his achievements.

1 Compare Plutarch's description of Alexander's response to the mutiny with the accounts of Arrian and Curtius (see note on p. 142). In what ways do they illustrate different aspects of Alexander's character?

2 Coenus died a few days after this mutiny. All sources that mention his death blame illness. Do you think it unreasonable to suspect poison, for his leadership during the mutiny? Why or why not?

3 Heracles was supposed to have built 12 altars to the gods in the far west. How much do you suppose that might have to do with Alexander's act?

4 Plutarch appears to take Androcottus' statement at face value, but what might have been Androcottus' reasons for saying this about the region's former ruler?

River voyage and the Malli

Alexander abandoned any further movement east and marched back again to Nicaea and Bucephala on the Hydaspes. From there he began, in November 326 BC, a voyage downriver to the Indus and on to the Arabian Sea. Along the way, he continued to campaign against any who resisted.

Plutarch 63   Alexander was now eager to lay eyes on the outer sea. He constructed many **oared transport boats and rafts**, and was carried along downriver on these. Although the pace was leisurely, this voyage was not without toil or fighting, for Alexander would assault the cities along the way, disembarking and attacking everything. In fact, he was very nearly killed when facing those people called the **Malli**, said to be the most warlike of the Indians. After scattering them from their walls with missiles, Alexander was the first one up a certain ladder set against the wall. Once he stood on the wall, however, the ladder fell to pieces, and he started to take blows from below by the barbarians standing inside along the wall's base. Although Alexander was virtually alone, he suddenly turned and leapt into the enemy's midst, and by good luck he landed on his feet.

---

oared transport boats and rafts   their construction was actually ordered before the mutiny, immediately after the victory over Porus. It is possible that Alexander intended all along not to reach the Ganges, but to travel down the Hydaspes and the Indus instead. The march east to the Hyphasis would then only have been an effort to stabilize the surrounding region. If this is so, then Alexander may have encouraged rumours about the East so that his soldiers would conveniently prevent him from continuing in that direction. The decision to quit his advance would then appear forced on him by his men and not a sign of his own weakness. The route downriver followed the Hydaspes into the Acesines, and the Acesines into the Indus.

Malli   a people dwelling to the east of the Acesines, just north of where the Hydraotes joins it.

When he brandished his arms, the barbarians thought some portentous blaze was hovering before his person, and so at first they scattered and fled. But once they saw he was with only **two Hypaspists**, they rushed him. Some tried at close range to pierce through his armour with sword and spear as he defended himself, but one man stood off a little and shot an arrow so well aimed and swift that it tore through his breastplate and lodged in the ribs of his chest. At this blow Alexander fell back and sank to his knees, but when his attacker drew his barbaric dagger and rushed at him, Peucestas and Limnaeus offered protection. Both of them were wounded; Limnaeus was killed, but Peucestas held his ground and Alexander killed the barbarian. But Alexander had received many wounds. When at last he was struck in the neck by a club, he leaned against the wall and faced his enemies. Then the Macedonians poured in around him. They seized him and carried him to his tent, already unconscious of his surroundings.

Right away, the word in the camp was that he had died. But with considerable and painstaking effort they sawed off the wooden arrow-shaft and managed with effort to remove Alexander's breastplate and began to cut out the arrowhead, which was driven into one of his ribs. This arrowhead is said to have been three fingers [5 cm/2 inches] wide and four fingers [7 cm/2¾ inches] long, so that during its extraction Alexander was afflicted with fainting spells and did very nearly die. Even after he escaped this danger, he remained weak and underwent a dietary regimen and medical treatment for some time. Still, when he realized from the noise outside that the Macedonians longed to catch sight of him, he grabbed his cloak and made an appearance. After sacrificing to the gods, he resumed **his voyage** and was carried downriver, conquering much land and great cities along the way.

---

1 Why do you imagine Alexander did not leap in the other direction, outside the wall? Was this bold act of his worth the risk?

2 In what other episode did Alexander make an appearance before his men after coming close to death (see p. 42)? What does such behaviour tell us about him? What do the episodes reveal about the relationship between Alexander and his men?

---

two Hypaspists   according to Arrian (6.11), all authors agreed that Peucestas was present with Alexander. Plutarch is the only extant author to name Limnaeus, but both Peucestas and Leonnatus would later receive golden crowns back at Susa for saving Alexander's life here.

his voyage   because of Alexander's wound, the expedition did not proceed downriver until seven days after the battle.

The Brahmins

During the voyage south, Sabbas, whom Alexander had made satrap of the Indian hillmen, revolted when he learned that Alexander had treated Musicanus, Sabbas' former enemy to the north, with clemency. According to Cleitarchus (Curtius 8.9), the Macedonians killed 80,000 of the Indians who revolted, and sold the captives into slavery.

Plutarch 64   Alexander captured those of the **Gymnosophists** who were largely responsible for persuading Sabbas to revolt and who had caused the greatest problems to the Macedonians. Ten of these men were noted for their shrewdness and concision in giving answers, and Alexander put impossible questions to them, declaring that he would execute first the one who answered most incorrectly, and so on with the rest in order. He commanded the eldest to judge the contest.

The first, when asked whether the living or the dead were more numerous, said that the living were, for the dead no longer 'were'. The second was asked whether the earth or the sea supported greater beasts. He replied that the earth did, for the sea was a part of the earth. The third, when asked which is the cleverest animal, said, 'The one humankind has yet to discover.' The fourth was asked his reasons for inciting Sabbas to revolt. He answered, 'I wanted him either to live nobly or to die nobly.' The fifth, when asked whether he thought Day or Night had been born earlier, said, 'Day, by one day.' When the king expressed amazement at this, he remarked that answers to impossible questions must inevitably be impossible. Moving on, then, Alexander asked the sixth how one might best become loved. 'By being most powerful, yet not feared,' he replied. There were three left. The first was asked how a human might become divine, and he answered, 'By doing what a human is unable to do.' The second was asked whether life or death was stronger, and he replied that life was, since it bears so many woes. The last, when asked how long it is good for a person to live, said, 'Until he no longer thinks that death is better than life.'

Alexander then turned to the judge and demanded the verdict. When the judge said that each spoke worse than the other, Alexander replied, 'You, then, will die first for such a decision.' 'Impossible, King,' he said, 'unless you spoke dishonestly when you claimed you would execute first the one who answered worst.' Alexander therefore let them go and even gave them gifts.

Gymnosophists   the true Gymnosophists followed Nature and led an ascetic life that included the rejection of clothing (hence the term, literally 'naked sophists'). Plutarch here wrongly uses this term of the Brahmins, not strictly philosophers in the Greek sense, but sage priests who served as advisers to Indian kings. Arrian (6.17) records that Alexander executed the Brahmins who had encouraged Sabbas to revolt. The competition described in this passage is generally believed to be a fiction composed by a Cynic philosopher.

1   How, precisely, is Alexander outwitted by the eldest of these thinkers?

2   Which of the philosophers' questions seem relevant to Alexander's own life experience?

3   What other episode features an exchange between Alexander and a Cynic (see pp. 25–6)? In what ways are the episodes similar?

The Gymnosophists

Plutarch turns at this point to address Alexander's interactions with Gymnosophists. Although his meeting with them would have occurred back in Taxila, Plutarch, perhaps following his source, breaks chronology to pair this episode with the preceding exchange between Alexander and the Brahmins.

Plutarch 65   The **sophists** of the highest regard lived by themselves in quiet repose, and Alexander sent **Onesicritus** to bring them to him. Onesicritus was one of those philosophers who studied with Diogenes the Cynic, and he records that Calanus ordered him with an altogether brusque and brutish manner to strip off his tunic and listen to him naked. In fact, Calanus refused to speak with Onesicritus otherwise, even if Zeus himself had sent him there.

But Onesicritus records that Dandamis was milder, and that once he had heard all about **Socrates**, **Pythagoras** and **Diogenes**, he said that he thought these men had

---

sophists   these Indian sophists are the true Gymnosophists. Greek tyrants such as Dionysius of Syracuse and Philip of Macedonia often invited philosophers to their courts, so that Alexander is following traditional practice in welcoming the respected thinkers of this foreign land. Greek Cynic philosophers (see p. 25) in particular appear to have found some connection between the ideas of the Gymnosophists and their own philosophy, so that they represented the Gymnosophists as very like themselves in the stories they recounted.

Onesicritus   the original source for this account, he claims to have met the Gymnosophists at Taxila. The doctrine of the Gymnosophists is clearly Cynic doctrine, so that Onesicritus probably supplied Cynic material himself.

Socrates, Pythagoras, Diogenes   all three of these Greek philosophers are famous not only for their sharp wits but also for their subversion of tradition. Socrates (c. 470–399 BC), who was the teacher of Aristotle's teacher and claimed to receive guidance from a divine spirit that led him to avoid politics, questioned pre-eminent Athenians in a manner that made them appear foolish, and was ultimately executed on charges of not believing in the gods and of corrupting the youth. Pythagoras (c. 570s–490s BC), perhaps best known for the theorem named after him, held that numbers were the ultimate reality – even the cause of gods – and founded a new religious movement based on these ideas. You have already seen the irreverence of Diogenes the Cynic (see pp. 25–6).

been born clever, but lived with excessive reverence for convention. Others say, however, that Dandamis said nothing but this alone: 'Why did Alexander come such a long way to this place?' Nevertheless Taxiles persuaded Calanus on the other hand to go to Alexander. Calanus' name was really Sphines. However, since he greeted people in the Indian tongue (with the word *cale* instead of *chairein*), the Greeks called him Calanus. They say it was he who laid out for Alexander the illustration of empire, by throwing down before him a dried and stiffened hide. Calanus stepped on its edge, and while the hide was pressed flat in that one spot, it rose up at other points. He showed how this continued to happen as he went around in a circle, pressing each part down in succession. But when he stood still at the centre of the hide, all its parts lay at rest. He meant to show by this presentation that Alexander would do best to hold down the middle parts of his empire and not stray far from those.

---

1   What is Onesicritus seeking to make of these Gymnosophists in having Dandamis criticize Socrates, Pythagoras and Diogenes as slaves to convention?

2   Calanus is a notable exception to the other Gymnosophists, for he agrees to join Alexander's court and travel with him, as one might expect a Brahmin to do. What is the political significance of Alexander's retaining a Gymnosophist rather than the Brahmins normally retained by Indian kings?

---

chairein   term meaning roughly in Greek 'to feel goodwill'. Greeks use the word in the imperative (*chaire*) in the sense of 'hello' and 'goodbye'.

6 Back towards Babylon

Gedrosia

> After reaching the mouth of the Indus River in 325 BC, Alexander decided to have his fleet sail west along the coast of Gedrosia while he himself crossed the desert along a route near the shore. You will recall that he followed a similar practice in traversing the desert between Gaza and Pelusium (see p. 62). By all accounts, this desert march through Gedrosia was far more difficult than Alexander had anticipated.

Arrian 6.23

Alexander marched through the land of the Gedrosians by a difficult route devoid of provisions. Among other things, there was no water for the army in many parts, and so they were forced to cover a lot of ground by night and further away from the sea. Alexander was eager to travel along the sea, however, both to discover the available harbours and to prepare for the **fleet** as much as possible along the way, either by digging wells or by providing a market or anchorage. But the Gedrosian land beside the sea was complete desert, so Alexander sent Thoas son of Mandrodorus to the sea with a few cavalry to see if by chance there was a harbour somewhere, drinkable water near the coast, or anything else that could meet their needs. On returning, Thoas reported that he found some **fishermen** living on the coast in stifling huts built of fitted shells and roofed with fish spines. These fishermen, he said, enjoyed what little water could be gathered by digging into the shingle. Yet even that water was not always fresh.

When Alexander reached a part of Gedrosia where food was more available, he distributed what he found among the pack animals, sealed it with his own seal, and ordered it to be conveyed to the sea. When he was going towards the station that was nearest to the sea, however, the soldiers made little of the royal seal. The guards themselves took the food and shared it with all those who were suffering most from hunger. They had been so defeated by their dire situation that they made a calculated decision to set their imminent death above the distant and less immediate threat from their king. When Alexander learned of their predicament,

---

fleet Nearchus was in charge of this fleet, which had orders in the autumn of 325 BC to sail west along the coastline. Because room for supplies on the ships was limited, Alexander's army marched along the coast in order to supply the fleet with food and water by whatever means possible.

fishermen known as the Ichthyphagi, or 'Fish-eaters'.

however, he **pardoned** those responsible. Raids into the countryside had failed to gather all the supplies needed for the army sailing with the fleet, and so Alexander sent Cretheus of Callatis to bring the rest. Alexander ordered the natives, too, to grind as much grain as they could, and to bring it along with palm dates and livestock down to the coast for the market to the army. He sent the Companion Telephus to yet another point with a little grain already ground.

6.24 Alexander next advanced towards the capital of the Gedrosians, a place called Pura, and reached it in a total of 60 days after setting out from Ora. Most chroniclers of Alexander's deeds record that together all the hardships the army suffered throughout Asia could not compare to the agonies suffered here. They record, too, that Alexander did not take this route in ignorance of its difficulty (Nearchus alone asserts this), but because he learned that no one had ever before crossed safely with an army – except **Semiramis** in her flight from the Indians. Yet even she, according to the natives, survived with only 20 of her army left. And then there was Cyrus son of Cambyses, who made it through with only seven still alive. Cyrus had actually traversed that region in order to attack India, but had lost the majority of his army on that desert and forbidding route before he could get there. These reports instilled in Alexander a desire to rival both Cyrus and Semiramis, and it was for this, as well as to provide necessities to the nearby fleet, that Nearchus says Alexander took this route.

The burning heat, **Nearchus** records, and the unavailability of water obliterated the majority of the army. The pack animals suffered in particular; they died from the deep and scorching sand, and often from thirst, too, as they came across towering

---

pardoned   this story is reminiscent of two tales in Homer's *Odyssey*. In one (10.1–79), the curious and envious crew open a bag they believe holds their king's gold. In the other (12.260–419), the starving crew kill and eat the Sun's sacred cattle against Odysseus' orders. All three tales highlight the self-control of the leader in contrast to the weaker will of his men.

Semiramis   legendary figure identified with the historical Sammu-ramat, queen regent of Assyria (810–806 BC). Greek tradition held that she was born of the Assyrian goddess Derceto, conquered Bactria and built the city of Babylon. Although Arrian names Semiramis here, he later records (*Indica* 5) that she died before she could attempt an invasion of India.

Nearchus   according to Plutarch (66) Alexander lost more than 75 per cent of his 120,000 infantry and 15,000 cavalry on this march. Nearchus (Arrian, *Indica* 19.5) records that Alexander had 120,000 soldiers in total when beginning his voyage down the Hydaspes, and this suggests that Plutarch exaggerates considerably. Alexander may well have emerged from the desert with less than a quarter of the 120,000, but we have to subtract from this also those who died in fighting during the river voyage, those sent west with Craterus, those left to garrison India and the land of the Oreitae and those who sailed with Nearchus. Regardless of the precise proportion of losses, the journey must have been catastrophic; Curtius (9.10) stresses Alexander's shame at having brought this calamity on his army.

---

hills of deep, loose sand that swallowed those walking on it like mud or, rather, untrodden snow. The path, therefore, which was both uneven and unstable, caused the horses and mules the greatest difficulty in both the ascents and downward climbs. The army itself suffered most from the long marches; because water was not available at consistent intervals, they were forced to march great distances as necessity required. When they were able to cover the necessary distance at night and come to water before dawn, their suffering was not completely intolerable. But when on long marches day came and they were caught still travelling, they suffered then, tortured by the heat and their unremitting thirst.

6.25   A great many of the pack animals died, with the army's complicity and support. Whenever food was lacking, the soldiers would together slaughter most of their horses and mules and devour their flesh, but then say that the animals had died from thirst or perished from exhaustion. There was no one to look into the truth of the matter, both because of the current hardship and because everyone was committing the same acts. This matter had not in fact escaped Alexander's notice, but he saw that it would be better to feign ignorance rather than to acknowledge what was going on and condone it.

Soon it was very difficult to bring along those afflicted with disease or falling behind from exhaustion; there were too few pack animals, and the soldiers were even breaking up the wagons, which the deep sand made impossible to pull. (In the first days of the march this factor had forced them to take not the shortest routes, but those that the teams could traverse.) Some men, therefore, were left behind owing to sickness, as were others who were overcome by exhaustion, heat or thirst. There was no one to help these men along, and no one to stay and tend to them, for the march was conducted with great haste, and the concern for the whole necessarily meant neglecting the needs of individuals. Still others were overcome by sleep along the journey, since most of the marching was done at night. Those who awoke and still had the strength followed along in the army's tracks. But of the great many only few survived; most, as if fallen overboard at sea, were lost in the sand.

Another calamity, too, befell the army, and was the greatest source of strife to soldiers, horses and pack animals alike. The Gedrosian land receives rain from seasonal winds, just as India does, but this rain falls in the mountains and not in the Gedrosian plains. The winds blow the clouds forward until they reach the mountain peaks, and there they stop and drop their rain. Once, the army was camped near a small stream-bed because of the little bit of water available there. But at about the second night watch this bed was suddenly filled with rainwater. The rain had fallen unseen by the army and rushed down from the mountains in such great quantity that it killed most of the women and children among the camp followers and swept away also the royal paraphernalia and all the surviving pack animals. The soldiers themselves barely survived, and salvaged their weaponry with difficulty, though by no means all of it. It was drinking water, however, that actually killed most of the men on the march, for the heat and their thirst drove them to ceaseless gulping whenever they happened on plenty of it. For this reason, in fact, Alexander usually did not place his camps near the water sources themselves, but as many as 20 stades [3.7 km/2.3 miles] away. That way, the men would not fall on the water as a mob and destroy themselves and the animals, and those most lacking restraint would be less likely to enter the springs or streams, and thereby ruin the water for the rest of the army.

6.26   There occurred during this march a noble deed, and of all Alexander's actions, this is the one that I think should not be forgotten, whether it in fact happened in this land or in **Parapamisadae**, as many have written. According to the story, the army was marching through the sand, and the heat of the day was already scorching, but they had to continue making their way towards the water, which still lay ahead. Alexander himself was afflicted with thirst, too; he led the way with great effort, but he did so on foot, so that – as is usual in this sort of situation – the rest of the soldiers would endure their toils more lightly because they shared the suffering equally with their leader. At that time, some of the light troops turned aside from the army to seek out water. They found only a scant bit pooled in a shallow gulley, but they quickly collected it anyway and hurried to Alexander, carrying the water as one would a great and precious thing. When they drew near, they poured it into a helmet and presented it to their king. He took the water, praised the men who brought it, and poured it out before everyone's eyes. That action bolstered the spirit of the entire army, so that you would have thought every soldier had drunk of the water that Alexander let fall to the ground. I applaud this act more than any other, a testament at once to the toughness and the generalship of Alexander.

---

1   Which do you believe was the greater reason for crossing this desert, provisioning the ships or rivalling Semiramis and Cyrus? Why?

2   Can you give an historical example from the past 20 years where (as here, **6.25**) the concern for the whole has required the neglect of individuals?

3   Arrian has worked hard to make this catastrophic and perhaps foolhardy desert march reflect well on Alexander. Reread the episode and list the various positive leadership qualities that Arrian has Alexander exhibit during this journey.

Parapamisadae   Alexander marched through Parapamisadae in his pursuit of Bessus, but Curtius (7.3) stresses the darkness and intense cold that claimed many lives on that march. Ancient authors locate this particular tale in a striking number of places. Curtius sets it in the deserts of Sogdiana (7.5), while Plutarch (42) records it as taking place during the pursuit of Darius. Yet another source, Frontinus (*Strategemata* 1.7), locates it in Africa. In Curtius and Plutarch, Alexander does not pour the water out, but tells the soldiers who brought it to give it to their sons.

The Carmanian procession

The following episode recounts Alexander's procession west across Carmania in 325–324 BC, after surviving the horrors of the Gedrosian desert.

Plutarch 67   Alexander refreshed his forces here and set out, indulging in a drunken carousal for seven days across Carmania. Horses pulled him slowly along – eight of them – as day and night he continuously enjoyed the sumptuous feast with his Companions above a **sacrificial altar** set on a lofty and conspicuous platform. Scores of wagons – some shaded by embroidered canopies dyed with purple, some by tree branches kept fresh-cut and green – followed behind bringing the rest of his Friends and commanders, all crowned and drinking. You would have seen no shield, no helmet, no sarissa, only wine bowls, rhytons and **Thericleian** vessels; the soldiers spent the entire march sousing themselves in wine from great casks and mixing bowls as they toasted one another, some leading the way on foot, others reclining. Strains from pipes and panpipes, songs and lyre music, and women's Dionysian revels filled every place, and following close on the heels of this march's disordered wandering were also games of Bacchic wantonness, as if the god himself were at hand and assuming a leading role in the revelry. Then, when Alexander came to the palace of **Gedrosia**, he again refreshed the army with festivities. And once, they say, while he was drunk and watching a competition of song and dance, his darling **Bagoas** won the contest, and then proceeded to walk

---

sacrificial altar   the Greek word, *thumelē*, was often used to refer to an altar to Dionysus in the theatre. The word here contributes to the spectacular quality of the march, but Plutarch may be hinting that Alexander's sitting *above* this altar might suggest some association with Dionysus as recipient of the sacrifices. Strabo (15.1) and Diodorus (17.106) in fact refer to this march as an imitation of Dionysus' triumphal return to the west on conquering the Indians. Drinking large quantities of alcohol was a requisite part of any such procession (*kōmos*) in honour of Dionysus. Curtius (9.10) harshly condemns the week-long drunken march, but Arrian (6.28) notably rejects the celebrations as a total fiction, since neither Ptolemy, Aristobulus nor any 'credible author' mentions them.

Thericleian   name given to certain expensive metal vessels supposedly invented by Theracles of Corinth.

Gedrosia   a mistake on Plutarch's part; Alexander has already crossed Gedrosia. Carmania is meant here.

Bagoas   Alexander enjoyed a sexual relationship with the eunuch Bagoas, as Darius had before him, according to Curtius (6.5). Nabarzanes, one of those who had plotted with Bessus to kill Darius (see p. 94), surrendered to Alexander and presented Bagoas to him as a gift, whereupon Bagoas successfully persuaded Alexander to pardon Nabarzanes.

This mosaic of the third century AD from Sousse, Tunisia, shows Dionysus (Bacchus) in a victorious procession after his conquest of India. His chariot is pulled by tigers, and Nike, the winged goddess of victory, stands behind him.

in full costume through the theatre and sit down next to Alexander. When the Macedonians saw this they clapped and shouted, demanding a kiss, until finally Alexander did embrace and kiss him deeply.

> 1 Why might festivities following the brutal march across the Gedrosian desert have been a practical decision?
>
> 2 How does this Alexander differ from other representations of him by Plutarch?
>
> 3 What might have been the political reasons behind the imitation of Dionysus? Do you find evidence for this in previous episodes?

Cyrus' tomb

> From Carmania Alexander returned to Pasargadae, roughly 32 kilometres (20 miles) north-east of Persepolis. It was the original capital of the Persian Empire under Cyrus the Great.

Arrian 6.29 The desecration of the tomb of Cyrus son of Cambyses upset Alexander, who discovered, as Aristobulus records, that it had been broken into and plundered. Cyrus' tomb, located in the royal park in Pasargadae, was surrounded by an irrigated grove with all kinds of cultivated trees, and deep grass grew in the meadow. The tomb itself was built of square-cut stone in the shape of a rectangle, and above it was set a roofed chamber of stone with an entrance narrow enough for a single small man to squeeze through, but then only with considerable difficulty. Inside the chamber sat a golden casket in which the body of Cyrus was buried, and beside the casket was a couch. The couch's feet were wrought with gold, a Babylonian tapestry covered it, and the bedding was of lush purple cloth. On it lay a Median cloak, other clothes of Babylonian making, loose-fitting Median trousers, robes of deep blue, as Aristobulus reports, some of purple, some of this or that colour, necklaces, short Persian swords and earrings fixed with gold and stones. A table stood there, too, and it was between this and the couch that the casket holding the body of Cyrus sat. Inside the precinct, beside the ascent up to the tomb there was a small chamber built for the Mages, who had passed the duty of guarding Cyrus' tomb from father to son ever since the time of Cyrus' son Cambyses. They received a sheep per day from the king, an appointed amount of flour and wine, and a horse to sacrifice to Cyrus every month. The tomb itself was inscribed in Persian: 'Mortal, I am Cyrus son of Cambyses. I founded the Persian Empire and ruled Asia as King. Do not, then, begrudge me my memorial.'

Visiting Cyrus' tomb was a priority for Alexander whenever he went to Persia, but he discovered that everything had been removed from it except the casket and the couch. Even Cyrus' body had been desecrated; the robbers had removed the lid of the casket and removed the body. They had tried to render the casket itself more portable by hacking off some pieces and breaking off others, but on failing left the

The tomb of Cyrus the Great at Pasargadae (under a more modern reconstruction here) is now known also as the Tomb of the Mother of Solomon.

casket in place and departed. Aristobulus records that he was commissioned by Alexander to restore Cyrus' tomb to its original order, to deposit in the casket all of the body that could be salvaged, to replace the lid, to fix the parts of the casket that had been damaged, to spread ribbons over the couch, to replace all the other embellishments one by one exactly as they were originally, to obscure the door by walling part with stone and filling part with clay and to impress that clay with the royal seal. Alexander arrested and tortured the Mages who guarded the tomb, hoping that they would give up the perpetrators. They, however, gave up neither themselves nor any other while under torture, nor were they proven privy to the act by any other evidence. For this reason Alexander **released** them.

---

1. What do the items in Cyrus' tomb reflect about the composition of his empire?

2. Given what you know of the Mages and their relationship with the Persians (see p. 12), why would they have been placed in charge of Cyrus' tomb?

3. Why would Alexander have made his visit to Cyrus' tomb such a priority?

4. Arrian names Aristobulus in this passage. Why was he likely to have been Arrian's source for all the details regarding the tomb?

Alexander's long-range plans

Arrian 7.1   Once Alexander had reached Pasargadae and Persepolis, a longing seized him to sail down the Euphrates and the Tigris to the Persian Sea. He wanted to see the mouths of those rivers, just as he had visited the mouth of the Indus and the sea there. Some have written also that Alexander planned to sail around most of **Arabia**, the land of the Ethiopians, Libya and the territory of the Nomadae

---

released   Curtius (10.1) records that, when the local satrap Orxines slighted Bagoas, the latter concocted an elaborate scheme (including seductively turning Alexander against Orxines and bribing other men to testify against him) that succeeded in having the satrap wrongly executed for looting the tomb of Cyrus. Arrian (6.30) simply records vaguely that Alexander executed Orxines for looting temples and royal tombs, and for illegally killing many Persians. Plutarch (69) complicates the issue further; he records that a Macedonian of status named Polymachus was executed for looting Cyrus' tomb.

Arabia   Arrian is describing the circumnavigation of Africa, beginning with a voyage south around the Arabian Peninsula. Ethiopia, Libya and the land of the Nomadae were not specifically defined nations, but vast regions of Africa unexplored by Greeks. Ethiopia lay to the south of Egypt. To Egypt's west was Libya, then Carthage and then the Nomadae. Mount Atlas, traditionally identified with the Titan who held up the sky, is located in modern Morocco. After sailing towards Gadeira (modern Cadiz, Spain), Alexander would have returned to 'our sea' (a typical way of referring to the Mediterranean) from the west, via the Strait of Gibraltar. Because many ancients did not view Africa as a continent separate from Asia, in the minds of some neither Alexander nor the earlier Persian kings could claim to have ruled the whole of Asia.

beyond Mount Atlas, towards Gadeira into our sea, so that after overthrowing Libya and Carthage he could justly be called the king of all Asia. The Persian and Median kings, after all, had ruled only a tiny portion of Asia and so had falsely dubbed themselves 'Great' Kings. From there, some say, he intended to sail into the **Black Sea** to the Scythians and Lake Maeotis; others say he meant to sail to Sicily and the Iapygian headland, since Alexander had already by that time been provoked by the name of the Romans, who were advancing towards greatness. I for one can neither surmise precisely the nature of Alexander's aims, nor am I interested in guessing at them. I do, however, think that I can assert with confidence that Alexander was planning nothing small or trifling, nor would he ever have remained quietly satisfied with what he had already conquered, even if he had added Europe to Asia and the **isles of the Brettanians** to Europe. Instead, Alexander would continue searching still further for whatever remained unknown, and on running out of rivals he would turn to contend with his very self.

> 1   Why do you suppose Arrian ends the rumoured list of planned conquests with the Romans?
>
> 2   What empire controls most of the lands named in this list of conquests? To what extent does Arrian present Alexander as a rival for this empire?

Executions and marriages

> From Persepolis Alexander travelled to Susa, the location of the following three episodes, which occurred in 324 BC.

Black Sea   while the preceding itinerary looked southward, the voyage to the Black Sea looks north. The third option, towards Sicily and Iapygia (Italy), looks west. Given that Alexander's campaign conquered eastern lands, this catalogue of possible future expeditions in essence proposes the other three cardinal directions, a fact that should probably lead us to consider all this to be speculation and rumour. The catalogue's final element is climactic; it juxtaposes Alexander's greatness with the growing power of the town that would later become the centre of Arrian's own Roman Empire. Alexander would in fact not have thought much of Rome; during his lifetime Rome was a small city occupied with wars against its Latin and Samnite neighbours. But just over 40 years later Rome would be fighting in southern Italy against Pyrrhus, king of Epirus, the homeland of Alexander's mother. In 264 BC Rome would begin to battle Carthage for control of Sicily, and that victory would prove essential to Rome's expansion east across the Mediterranean.

isles of the Brettanians   in naming the British Isles, Arrian hints at the limits of Roman conquest and beyond. The Roman province Britannia did not include even the whole of the island of modern Great Britain.

Arrian 7.4   Once Alexander had reached Susa, he sent **Atropates** to his satrapy, but arrested and executed **Abulites** and his son **Oxathres** for governing the Susians poorly. The men overseeing those regions conquered by Alexander had in fact perpetrated many crimes, violating temples, tombs and their own subjects. This was because the king's expedition against the Indians had taken a long time. It seemed impossible that Alexander could return from facing so many peoples (and so many elephants!) without dying beyond the Indus, the Hydaspes, the Acesines or the Hyphasis. The misfortunes, too, that Alexander suffered in Gedrosia had induced the western satraps to doubt still further that he would ever return home. But they say that Alexander himself had grown harsher at that time, too, inclined to believe accusations as if fully trustworthy in every case, and to punish severely those convicted of even small offences, because he thought that those same intentions would lead them to commit great crimes.

Alexander held weddings also at Susa, for both himself and his Companions. He married Barsine, the eldest of Darius' daughters, and, according to Aristobulus, he married **Parysatis** as well, the youngest of the daughters of Ochus. (Already Roxane, the daughter of Oxyartes the Bactrian, had been wedded to Alexander.) Alexander gave Drypetis to Hephaestion; she too was a daughter of Darius and sister to Alexander's own wife, and Alexander wanted his own children to have Hephaestion's as first cousins. To Craterus he gave Amastrine, daughter of Darius' brother Oxyartes. To Perdiccas he gave a daughter of Atropates, the satrap of Media. To Ptolemy the bodyguard and to Eumenes the royal secretary, he gave the daughters of Artabazus, Artacama and Artonis; Nearchus received the daughter of Barsine and Mentor; Seleucus, the daughter of Spitamenes the Bactrian. And Alexander likewise gave the rest of his Companions the noblest daughters of the Persians and Medians – as many as 80 brides. The weddings were held in accordance with Persian custom; seats were provided for the grooms in succession, and after the drinking, the brides came and sat beside their respective grooms, who took them by the hand and kissed them. Everyone was being married at the same time, and the king was the first to begin this ritual. This act more than anything else was thought to exemplify best Alexander's goodwill and fellowship. Each groom then took his bride and led her away. Alexander provided a dowry for all of them and ordered that the names of all Macedonians who had married Asian women be recorded. There were over 10,000 of these marriages, and Alexander gave all the couples wedding gifts.

Atropates, Abulites, Oxathres   satraps of Media, Susiana and Paraetecene. Plutarch (68) states that Alexander ran Oxathres through with a sarissa. Curtius (10.1) records that Autophradates, satrap of the Tapurians, was executed as well, for seeking the throne himself.

Parysatis   her father, Artaxerxes III Ochus, was king of Persia from 359 to 338 BC. He and Darius represented two sides of the Persian royal family.

This detail of a Roman wall-painting from Pompeii depicts Alexander (accompanied by a Persian bodyguard) and Barsine, with Winged Cupid standing between them. Cupid has stripped Alexander of his shield, and his helmet lies on the floor at Barsine's feet, suggesting that Alexander's passion for her has led him to abandon his martial goals. The pair's clothing would have prompted the viewer to identify them with Ares and Aphrodite, the gods of war and love.

1. Why might Alexander have felt the need to take such strong action on his return from the East?

2. How close were the satraps to being right in their expectation that Alexander would not return?

3. Curtius (10.3) has Alexander say that he held these marriages to erase every difference between conquered and conqueror. Do you believe this was Alexander's plan? If not, what was?

4. In marrying both Barsine and Parysatis, Alexander not only joins the royal family, but also effectively reconciles both sides through himself. Whom else does Alexander notably marry into this Persian royal family?

5. Almost all of the Companions left their Persian wives after Alexander's death. Why do you suppose they and 10,000 other Macedonians would have married Persian women in the first place?

6. Given Alexander's love of the *Iliad*, this mass marriage might recall the Homeric system of concubinage and the division of noble Trojan women among the Greek kings after the sack of Troy. Do you believe this forced intermarriage by Alexander is a genuine effort to surmount ethnic differences, or might it be considered a war crime, that is, an attempt to eradicate pure Persian noble stock?

Alexander eliminates debt

Arrian 7.5   This seemed to Alexander the right time to clear any and all **debts** that the soldiers had incurred, and to this end he ordered each to record how much he owed. In the beginning few recorded their names, for they were afraid that this might be some ruse of Alexander's, an attempt to discover who had lived in extravagance and beyond his soldier's wages. When Alexander received report that many were not registering themselves but hiding what they owed, he criticized the soldiers' mistrust. He said that a king should speak nothing but the truth to his subjects, and that none of his subjects should suppose that his king speaks anything but the truth. He then placed banking tables in the camp with gold upon them and ordered those in charge of the disbursement to stop registering names altogether and to relieve the debts of any who presented a certificate of debt. At this, they did indeed believe that Alexander spoke the truth, and they were cheered more by the gift of anonymity than by the payment of their debts. They say that the total of this gift to his soldiers was 20,000 talents.

> • What does this tale reveal about the relationship between Alexander and his army at this point?

The 30,000 Epigoni

Arrian 7.6   The satraps from Alexander's newly founded cities and from the other conquered territory came to Alexander with about 30,000 youths of the same age, whom Alexander called the **Epigoni**. They had been equipped with Macedonian arms and trained for war in the Macedonian style, and it is said that their arrival disturbed the Macedonians, who thought Alexander was scheming to end his prior dependence on them. After all, Alexander's Median dress was a great source of distress for the Macedonians who saw it, and the weddings held in accordance

---

debts   soldiers could accumulate debt quite easily, for merchants selling all manner of luxury items would have followed the army through much of the campaign. Arrian's record of the total debt cleared is twice that given by Plutarch (70), Curtius (10.2) and Diodorus (17.109).

Epigoni   Alexander had ordered the formation of this force back in Bactria in 327 BC (see p. 111), so that they now had roughly three years of training. According to Plutarch (71), Macedonian critics of this corps called them *pyrrhikhistai*, or 'war-dancers'. War dances were not uncommon in Greek culture. They had a ritual function, but also involved rigorous physical training under arms. Such ritualized practice had probably also been a part of the training for Epigoni, so that the term probably acknowledged these youths' exceptional preparation in the Macedonian style, but stressed their utter lack of experience.

with Persian custom displeased most of them, too – even the grooms themselves, despite their receiving a great honour on a par with the king. Peucestas, the satrap of Persia, distressed them too. He adopted the Persian dress and language, and Alexander was pleased at Peucestas' turning barbarian. Furthermore, the cavalries of the Bactrians, Sogdianians, Arachotians, Drangians, Arians and Parthians, and also those Persian cavalry called the **Euacae** – all those who seemed outstanding in reputation, physical beauty or some other area of excellence – had been incorporated into the Companion Cavalry. A fifth **hipparchy** had actually been added to it. This new hipparchy itself was not entirely barbarian in composition, but barbarians were enlisted throughout the cavalry as a whole when Alexander increased its size. Meanwhile Alexander had enlisted the following men into the *Agema*: Cophen, son of Artabazus; Hydarnes and Artiboles, sons of Mazaeus; Sisines and Phradasmenes, sons of Phrataphernes, satrap of Parthia and Hyrcania; Itanes, son of Oxyartes and brother of Roxane, Alexander's wife; and Aegobares and his brother Mithrobaeus. Hystaspes the Bactrian was named their commander, and they were issued Macedonian spears instead of the barbarian sling-javelins. All this distressed the Macedonians, who felt Alexander was in fact turning wholly barbarian in purpose and reducing Macedonian tradition – and the Macedonians themselves – to a position of dishonour.

---

1 Do you think this sort of integration would have been more offensive to the Macedonians than giving the barbarians a distinct corps? Why or why not?

2 How fundamental to Alexander's overall objectives do you think this policy of integration was?

3 Arrian makes a lot in this passage of Alexander's supplying the barbarians with Macedonian weapons. What practical reasons would Alexander have had for doing this? Why did this act upset the Macedonians so?

4 On reading this passage closely, do you believe Alexander's policies are an attempt to make the Macedonian army more Persian or the Persians more Macedonian?

Euacae   the identity of this group of Persians is unknown.

hipparchy Arrian is careful to clarify that Alexander did not introduce a distinct barbarian unit into the Companion Cavalry. Instead, he had increased the overall cavalry size by one hipparchy, and then integrated barbarians into all of them, including the previously existing four.

Dissent and the dismissal of the unfit

From Susa Alexander sailed down the river Eulaeus to the Persian Gulf, and then up the Tigris River. On reaching Opis, Alexander announced to his Macedonian soldiers the discharge of all those who were either disabled or too old to fight. The news sparked an angry response from the Macedonians, who were already upset by some of Alexander's earlier policies. In this so-called 'Mutiny at Opis', they went so far as to demand that Alexander simply discharge them all and take his father Ammon (a sarcastic reference to events at Siwah – see pp. 67–8) with him on future expeditions. Alexander reacted immediately by pointing out 13 ringleaders in the crowd for execution and addressed the cowed Macedonians with a lengthy speech (Arrian 7.9–10). According to Curtius (10.2), Alexander first delivered the speech, then arrested 13 ringleaders and handed them over to his Bodyguards. The excerpt below follows Alexander's speech in Arrian.

Arrian 7.11 Alexander leapt swiftly down from his speaker's platform and entered the palace. There he neither cared for his person nor was he seen by any of his Companions. But on the third day he invited certain select Persians to him and made them the new battalion commanders. He also determined that only those men he named Kinsmen could kiss him. On first hearing Alexander's speech, the Macedonians stood dumbstruck before the speaker's platform, and not a single person followed the king as he left, except his attendant Companions and the Bodyguards. The majority remained; they did not have anything particular to do or say, but were simply unwilling to leave. But then news about the Persians and the Medians reached them, that the Persians had been made battalion commanders, that the barbarian force had been integrated into the units, and that Macedonian terms were now being applied to Persians: there was an *agema* called 'Persian'; there were Persians as new *pezetairoi* and *astheteroi*; there was a Persian battalion of *argyraspides*, and a fresh Royal *Agema* in the Companion Cavalry. At this news, the Macedonians lost all restraint. They ran *en masse* to the palace, threw down their arms, and pleaded with the king. There they stood before his doors shouting and begging to be let in, and they expressed their willingness to hand over both those behind the recent disturbance as well as those who had actually instigated

---

pezetairoi, astheteroi, argyraspides   units that by tradition were exclusively Macedonian. *Pezetairoi* were literally 'Companion foot-soldiers', probably from Lower Macedon, while *astheteroi* were probably some sort of Companions from Upper Macedon. *Argyraspides*, 'Silver Shields', was applied to the Macedonian Hypaspists (see pp. 2, 35 and note), perhaps as early as the battle of Gaugamela (Diodorus 17.57); the term probably originated with the distribution of new shields to them, but it was clearly honorary as well.

the uproar. Nor did they intend to leave the palace doors, they said, day or night, until Alexander showed them some compassion. When these events were relayed to Alexander, he quickly emerged. And when he saw their grovelling and heard most of them shouting and wailing, tears came to his eyes as well. He acted as though about to say something, but even then they continued pleading. Finally one Callines, a Companion Cavalryman of venerable age and high rank, spoke along these lines:

'King, the Macedonians are distressed because you have now made some of the Persians your "Kinsmen", so that while Persians are called "Kinsmen" and kiss you, none of the Macedonians has yet tasted of this honour.' 'But I,' replied Alexander, 'consider all of you my kinsmen, and from now on I shall call you so.' Once he said this, Callines stepped forward and kissed him, as did any others who wished to do so. And so they took up their arms again and returned to the camp, shouting and singing in triumph as they went.

After this, Alexander sacrificed to all the gods to whom he usually sacrificed and held a public feast. Those seated immediately around him were Macedonian. The Persians were seated beyond these, and after the Persians were those from the other peoples, men of high repute or of particular distinction in some other quality. Alexander himself and those with him drew water from the same bowl and poured the same libations, as the Greek seers and the Mages together began the ceremony. Alexander prayed for all good things, but particularly for concord and fellowship in governance between Macedonians and Persians. The tale holds that there were 9,000 participants at the feast, and that all of them poured the same libation as they sang triumphantly.

7.12   Afterwards, all those Macedonians who were unfit for service owing to age or some other condition were in fact now ready to leave Alexander for home. These numbered as many as 10,000, and Alexander paid them not only for the time each had then served, but also for the time spent getting home. And on top of this he gave them each a **talent**. He did command, however, that any children of theirs by Asian women be left with him, so that they would not introduce discord to Macedonia, namely between foreigners or children by barbarian women and those other children and mothers the soldiers had previously left behind. He himself, Alexander said, would make sure these children were raised in the Macedonian style in all respects, especially in their outfitting for war. He would bring them to Macedonia and deliver them to their fathers himself once they had become men. These were the dubious and vague promises Alexander made to the newly discharged. He decided, however, also to demonstrate beyond

---

talent   according to Plutarch (71), these men were also to have front-row seats and sit crowned with garlands at all competitions and theatrical performances, a great honour commensurate with the large sum given them. Additionally, the orphans of any who had died would receive their father's pay.

all doubt his affection for them and his deep concern for their welfare, and so he sent the man he trusted most and valued equal to his own life, namely Craterus, to serve as protector and commander on their march. After bidding them all farewell, he tearfully sent them on their way, and they departed in tears themselves. Alexander ordered Craterus in fact not only to lead these men, but also to assume on his arrival the management of Macedonia, Thrace, Thessaly and the **freedom of the Greeks**. Alexander commanded Antipater to bring him fresh Macedonian recruits of fighting age to replace those being sent home. He sent Polysperchon along, too, as Craterus' second-in-command, so that if during the journey anything happened to Craterus, who was ill on departure, the men would still have a general.

The following rumour was passed quietly among those who report royal actions with an enthusiasm matching the secrecy of a king's motives, and who, led by guesswork and their own depravity, take a reliable piece of information in the wrong direction rather than towards the truth. This rumour claimed that Alexander had by that point been won over by his mother's slandering of Antipater and wanted to remove him from Macedonia. It is possible, however, that Antipater's summons held no dishonour, but was intended to prevent the differences between Antipater and Olympias from leading to any ill feeling that Alexander would not be able to resolve. The two of them, in fact, had been writing to him without cease. Antipater would describe Olympias' wilfulness, her temper and her meddling – hardly befitting the mother of Alexander. According to one story, when Alexander learned of his mother's actions he remarked that she was charging him steep rent for a mere **ten-month stay**. Olympias in turn criticized Antipater for being haughty about his high distinction and the attention he was given in general, and for failing to remember how he was appointed to his position in the first place. Instead, she alleged, Antipater considered himself foremost among all Macedonians and Greeks. These latter allegations, the criticisms of Antipater, tended to hold more weight for Alexander, since frankly those kinds of action are more **threatening to a kingship**. Nothing clear, however, no deed or word, was ever reported of Alexander that should have led someone to suppose that Antipater pleased him any less than **before ...**

---

freedom of the Greeks refers to the Macedonian responsibility of enforcing the oath taken by member states of the Corinthian League. The Greek freedom referred to here is not the freedom of all Greeks from a foreign power, but the freedom of all the Greek city-states from one another.

ten-month stay refers to Alexander's time in Olympias' womb. The ancients regularly referred to the 40-week human gestation as a ten-month period.

threatening to a kingship you will recall that, according to Plutarch, Antipater had already been treating with the Aetolians (see p. 102).

before ... a large lacuna begins at this point in the extant text of Arrian.

1   What is the significance of Alexander's limiting his kiss to Kinsmen only?

2   How does Alexander's reaction to this mutiny compare with his reaction to the mutiny on the Hyphasis (see pp. 141–2)?

3   What is the symbolic significance of the term 'Kinsman'? What appears to define a Persian as a Kinsman? How does a Macedonian now seem to become one?

4   According to Arrian, Alexander prayed for 'concord and fellowship in governance between Macedonians and Persians' (7.11). How much weight should be given to the phrase 'in governance'? Does Alexander seem to you to be seeking equality between these two peoples? Support your answer.

5   Of which nationality in the new empire would you wish to be a member at this time of the campaign? Why?

6   Who would you say won this standoff between Alexander and the veteran soldiers? Explain why you believe so.

7   Given what you know of Craterus (pp. 101, 102 note, 112), why do you think Alexander chose to send him with the discharged to Macedonia? Why would he be an appropriate choice as the new regent of Macedon?

8   Are you convinced by Arrian's argument against the rumour regarding Antipater? Why or why not?

Death of Hephaestion

From Opis Alexander travelled north-east to Ecbatana, where an enormous festival was eclipsed by the death of his closest friend.

Plutarch 72   When Alexander came to Ecbatana in Media and had dealt with urgent matters there, he resumed theatrical performances and festivals, because 3,000 **performers** had arrived fresh from Greece. During those days Hephaestion happened to be ill with fever, but that young and soldierly fellow could not stick to a strict regimen. As soon as his doctor Glaucus left for the theatre, Hephaestion ate a boiled rooster for breakfast and drained a **cooler** of wine. He then began to feel poorly and died shortly after. In his grief at Hephaestion's death, Alexander abandoned all reason. He immediately ordered all **horses and mules** shorn in

---

performers   Arrian (7.14) records that Alexander honoured Hephaestion after his death with literary and athletic contests by 3,000 artists and athletes. They were probably these performers, and they would soon perform yet again at Alexander's own funeral.

cooler   this *psykter*, if similar in volume to the one that Alcibiades and Socrates finish together in Plato's *Symposium* (213e), would have contained about 2 litres (2 quarts). It may have been bigger.

horses and mules   shearing horses in mourning appears to be a Thessalian and Persian practice, but clipping mules would probably have been viewed as extreme. Banning the pipe, or *aulos*, is remarkable as well. The instrument was probably often played during repetitive group activity, such as rowing or marching, and likely also during certain religious ceremonies.

mourning; he stripped the cities completely of their battlements; he crucified the unlucky doctor; and he banned pipe-playing – all music, in fact – from the army for a long time, until an oracle came from Ammon commanding that Alexander honour and sacrifice to Hephaestion as a **hero**. Using war as a consolation for his grief, Alexander set out to hunt and track people as if they were animals. After subduing the **Cossaeans**, he slaughtered all their adult males, and he called this an offering to Hephaestion. He was planning, too, to spend 10,000 talents on Hephaestion's tomb and burial with all its embellishments, and hoped even to surpass this expense by the artistry and extravagance of the preparations. For this reason he hoped specifically to retain the services of the artist Stasicrates, whose artistic innovations lent a certain magnificence, boldness and ostentation. Stasicrates had once before told Alexander that Mount Athos in Thrace could be sculpted and shaped into a human likeness better than any other mountain, and that, if Alexander liked, he could fashion **Athos** into the most lasting and conspicuous of statues for Alexander – its left hand holding an inhabited city of 10,000 and its right pouring as a libation the plentiful flood of a river streaming forth into the sea. This offer, in any case, Alexander had declined, but now he began devoting time with his artists to concocting and developing things far more outlandish and expensive.

---

1   What aspects of Alexander's behaviour in particular does Plutarch appear to criticize?

2   Based on discrepancies with other sources, what might Plutarch have exaggerated to make his point?

---

hero   cult worship of heroes had in the centuries before generally been reserved for the likes of Heracles, Theseus or Orestes, traditional (and usually mythical) heroes of the distant past. Hephaestion's body was to be carried to Babylon, where his pyre would be built. Construction of the pyre was never finished, because of Alexander's own death, but the tomb was constructed. It is described by Diodorus (18.4). Remarkably, the tomb was modelled on Babylonian architecture. Human sacrifice, suggested by Alexander's 'offering to Hephaestion', was not a normal practice among Greeks, but there is a precedent for it in the *Iliad*, where Achilles sacrifices Trojan youths at the funeral of his close companion Patroclus (23.175–6). Is this a further attempt to associate Alexander with Achilles?

Cossaeans   a mountain tribe of brigands south-west of Ecbatana who had in the past managed to keep their independence – and even exact tribute – from the Persian kings. Other sources (Arrian 7.15; Arrian, *Indica* 40.6–8; Diodorus 17.111; Strabo 11.13) do not mention a massacre, but record instead that they were settled in cities.

Athos   although less elaborate than this proposal, the sculpting of Mount Rushmore in the United States is a modern example of Stasicrates' vision actually carried out.

Alexander's death

After Hephaestion's funeral and the campaign against the Cossaeans in 324–323 BC, Alexander turned towards Babylon, the former capital of the Persian Empire and the site of his impending death.

Plutarch 73   While Alexander was heading for Babylon, Nearchus (who had by this point returned from his voyage through the Great Sea to the Euphrates) told him that he had met some **Chaldaeans** who recommended that Alexander should stay away from Babylon. Alexander ignored this advice and marched on. But on reaching the walls of the city, he saw many crows quarrelling and clawing at each other, so that some of them fell dead on the ground next to him. Later, intelligence against Apollodorus, who was stationed at Babylon, revealed that that general had had the seer **Pythagoras** conduct sacrificial auspices regarding the king's fate. When Alexander demanded that the seer come before him, he did not deny the act, and Alexander asked him about the outcome of the sacrifice. When Pythagoras replied that the liver had no lobe, Alexander cried, 'Oh no! A powerful omen!' He did no harm to Pythagoras, however, but was instead annoyed that he himself had failed to listen to Nearchus. He then began spending most of his time outside Babylon, either staying in his tent or sailing on the Euphrates. But many omens troubled him. Once, a tame donkey attacked and killed with a kick the largest and most beautiful lion in Alexander's menagerie. At another time, Alexander took off his **clothes** for exercise and was playing ball. When the young men with him went to retrieve their cloaks after play, they found a man sitting on the throne in silence and wearing Alexander's diadem and the royal robe. They asked this man who he was, but he was mute for some time. When he fully regained his senses, however, he said he was a Messenian named Dionysius. He had been charged with a certain crime, brought here from the sea, and had spent a long time in

---

Chaldaeans   highly respected astrologers with access to continuous celestial records that were ancient and accurate. They had received revenues from the temple of Bel (Marduk) meant for its renovation, and according to Aristobulus (Arrian 3.16, 7.17) Alexander suspected the Chaldaeans wanted to prolong construction so that they could continue to have free access to these funds. In Arrian, however, Alexander does take the Chaldaeans' advice more seriously than in Plutarch.

Pythagoras   this prophecy may have been a career-making one for the seer. He is credited with successfully prophesying the later deaths of Perdiccas (in 321 BC) and of Antigonus (in 301). The details of the liver's lobe were vital to the reading of sacrificial entrails. The utter absence of the lobe is never a good sign.

clothes   there are a couple of other variants for this story. In one, Alexander is not playing ball, only being rubbed down with oil (Diodorus 17.116). In the other, Alexander simply leaves the throne unattended and does not disrobe at all (Arrian 7.24).

chains. But just now, he said, **Serapis** had stood before him and freed his bonds. The god then brought him here and ordered him to put on the robe and diadem, and to sit in silence.

74   On hearing this Alexander executed the man, as his seers commanded, but he began to grow dispirited, unsure of divine favour and suspicious of his Friends. He feared Antipater and his sons in particular. One of them, Iolas, was his head cupbearer, and the other, Cassander, had recently arrived. The latter had witnessed some barbarians prostrating themselves before Alexander. Because he had been raised according to Greek tradition and had never seen such a thing before, Cassander roared with laughter. Alexander was enraged at this behaviour; he seized Cassander's hair violently with both hands and drove his head against the wall. On another occasion, when men were bringing charges against Antipater, Cassander sought to rebut them. But Alexander stepped in: 'What do you mean? Would people who have not been wronged make such a long journey to bring false charges?' When Cassander then replied that the journey itself was a sign of false charges because the men had travelled far from the evidence, Alexander burst out laughing: 'These are the sophisms of **Aristotle's ilk** that may be applied to either side of an argument! If any of you even appears to harm these men in the slightest, you will wail aloud in your agony.' And Cassander, they say, continued always to harbour a terrible and deep-rooted fear of Alexander. Many years later, as king of the Macedonians and ruler of Greece, Cassander was walking about in Delphi viewing the statues, when suddenly his eyes fell on one of Alexander. The very sight afflicted him on the spot; he shook with convulsions and scarcely recovered from his dizziness.

75   By this point, Alexander had resigned himself so completely to divine will and was so troubled and fearful in pursuing his aims, that he interpreted anything

---

Serapis   mentioned only in Plutarch's version of events, this god is of Egyptian origin and combines the elements of Osiris and Apis (Hapi): Osiris-Hapi = Serapis. Alexander probably embraced the cult of Serapis after encountering it at Rhacotis, the site of Alexandria in Egypt. Ptolemy and his successors made Serapis a very important deity; according to Ptolemaic tradition, Serapis was the guarantor of kingship.

Aristotle's ilk   an intriguing reference to Aristotle. In embracing certain barbarian customs, Alexander appeared to defy a major assumption of Aristotle's, that the Greeks were the best and most civilized of all peoples. Although Aristotle had been a teacher of Alexander, the two were by this time no longer on close terms. Many Greeks had heard about Alexander's policies to the east, and there was widespread concern throughout the Corinthian League. It is very possible that when Cassander attempts to intervene on behalf of his father, he is arguing against accusations that might have led to (or justified) Alexander's replacing Antipater with Craterus (see p. 163). Alexander's accusation here is somewhat unfair. It is an allegation long levied against sophists generally, notably in *Clouds* by Aristophanes, the Athenian comic playwright, but Greek students of rhetoric regularly practised their art by defending both sides of a given argument.

slightly irregular or out of place as a portent or sign. His palace was filled with men sacrificing, purifying and prophesying. While it is true that disbelief and contempt for divine matters is a terrible thing, the fear of divine forces is terrible as well. Like water that flows ever downward to the lowest depths, this fear was filling a now thoroughly frightened Alexander with folly.

When divine oracles were brought regarding Hephaestion, Alexander did **quit his grief**, at least, and returned again to festivals and drinking-bouts. Then one day, after hosting Nearchus and his men in splendid fashion, Alexander took a bath as he usually did before sleeping. But he then left to go drinking, at **Medius'** invitation. While carousing at Medius' all the next day, Alexander began to have a fever. It did not come from gulping down a **cup of Heracles**, nor did he suddenly feel a pain like a spear wound in his back. Some have felt compelled to write these things, as if composing a tragic and heart-rending conclusion to a great drama. But Aristobulus records only that Alexander was out of his mind with fever and continued drinking wine to slake an intense thirst. This then led to delirium, and he expired on the thirtieth day of the month of Daesius.

76   The *Ephemerides* record the following about his illness. On the eighteenth of the month of Daesius Alexander was sleeping in his bathing-room because of fever. On the next day he washed and moved to his bedroom, where he spent the day playing dice with Medius. He then took a late bath, sacrificed to the gods, ate a bit, and suffered from fever throughout the night. On the twentieth he performed the usual sacrifice, and while lying in the bathing-room gave his attention to Nearchus, listening to the account of his voyage through the Great Sea. He did the same on the twenty-first, but grew increasingly feverish. He spent that night terribly ill, and the intense fever continued through the next day. He was carried to the great plunge-bath so that he could lie beside it, and there he actually met with his commanders to discuss how the vacancies in command posts might be filled most judiciously. On the twenty-fourth he suffered from intense fever and sacrificed only on being carried to the victims. He ordered his top commanders to spend their time in the palace courtyard, and his squadron and division leaders to spend the night just outside. He was carried to the palace across the river on the

---

quit his grief   Alexander is consoled by the oracles of Ammon to which Plutarch earlier referred (p. 165). While the oracle did not grant Alexander's wish that Hephaestion be deified, it did allow his worship as a hero.

Medius   there is no record of this man, a Thessalian from Larisa, holding a military post, but he was one of the ship captains during the river voyage in India and appears to have been a close personal friend of the king's. Not surprisingly, his relationship with Alexander led to allegations of murder directed at him after the king's death (Arrian 7.27).

cup of Heracles   according to Diodorus (17.117), drinking deeply from this special cup was part of a ritual commemoration of that hero's death, which occurred on Mount Oeta in Thessaly. The ritual would therefore have been very familiar to Medius.

twenty-fifth, and he slept a little there, but his fever did not subside, and when his commanders visited him he could not speak. The same was true on the twenty-sixth. The Macedonians, therefore, supposing he was dead, came to the palace doors and began shouting and threatening the Companions violently until they succeeded in overpowering them. Once the doors had been opened, they all one after another stripped to their **tunics** and passed alongside his couch. During that day Python and Seleucus were sent with their units to the temple of Serapis to ask whether they should convey Alexander there, but the god answered that they should leave him where he was. In the afternoon of the **twenty-eighth**, Alexander died.

77 Most of the above has been quoted word for word from the *Ephemerides*. No one suspected poison at the time, but they say that five years later, after receiving some piece of intelligence, **Olympias** executed many men and had Iolas' remains scattered in the belief that he was the one who administered the poison. Some record that a certain Hagnothemis heard from the king Antigonus that Aristotle himself procured the poison and advised Antipater to administer it to Alexander. According to this account the poison was water – cold and icy – from a certain cliff in **Nonacris**. It was collected like fine dew and stored in a donkey's hoof, since the cold and pungent poison would have eaten through any other container. Most believe, however, that such tales of poisoning are wholly **fabricated**, and there

---

tunics the soldiers' stripping to their tunics may in part have been a measure against any assassination attempt, but it was more likely to have been a gesture of respect. When, after the dismissal of the unfit (see p. 161), the soldiers threw down their arms, which included their weapons and armour, they would have been wearing only their tunics.

twenty-eighth Alexander's death may be dated precisely to 10 June 323 BC, based on a contemporary tablet from a Babylonian astronomical diary. The contradiction in Plutarch's dates for Alexander's death (see p. 168) results from his using different sources (first Aristobulus and then the *Ephemerides*).

Olympias propaganda started by Olympias against Antipater has probably influenced the Alexander tradition. Cassander later avenged his younger brother Iolas by having Olympias murdered and preventing her burial.

Nonacris small town in the northern Peloponnesus. The water is from the river Styx, frequently identified with the mythological river of the Underworld. According to Hesiod (*Theogony* 775–806), gods could safely drink the water as long as they did not swear a false oath while doing so.

fabricated it is clear from all the controversy that the true cause of Alexander's death was unknown in antiquity, but recent scholars have continued with the speculation, combing the ancient sources for evidence of injury and symptoms. Modern proposals include poison (strychnine or hellebore), medication (an impatient overdose of hellebore), syphilis, scarlet fever, alcoholism, malaria (perhaps contracted at the river Cydnus, see p. 41), typhoid fever, flu, acute pancreatitis, West Nile virus and the serious injury Alexander sustained among the Malli (see pp. 143–4). We can look forward to others.

is plenty of evidence to support this. As the commanders quarrelled for many days, Alexander's body lay uncared-for in a hot and stifling environment. Yet the corpse remained pure and fresh, and bore no sign of the damage one would expect from poison.

---

1 From a strictly political perspective, why might there have been a real source of tension between Alexander and Antipater's family (**74**)?

2 It is a standard element in ancient biography to include omens presaging the subject's death. Why do you suppose this is the convention? How does it contribute to the reader's understanding of Alexander's character?

3 What might a death by drinking from a cup of Heracles have symbolized to an ancient? What about the 'pain like a spear wound in his back' (**75**)?

4 Does the way in which Alexander died seem to suit the manner in which he lived his life?

5 Here Plutarch records material from the rather tedious *Ephemerides*. Is there any way in which the information enhances one's understanding of Alexander's character?

6 Plutarch writes that most of this material (**76**) comes directly from the *Ephemerides*. What detail(s) do you suppose did not? Support your answer.

7 The water of the river Styx (**77**) was supposed to be poisonous to mortals. What symbolic relevance for Alexander might ancients therefore have found in this choice of poison?

Obituary

Arrian 7.28   Alexander died in the one hundred and fourteenth Olympiad, during the archonship at Athens of Hegesias. He lived for **thirty-two** years and eight months, according to Aristobulus, and he ruled for the last twelve years and eight months of his life. He had a most handsome physique and an unparalleled liking for labour. He was especially shrewd, particularly courageous in judgement, exceedingly desirous of honour and danger, and most attentive to the divine. When it came to bodily pleasures, he was unsurpassed in self-restraint. He had the greatest talent for determining what was necessary even in an uncertain situation, and was superior at inferring what was likely from what was observable. He was a champion at marshalling an army, as well as arming and outfitting it. And when it came to firing the army's spirit, injecting it with optimism, and dispelling fear in the face of danger by his own fearlessness, he was most magnificent in every way. Furthermore, he did with greatest courage all that clearly needed doing, and whenever he had to steal victory from the enemy, he was most adept at gaining the advantage on them before they even began to fear what was coming. He

---

thirty-two   if Plutarch is right in dating Alexander's birth, then Alexander was just under a month short of 33 years.

was especially faithful to treaties and agreements, and particularly immune to those who attempted to deceive him. He spent money most sparingly on his own pleasures, but for the welfare of his fellow man he was especially indulgent.

7.29   If Alexander erred at all out of impulsiveness or in anger, or if he was led on to behave rather excessively like the barbarians, I myself do not make much of it, nor would any who reflect objectively on these facts: that he was young, that he enjoyed unremitting good fortune and that he was surrounded by those men who have and will always attend kings for base purposes and so strive to please them rather than to advise what is best. But I am certain that Alexander alone of the ancient kings had the character to repent of his wrongs, and that this was because of his noble nature. Most people, even if they recognize their error at all, think to conceal their wrong by defending it as though done for the best. They do this in poor judgement. The only remedy for wrongdoing, in my opinion, is to confess to it and to demonstrate unmistakable remorse; he who has injured others through his lack of discretion can avoid aggravating their sense of injury, if only he concedes that he has behaved poorly. Furthermore, if his errors have truly pained him, he may have confidence that he will never again commit any such error in the future.

Alexander did assign his own birth to a god, but I do not consider that much of a crime, particularly if it was only a ploy aimed at securing the reverence of his subjects. Furthermore, he was no less obscure a king, I think, than **Minos**, **Aeacus** or **Rhadamanthus**, and these men were called sons of Zeus long ago without risk of appearing insolent. The same is true for **Theseus**, son of Poseidon, and for **Ion**, son of Apollo. Alexander's Persian attire, I think, was an effort to keep the king from seeming wholly foreign to the barbarians, and at the same time to distance himself a bit from the impulsive and insolent behaviour typical of the Macedonians. It was this same reason, I believe, that led him to introduce the Persian *Melophoroi* and Persian nobles into his battalions and divisions. Finally, he engaged in lengthy drinking-bouts, as Aristobulus records, not for the wine, since Alexander did not drink much, but for the fellowship with his Companions.

7.30   Whoever would criticize Alexander, let him list all those actions that deserve criticism. But first let him gather together the whole sum of Alexander's deeds, and then let him reflect on who he is himself and what sort of fortune he enjoys who would criticize a man who became what he did and who attained that pinnacle of mortal good fortune. Alexander was undisputedly king of both continents and his name reached every corner of the earth, while any who would criticize him

---

Minos, Aeacus, Rhadamanthus, Theseus, Ion   the first three were sons of Zeus. They were kings during their lives and became judges in the Underworld after death. Theseus was a mythical civilizer, and king of Athens; Ion was the mythical founder of the Ionians. All five figures were sons of gods, but mortal. Heracles is notably absent from this list, perhaps because he was not a king, and because he did in fact become immortal.

is himself rather trivial, toiling to trivial ends and yet failing even to set those matters straight. I for one believe there was no race of humankind, no city at that time, no individual unvisited by Alexander's name. Nor do I think that such a man, one unlike any other mortal, could be born of other than divine origins. Oracles, they say, indicated this at Alexander's death, and there are other signs: the various visions seen by some, the dreams had by others, the honour still paid him by humankind, the immortal memory of him, and even now after so much time the various oracles that bid the race of Macedonians to honour him. While even I myself have condemned some of Alexander's actions in my history, still I feel no shame in my awe at the man. My criticisms of his deeds emerge from my sense of candour, but I offer them also for the benefit of humankind. The same reason drove me to write this history, and in doing so I myself enjoyed the help of a **god**.

---

1   What statements in the first paragraph (**7.28**) can you dispute with evidence from your reading?

2   Why is Arrian careful to write 'of the ancient kings' (**7.29**)?

3   What errors of Alexander is Arrian defending by pointing to Alexander's remorse (**7.29**)?

4   Do you agree about the reasons Arrian gives for Alexander's introduction of the Persian *Melophoroi* and nobles into his army?

5   At the conclusion of his obituary, Arrian discusses the claim for Alexander's divinity. What sort of relationship with the divine does Arrian appear to believe Alexander had?

6   Do you think that Arrian's concluding comments are a fair assessment of Alexander, or are they an exaggerated eulogy?

---

god   in referring to divine assistance after a discussion of Alexander's divinity, Arrian implies a close relationship between author and subject. You will also recall earlier discussions by Arrian about his work (pp. 28, 31–2), where he claims to be glorifying Alexander's deeds just as Homer celebrated Achilles. The Homeric bard would traditionally invoke the Muse for inspiration in reciting an epic poem, and Arrian here applies that convention to his much later literary and historical genre, one characterized by rivalry between authors who tended to talk up their subject-matter.

Epilogue

Most of our ancient sources report that as Alexander lay dying in Babylon his Friends asked him to name his successor. He replied, 'The best man, since I foresee that my funeral games will be a great contest between my Friends' (Diodorus 18.1). Alexander may well have felt that naming an heir was pointless. Many pretenders to the throne would, as he predicted, soon emerge from among those closest to him, and it is doubtful that a name uttered by him in a fever on his deathbed could have curbed their ambitions.

Alexander's 'Successors'

Alexander was survived by two legitimate male blood-relatives, but neither was a promising successor. Roxane's son Alexander IV, born two months after Alexander died, was only an infant, while Alexander's half-brother Philip III Arrhidaeus was mentally unfit to rule. While Arrhidaeus did claim the throne, he reigned only as a figurehead under the supervision of others. Antipater continued to control Macedonia as regent there, while Perdiccas, who had been Alexander's second-in-command, now effectively ruled the new empire.

Almost immediately other generals and administrators of the deceased Alexander began to lay claim to smaller portions of the realm. Craterus had control of the Cilician navy. Eumenes, Alexander's secretary, ruled Cappadocia. Antigonus, Alexander's satrap in Phrygia, was extending his power southwards. Lysimachus, a general and Bodyguard of Alexander, assumed control of Thrace and north-west Asia Minor. Finally, Ptolemy, who was ordered to govern Egypt on behalf of Arrhidaeus, took that land for himself. While Alexander's corpse was en route to burial at either Aegae or Siwah (sources disagree), Ptolemy acquired possession of it at Damascus and gave it a Macedonian burial in Memphis – an unmistakable bid for Alexander's legacy.

War followed between these so-called 'Successors'. Within three years of Alexander's death Craterus died in battle against Eumenes, and Perdiccas was killed by his senior officers after failing to wrest Egypt from Ptolemy. Both of Alexander's legitimate heirs (Arrhidaeus and Alexander IV) came under the supervision of Antipater, who still controlled Macedonia. A few years later Eumenes too was executed by his own troops, Antigonus had command of the Macedonian army in Asia, and Seleucus, another of Alexander's generals, was quickly establishing his rule in Babylon and the eastern regions of the empire.

The next years saw the extinction of Alexander's legitimate heirs. Two years after Antipater died in 319 BC, Olympias managed to gain control of Macedonia and executed Arrhidaeus. Alexander IV became king at four years old, and Olympias ruled through him. But when Cassander conquered Macedonia the following year, he in turn executed Olympias and soon dispatched Roxane and the young Alexander as well. By 304 Antigonus, Ptolemy and Seleucus had all assumed the name 'King', a title that asserted their competing claims to Alexander's empire.

More war followed. By 277 BC – after over four decades of fighting between the 'Successors' – Ptolemy, Antigonus, Seleucus, Cassander and Lysimachus were all dead, and three major kingdoms had emerged from the fray. The Ptolemies ruled Egypt and Libya. The Antigonids (descendants of Antigonus) now controlled Macedonia and parts of Greece. The Seleucids ruled the vast territory extending from the eastern Mediterranean to roughly the border of modern Pakistan. Alexander had taken ten years to build his empire, but he had governed the whole for fewer than two when he died. Now the emergence of these three powers after so many years made it clear that his short-lived empire would never be restored to any single successor.

The Hellenistic Age

Alexander's legacy is greater than his conquests. He and his father before him had garnered Greek support for the invasion of Persia in part by casting the venture as a Panhellenic enterprise, a war of revenge by Greeks against barbarians. Alexander's 'Successors' – Antigonus, Seleucus, Ptolemy and their descendants – likewise established their authority by defining their kingdoms as Greek kingdoms. Alexander's extensive conquest combined with this primacy given to Greek culture during and after it thus gave birth to what has been termed the Hellenistic Age (323–30 BC).

Many have considered the age a period of decline, a transitional stage between the glory of Greece and Rome's Golden Age. But the influence of Greek culture in Europe and Asia was never greater; it was consciously adopted and promoted by the Hellenistic kings with an enthusiasm reminiscent of the Macedonian court of Philip II. While the territory of Alexander's empire was not to be united again under a single king, Greek peoples throughout the known world felt a common bond. Greek became the lingua franca across the eastern Mediterranean and the Middle East. Cities from Spain to Pakistan built Greek theatres and gymnasia. Kings invited Greek poets, playwrights, musicians, philosophers and athletes to their courts. Royal libraries soon emerged, most famously the Library of Alexandria, which was inspired by and modelled on the personal library of Aristotle himself. These aimed to collect and catalogue all the learning of the known world (poetry, drama, geography, philosophy, mathematics, history and the rest) in an initiative perhaps not rivalled in innovativeness, scope and sophistication until our own modern Information Age.

Man versus myth

The very power of Alexander's name is another key facet of his legacy. Cyrus II, founder of the Persian Achaemenid dynasty, was the first king to assume the title 'Great'. When Alexander himself took the title, as he probably did during his lifetime, it was most likely in order to legitimate his claim to the Persian throne. But over time his title 'Great' has come to be understood, I think, more as an epithet than a title; it suggests that Alexander had within himself an innate greatness or transcendence that his deeds demonstrated to the world. Subsequent leaders have since attached the epithet to their own names like a talisman meant to evoke the famous Alexander. Still others have received the honorific title posthumously, and in each case the recipient of this distinction seems suddenly and indisputably elevated to a plane well above the rest of us.

Our greatest leaders regularly become legends, of course, sometimes even at the expense of their historical selves. A 2008 poll, for example, found that 23 per cent of the British public believed Winston Churchill a mythical figure. If the road from man to myth is so short today, it was even shorter in antiquity. Already during Alexander's lifetime people were relating fanciful tales about him, many of which were gradually combined to form the *Alexander Romance*. According to this account, he won a victory in the Olympic games, conquered Rome, explored the depths of the sea and rode into the sky on a bird-drawn chariot. Such stories were popular in antiquity, and the *Alexander Romance* was a favourite across Europe through the Middle Ages and the Renaissance. That popularity has helped him to become a legend for the world. For many he has represented a superhuman determination to accomplish the truly impossible. For others, he has been a virtuous and courageous king ultimately undone by personal vices or by Fortune herself. Still others have found in him a brutal and unscrupulous tyrant. The real, historical Alexander may remain elusive, but he welcomes all to find in him whatever they would like or need to find – just the ingredient to keep a legend alive.

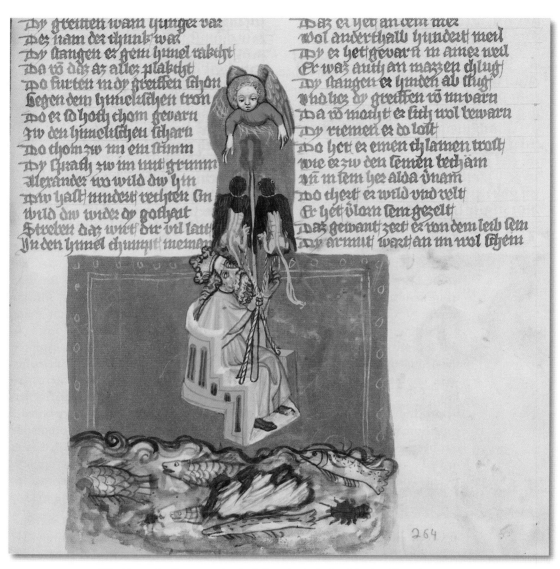

The Alexander Romance *inspired the episode depicted in this fifteenth-century German illumination. As the Alexander of the* Romance *explores impossible regions such as the depths of the sea or the Isles of the Blessed, divine forces invariably and emphatically turn him back. At one point (2.41), he rides a makeshift chariot drawn by two large birds that he entices into the air with horses' livers affixed to spears. As soon as he reaches the sky, 'a flying creature in the form of a man' orders his return to earth. Here the artist notably captures this tension between mortal and divine: an enthroned Alexander drawn by sphinxes begins to break the frame of the miniature as he threatens to ride into Heaven itself.*

Ancient sources

Extant

The following are the most important ancient sources for Alexander's campaign that survive from antiquity. (There are many other anecdotal sources as well.)

Alexander Romance a wholly romantic account of Alexander's campaign attributed falsely to his court historian **Callisthenes**. It offers little accurate information, but does provide insight into how Alexander was popularly perceived in his time and in the centuries following his death. It draws some of its material from oral accounts that began as early as Alexander's own day, but it took roughly its present form around the third century AD. Originally written in Greek, there were Syriac and Arabic versions as well. It became widely popular during the medieval period, when it was translated into most major European languages.

Arrian Flavius Arrianus Xenophon, AD *c.* 86–post 146, who wrote the *Anabasis of Alexander* in Greek. His main sources were the now-lost works of **Aristobulus** and **Ptolemy**. See Introduction (p. 5).

Curtius Quintus Curtius Rufus, first century AD, who wrote a highly rhetorical ten-book *History of Alexander the Great* in Latin. The first two books (up to the spring of 333 BC) are lost. He composed lengthy speeches for the work and often presents characters' thoughts and motivations. These aspects of the work are highly interpretive, but Curtius did base them on evidence from his sources. He may well be the same Curtius Rufus who had an extensive public career, ending up as proconsul of Africa. He followed **Cleitarchus** among others for his history, and expresses strong criticism of Alexander's behaviour at many points.

Diodorus Diodorus Siculus, mid-first century BC, who wrote the 40-book *Library* (an ambitious universal history spanning from mythical times to 60 BC) in Greek. Book 17 treats Alexander, and has survived in almost its entirety. He followed **Cleitarchus** closely, and highlights Alexander's moderation and self-restraint.

Justin Marcus Iustinianus Iustinus, *c.* second–fourth century AD, author of a summary in Latin of the lost Greek work by **Pompeius Trogus** which he interspersed with his own moralizing passages.

Plutarch Mestrius Plutarchus, AD *c.* 46–120, moral philosopher who wrote a *Life of Alexander* in Greek as part of his series of 'parallel lives' (see Introduction, pp. 4–5). He wrote the biography with a variety of earlier sources at his disposal, including a collection of **Letters** attributed to Alexander.

Lost

The works by the following authors are no longer extant, but their writings were vital to authors of the surviving works listed above.

Aristobulus (from Cassandreia) engineer and officer during Alexander's campaign, who began writing his history when he was 83. It was criticized in antiquity for its flattering portrait of Alexander, but **Arrian** used it as one of his two major sources.

Callisthenes (from Olynthus) Aristotle's nephew and student who served as Alexander's court historian and wrote the court's official *Deeds of Alexander*. His job was to present Alexander in a manner agreeable to the Greeks while at the same time suggesting his divine paternity. His arrest in 327 BC, apparently because of his opposition to *proskynesis*, prevented him from finishing his work, which ended at around 329.

Chares (from Mytilene) Alexander's chamberlain after the death of Darius. He wrote scandalous and romantic anecdotal memoirs of the campaign and life at court.

Cleitarchus though probably never on the campaign, he wrote a 12-book history in *c.* 310 BC based on eyewitness accounts. Though criticized by some for fabrications, it was nevertheless the most widely read account of Alexander in antiquity and the primary origin of the so-called 'vulgate' tradition preserved by the extant sources **Curtius**, **Diodorus** and **Justin**.

Nearchus (from Crete) chief admiral of Alexander's fleet that sailed the Hydaspes and Indus rivers and then the Arabian Sea. He was a boyhood friend of Alexander and was close to him in his last year. He wrote a memoir of events in India and his voyage from the Indus River to the Persian Gulf. **Arrian** used this work extensively for his *Indica*, and doubtless drew from it also for his history of Alexander.

Onesicritus (from Astypalaea) Alexander's chief helmsman and lieutenant to **Nearchus** during the ocean voyage. He was schooled in the Cynic philosophy of Diogenes and famous in antiquity for his highly embellished account.

Pompeius Trogus (from Transalpine Gaul) a Romanized member of the Gallic Vocontii tribe, he wrote the *Philippic Histories* in 44 books in about the first century BC. Preserved today in summary form thanks to **Justin**, this work treated Macedonia (including the reigns of Philip and Alexander) in Books 7–12. He cast Alexander as a brutal tyrant corrupted by his conquests.

Ptolemy Ptolemaeus I Soter, 367/6–282 BC, Alexander's friend from childhood and an important commander during the campaign. After Alexander's death he became governor of Egypt, then king and founder of the Ptolemaic dynasty. His history of Alexander tends to present him in a good light and to highlight Ptolemy's own contributions to the campaign, so that while full of accurate technical detail, it was at least in part propaganda. It served **Arrian** as a chief source for his own history.

Other written sources

The following are other written documents, some perhaps authentic, from which many of the above ancient sources drew.

Bēmatist **records**   the logs of Alexander's *bēmatists* (surveyors), these would have provided distances travelled and other technical information throughout the campaign.

Ephēmerides   ascribed to Alexander's royal secretary Eumenes, these were probably literary compositions that purported to be the official royal journals. Material quoted from them treats primarily the last days of Alexander's life and is consistently occupied with his personal habits, not military or administrative affairs.

Hypomnēmata   literally 'memoranda', these were the personal notes of Alexander. **Diodorus** (18.4) records that after Alexander's death Perdiccas read an account of Alexander's future plans from them to the Macedonian infantry.

Letters   correspondence to and from Alexander apparently available in antiquity as a collection. **Plutarch** frequently refers to them. Some reproduced by the extant authors are clearly spurious. The authenticity of none is certain.

Further reading and references

Reference works

Waldemar Heckel, *Who's Who in the Age of Alexander the Great: Prosopography of Alexander's Empire* (Oxford, 2006).

The place to turn for more detail on any individual relevant to Alexander's life and campaign.

Simon Hornblower and Antony Spawforth (eds), *The Oxford Classical Dictionary* (3rd edn, Oxford, 1996).

An essential resource for any student of Classics.

C.A. Robinson, *The History of Alexander the Great: A Translation of the Extant Fragments*, 2 vols (Providence, 1953–1963). A translation of most of the historical fragments pertaining to Alexander in Felix Jacoby's *Die Fragmente der Griechischen Historiker* (Leiden, 1923–1958), with commentary.

Richard J.A. Talbert (ed.), *Barrington Atlas of the Greek and Roman World* (Princeton, 2000).

The most splendid and detailed atlas available for the ancient world.

Historical biographies

A.B. Bosworth, *Conquest and Empire: The Reign of Alexander the Great* (Cambridge, 1988).

Studiously avoids the ancient evidence from more legendary accounts and presents an opportunistic, often ruthless, Alexander.

Peter Green, *Alexander of Macedon 356–323 BC: A Historical Biography* (Berkeley, 1991).

Originally written in 1970 with an axe to grind, this highly readable account seeks to debunk the overly idealistic views of Alexander that preceded it.

Ian Worthington, *Alexander the Great: Man and God* (Harlow, 2004).

A more recent biography that interprets Alexander's life largely in terms of his notions of personal divinity.

Macedonia and Philip II

Eugene N. Borza, *In the Shadow of Olympus: The Emergence of Macedon* (Princeton, 1990).

Traces Macedonia's early history and institutions from pre-historic times to the reign of Philip II, suggesting that the Macedonians distinguished themselves culturally from their Greek neighbours.

R.M. Errington, *A History of Macedonia* (Berkeley, 1990).

A broader and quite accessible introduction, interesting in part for its rather negative assessment of Alexander's impact on Macedonia's history.

N.G.L. Hammond, *The Macedonian State: Origins, Institutions, and History* (Oxford, 1989).

A comprehensive yet accessible history – a rich and highly recommended resource.

The Persians

Maria Brosius, *The Persians: An Introduction* (London, 2006).

A broad overview of the history and culture of the Parthians, Sasanians and Persians from the sixth century BC to the seventh century AD. The first chapter covers the Achaemenids.

J.M. Cook, *The Persian Empire* (New York, 1983).

Long the standard work on ancient Persia, this is a well-illustrated introduction to the Persian Empire, including detailed discussion of its religion and administration.

Amelie Kuhrt, *The Persian Empire*, 2 vols (London, 2007).

A splendid collection of ancient sources relevant to the Achaemenid Persian Empire (Greek and Latin, but also Akkadian, Aramaic, Egyptian, Hebrew and Old Persian), all translated into English and with introductory discussion.

Bruce Lincoln, *Religion, Empire, and Torture: The Case of Achaemenian Persia, with a Postscript on Abu Ghraib* (Chicago, 2007).

Discusses the relationship between empire and religion in ancient Persia, with an intriguing glance at the American empire of today.

Alexander's 'Successors' and the Hellenistic Age

A.B. Bosworth, *The Legacy of Alexander: Politics, Warfare, and Propaganda under the Successors* (Oxford, 2002).

An account of the years after Alexander's death which emphasizes the posthumous role of Alexander as an example of heroism that the Successors sought to imitate to legitimize their rule.

Graham Shipley, *The Greek World after Alexander, 323–30 B.C.* (London, 2000).

Provides objective and fairly full coverage, breaking up historical survey with discussion of important topics such as the philosophy, literature or science of the period.

F.W. Walbank, *The Hellenistic World* (Cambridge, Mass., rev. 2006).

Originally published in 1981 and now newly revised, a brief (for this complex period), accessible and very useful introduction to events from the death of Alexander to 146 BC.

Ancient works in translation

Arrian, *The Campaigns of Alexander*, trans. Aubrey de Sélincourt (Baltimore, 1971).

Diodorus, *The Library of History*, Loeb Classical Library, vols 8 (Books 16.66–17) and 9 (Books 18–19.65), trans. C. Bradford Welles (Cambridge, Mass., 1997).

Justin, *Epitome of the Philippic History of Pompeius Trogus*, vol. 1 (Books 11–12: *Alexander the Great*), trans. J. C. Yardley, with commentary by Waldemar Heckel (Oxford, 1997).

Plutarch, 'Life of Alexander', in *Age of Alexander*, trans. Ian Scott-Kilvert (London, 1973).

Pseudo-Callisthenes, *The Greek Alexander Romance*, trans. Richard Stoneman (London, 1991).

Quintus Curtius Rufus, *The History of Alexander*, trans. John Yardley (London, 2005).

Glossary

Terms

Achaemenid the dynasty ruling the Persian Empire from **Cyrus II** (Cyrus the Great) to **Darius III**.

Aegae ceremonial capital of Macedonia and site of Philip's assassination.

Agēma generally any division or corps of an army, but in the Macedonian army the Royal *Agema* is a special unit of the **Companion Cavalry**. It served as Alexander's personal guard and had replaced the **Royal Squadron** by the time of the battle against **Porus**.

baggage train strictly, the pack animals and all they carried to support the army, but would also have included non-fighting members of the campaign and other hangers-on such as vendors and prostitutes.

barbarian an often pejorative term used of non-Greeks.

battalion a unit of infantry.

Bodyguards more than mere protectors of the king's person, these seven (later eight) **Companions** were hand-picked by the Macedonian king and formed his most intimate circle.

Brahmins sage priests who served as advisers to Indian kings.

Chaeronea site of an important battle in 338 BC through which Philip established a thinly veiled sovereignty over the Greek **city-states**. Alexander fought as commander of the Macedonian left **wing**.

Chaldaeans when the Persians absorbed the Chaldaean Empire into their own, the term Chaldaean ceased to refer to the people of Babylonia, and was applied instead to a learned priestly class, strictly priests of Babylonian **Bel-Marduk**, famed for their knowledge of the magical arts and their prophetic wisdom.

chiliarch literally 'commander of 1,000' in Greek, this term refers to Greek cavalry commanders of approximately 1,000 men, but also to the Persian king's second-in-command, the Grand Vizier, who originally commanded a palace guard of 1,000.

city-state *polis* in Greek, one of many independent and sovereign Greek territories comprising a city and the lands surrounding it.

Companion one of a group of noble cavalrymen hand-picked by the Macedonian king.

Companion Cavalry composed of elite **Companions**, frequently fought alongside Alexander himself.

Corinthian League confederation of Greek **city-states** and Macedonia established after the battle of **Chaeronea** in 338 BC. A declaration of war on **Persia** was one of the League's first acts under Philip, and all members of the League were required to contribute money or forces to the effort.

Cynic school of philosophy that advocated self-sufficiency and happiness through a virtuous life lived in accordance with Nature and through the rejection of power, wealth and glory.

Delphi   home to the famous **oracle** of **Apollo**. People from all over the Greek-speaking world would come here to seek the oracle's guidance and support.

diadem   a purple ribbon with a white stripe traditionally worn by Persian royalty, and then adopted by Alexander. Whereas Persian kings typically wore it around the Median **tiara**, Alexander wore it around the *kausia*, the felt hat worn by Macedonian kings.

Ephēmerides   Macedonian court journals to which ancient writers refer for evidence of daily royal activity. Their authenticity, however, is not entirely certain.

Epigoni   literally 'Successors', these 30,000 Persian boys were trained as soldiers in the Macedonian tradition. This training displeased many of the older Macedonian soldiers, who wished to maintain a clear distinction between Macedonians and barbarians.

Friend   originally a Persian title enjoyed by nobles of the king's choosing. As part of his policy of orientalism, Alexander bestowed the title on a select number of his **Companions**.

groom   probably a member of the **Royal Pages**, he was in charge of helping the king mount his horse and accompanied him in battle.

Gymnosophist   one of a group of Indian thinkers who followed Nature and led an ascetic life that included the rejection of clothing; hence the term, literally 'naked sophist'.

hipparchy   any of several **Companion Cavalry** divisions created after the execution of the prominent commander **Philotas** (and his father **Parmenion**) in 330 BC to replace the regionally defined squadron.

hoplites   heavily armed infantry soldiers, typically arranged in **phalanx** formation.

Hypaspists   a corps which typically fought on the Macedonian front line, between the infantry to the left and the **Companion Cavalry** to the right. Fighting at the seam between infantry and cavalry required experience and versatility, and this corps was the most respected of the Macedonian infantry.

Ilium   another name for Troy, the city against which, according to legend, Agamemnon led an invasion as commander-in-chief of the Greek peoples. It is the source for the name of **Homer**'s epic *Iliad*, which treats events during the Trojan War.

kandys   purple long-sleeved wool shirt traditionally worn by Persian kings. Like the **tiara**, it was of Median origin, and Alexander appears not to have adopted it as part of his attire.

Kinsmen   elite Persian cavalry squadron of 1,000. Not necessarily blood-relatives of the king, they were members of the noblest class. They alone were permitted to kiss the king when performing *proskynesis* before him.

League of Corinth   see **Corinthian League**.

Mages   members of a priestly class of Medians who continued to play a fundamental role in religious matters under Persian rule, including sacrifice and the interpretation of omens.

Mēlophoroi   literally 'Apple-bearers', a group of 1,000 infantry selected from the so-called Immortals, a Persian infantry corps of 10,000. Each *melophoros* carried a spear with a golden apple on the butt as counterweight and butt spike.

mercenaries   Greek males with battle experience who offered their service as soldiers for pay. Both Alexander and Darius hired mercenary forces.

Ocean   Greeks believed that the river Ocean encircled all the world's lands.

Olympic games   **Panhellenic** games held in honour of **Zeus** at Olympia.

oracle   a place where a deity was believed to offer advice or prophecy through an intermediary. The most famous oracles in Alexander's day were at **Delphi** (sacred to **Apollo**), Dodona (sacred to **Zeus**) and Siwah (sacred to Zeus **Ammon**).

Pages   see **Royal Pages**.

Panhellenic   concerning all Greeks.

Patroclus   see **Achilles**.

Pella   administrative capital of Macedonia.

Peloponnesian War   a lengthy conflict (431–404 BC) between the empire of Athens and the Peloponnesian League led by Sparta. Virtually all of the Greek **city-states** (and even the Persian Empire) were involved and/or affected.

Persia   properly the native land of the Persians, north of the Persian Gulf and the location of the cities Persepolis and Pasargadae, but the name frequently refers to the whole of the **Achaemenid** Empire.

Persian Wars   invasions of Greece by **Persia** under **Darius I** (Darius the Great) in 490 BC and **Xerxes** in 480–479 BC. The **Corinthian League** pointed to the latter invasion in particular as justification for the Macedonian-led war of revenge against Persia.

phalanx   a formation composed of rows of **hoplites** facing in the direction of the enemy. The Macedonian phalanx was highly trained, able to change directions quickly and to expand its width as needed by reducing the number of its rows. The term may also refer more generally to an army's front line, or any part of an army in fighting formation.

proskynēsis   'bestowing a kiss upon' in Greek, the term refers to a range of acts, from kissing one's own fingertips to bending forward prostrate on the ground. Greeks associated such behaviour with the worship of a god, but among peoples of the Near East such gestures were formalized acknowledgement of another's social superiority.

Royal *Agēma*   see *Agēma*.

Royal Guard   see **Royal Hypaspists**.

Royal Hypaspists   also called the Royal Guard, the most distinguished unit of the **Hypaspists**, the infantry units fighting closest to the **Companion Cavalry**. Traditionally, these were infantry shield-bearers for the king himself in battle, and this unit continued to protect the king when he fought on foot.

Royal Pages   noble Macedonian youths who tended to the king's person and prepared his horse for battle. They enrolled at 14 and served for perhaps four to six years. An alleged conspiracy by the Pages was led by Hermolaus.

Royal Squadron   the most elite unit of the **Companion Cavalry**, it protected the king when he fought on horseback.

sarissa   a Macedonian cornel-wood pike remarkable for its great length (5–6 metres/15–18 feet). The first three rows of a **hoplite** unit would lower their sarissae so that an approaching enemy would encounter three rows of these pikes before reaching the first row of Macedonian infantrymen.

satrap   ruler of a satrapy, one of the more than 20 tribute-paying regions of the Persian Empire.

scythe chariot   these had long blades extending outward from the wheels that were meant to cut down any soldiers (and horses) in the chariot's path.

squadron   a unit of cavalry.

stade   a measure of distance approximately 185 metres (about 200 yards) and the length of a Greek athletic stadium.

talent   1 talent was the equivalent of 6,000 drachmas. By Alexander's day, a single day's work by a skilled labourer earned him 2–3 drachmas. Modern inflation and the fact that a talent was, strictly speaking, a measure of weight (in gold, but more often silver), make it all but impossible to assign a modern equivalent to the talent. At the present time, roughly £300,000 (about $600,000) may approximate its value.

Taxiles   title for any ruler of the region around Taxila, the largest city between the Indus and Hydaspes rivers. During Alexander's conquest, this ruler's name was Omphis.

tiara   the tall, conical headdress of the Persian kings. It was Median in origin, however, and Alexander avoided wearing it.

Troy   see **Ilium**.

wedge   an offensive cavalry formation (though sometimes including infantry) in the form of an upside-down 'V', designed to punch through and sever an enemy line.

wing   the left and right wings, and the centre, are the usual ancient terms for the three major portions of an army in battle formation. The terms 'left' and 'right' are always applied from the perspective of the army described, so that an army's right wing typically faces its enemy's left, and vice versa.

People, gods and heroes

Achilles   the most formidable Greek hero during the Trojan War. **Homer**'s *Iliad* recounts the death of his close friend and comrade Patroclus, and Achilles' vengeful retribution for his death. Alexander was, through Olympias, thought to be a descendant of Achilles himself.

Ammon   a Libyan and Egyptian sky god whom the Greeks identified with **Zeus**. His oracular shrine was at Siwah in Libya.

Anaxarchus   a philosopher from Abdera (northern Greece) described by Plutarch as having an unorthodox approach to philosophy. He generally receives a negative portrayal in the Alexander sources, mainly as a luxury-loving and sophistic sycophant, in contrast to **Callisthenes**.

Antipater   a noble Macedonian whom Alexander left as regent in Macedonia during the eastern invasion.

Apis   regularly identified by the Greeks with Epaphus, a legendary king of Egypt and son of **Zeus** and Io. The Egyptians recognized the Apis bull as a corporeal manifestation of their creator-god Ptah.

Apollo   the god of prophecy, the lyre and poetry. His most famous **oracle** was at **Delphi**.

Aristander   a prophet who hailed from Lycian Telmessus (in modern Turkey), Alexander's most important seer during his campaign against **Persia**.

Aristobulus   Alexander's chief engineer throughout the campaign. His account of the campaigns was written at least 20 years after Alexander's death in 323 BC.

Aristotle (384–322 BC) student of Plato, uncle of **Callisthenes** and founder of the so-called 'Peripatetic' school of philosophy (at the Lyceum in Athens) in 336. **Philip II** invited Aristotle to Macedonia to educate the young Alexander.

Attalus a politically powerful and noble-born Macedonian. Philip's marriage to Attalus' niece **Cleopatra** caused Alexander and **Olympias** considerable distress.

Bagoas a Persian eunuch renowned for his beauty. First **Darius III**'s lover then Alexander's after the death of Darius. By 325 BC he was believed to exercise considerable influence over Alexander.

Barsine (1) the name assigned wrongly by Plutarch to **Memnon**'s widow, with whom Alexander had sexual relations (but not a formal marriage) on **Parmenion**'s advice.

Barsine (2) the name of **Darius III**'s eldest daughter (also called **Statira** through confusion with Darius' wife) whom Alexander married at the Susa mass wedding in 324 BC.

Bel-Marduk the Babylonian god equated with Syrian Baal and Tyrian **Melcarth**. The Greeks identified him with **Heracles**. His priests were the **Chaldaeans**, famed for their knowledge of the magical arts and their prophetic wisdom.

Bessus satrap of Bactria under **Darius III**. After deposing Darius in 330 BC and assuming the name of King Artaxerxes V, he was captured and executed in 329 by Alexander.

Bucephalas Alexander's favourite horse, notably mastered by him while still a boy. Bucephalas died in India, and Alexander founded a city in his name.

Callisthenes a philosopher and nephew of **Aristotle**, he served as Alexander's official court historian, but opposed divine honours for Alexander and was critical of his policy of orientalism. He famously refused to perform *proskynesis* and was arrested during the **Pages'** conspiracy. Although his complicity in that conspiracy was never proven, he was either executed outright or died during custody.

Cambyses II son of **Cyrus II** (Cyrus the Great) and king of **Persia** 530–522 BC, known for his conquest of Egypt. According to Herodotus, he slew an **Apis** bull and sent a force of 50,000 to destroy the **oracle** of **Ammon** in 525.

Cassander son of **Antipater**, sent to Alexander at Babylon in 323 BC. His brother Iolas was Alexander's cupbearer. Alexander's relationship with this family was uneasy in the year prior to Alexander's death.

Cleitus an experienced general who served Alexander's father **Philip II**. His sister was Alexander's wet-nurse and he himself saved Alexander's life during the fighting at the Granicus River. Cleitus was outspoken in his disagreement with Alexander's lofty behaviour and his policy of orientalism, however, and during a drunken argument at Maracanda Alexander killed him.

Cleopatra niece of **Attalus** and a pure-blooded Macedonian. **Philip II**'s marriage to her might have presented a threat to **Olympias** and her status within the palace, and a child by her might naturally have replaced Alexander as heir to the kingdom.

Coenus Macedonian commander who notably led the left cavalry against **Porus** at the Hydaspes in 326. He died not long after publicly addressing Alexander on behalf of the Macedonians during the mutiny at the Hyphasis.

Craterus high-ranking Macedonian officer and son-in-law of **Antipater**; he held important commands in Sogdiana and India. Craterus was in charge of leading home the 10,000 Macedonian unfit and was probably meant to replace Antipater as regent there in 323 BC.

Cyrus II (Cyrus the Great) son of Cambyses I and father of **Cambyses II**. King of **Persia** (559–530 BC), he defeated the Median and Lydian Empires and Babylon, expanding the **Achaemenid** Empire so that it stretched from Turkey to the Indus River. According to Herodotus, Cyrus died in battle against Tomyris, queen of the Massagetae, a people the Greeks associated with the Scythians. Alexander restored his tomb on his return to Pasargadae in 324.

Darius I (Darius the Great) king of **Persia** (522–485 BC) and father of **Xerxes**; he led a number of failed expeditions against Greece that included the famous battle of Marathon in 490.

Darius III royal name of Artashata, who became king of **Persia** (336–330 BC) after the assassination of Artaxerxes IV. He was present and defeated at the battles of Issus (333 BC) and Gaugamela (331 BC). In 330 **Bessus** deposed him and abandoned him in the desert east of Rhagae.

Diogenes important **Cynic** philosopher.

Dionysus the Greek god of wine. There was a tradition, perhaps established during Alexander's campaign, that Dionysus had himself led a campaign against India.

Hephaestion a close friend of Alexander's throughout his life, thought to have been his lover early on. He enjoyed significant promotion and honours in the latter half of the campaign. Alexander's extraordinary mourning at Hephaestion's death is legendary.

Heracles a Greek hero more familiar today by his Roman name Hercules. He was generally recognized as a culture hero, associated with colonization and the spreading of Greek customs. The royal house of Macedonia traditionally traced its lineage back to this son of **Zeus** and Alcmene.

Homer the name attributed to the poet of the epics *Iliad* and *Odyssey*, works that are in fact products of a lengthy oral tradition.

Isis the Egyptian fertility goddess associated with the annual flooding of the Nile and the agricultural boon that the flooding brought.

Lysippus an outstanding sculptor; one of the many outstanding Greek artists, writers, engineers and philosophers invited to the Macedonian royal court. According to Plutarch, Lysippus was the only sculptor Alexander deemed worthy of depicting him.

Mazaeus satrap of Cilicia and/or Syria, he led the Coele and Mesopotamian Syrians for **Darius III** in the battle of Gaugamela. After he later surrendered Babylon, Alexander appointed him satrap of Babylonia, making him the first Persian satrap in Alexander's empire.

Melcarth the main deity of Tyre, equated with Syrian Baal and Babylonian **Bel-Marduk**. The Greeks called Melcarth the Tyrian **Heracles**.

Memnon a Greek general from Rhodes who was put in charge of the entire Persian fleet and made head of operations against Macedonia itself during Alexander's campaign eastward. Memnon's death in 333 BC at Mytilene was a major blow to **Darius III**'s strategy.

Nearchus a life-long friend of Alexander's, he served as chief admiral of Alexander's fleet on the journey down the Indus River and through the Persian Gulf.

Olympias Alexander's mother, from Epirus, south-west of Macedonia. She exercised considerable power in Macedonia during Alexander's campaign, famously writing to her son in criticism of **Antipater**'s behaviour as regent there.

Parmenion Alexander's second-in-command for much of the campaign. He was an experienced general and very popular with the army, but Alexander had him executed after his son **Philotas** was found guilty of conspiracy.

Pausanias a Bodyguard who assassinated **Philip II**, his former lover, after he failed to receive justice from him for abuses suffered at the hands of **Attalus** and **Cleopatra**.

Philip a doctor from Acarnania in western Greece who cured Alexander of his illness at the Cydnus River in Cilicia.

Philip II king of Macedonia (359–336 BC) and Alexander's father. During his rule he established Macedonia as a major power and formed the **Corinthian League** before his very public assassination in **Aegae**.

Philotas son of **Attalus'** son-in-law **Parmenion**, this important commander was tried in Phrada for allegedly leading a conspiracy to assassinate Alexander.

Porus Indian ruler of the region between the rivers Hydaspes and Acesines.

Ptolemy one of Alexander's generals who went on to rule the kingdom of Egypt, initiating the Ptolemaic dynasty that lasted for three centuries until Cleopatra's suicide brought it to an end. Ptolemy, keenly interested in linking Alexander to his own Egyptian kingdom, commandeered Alexander's corpse and brought it to Memphis. He also composed his own account of Alexander's campaign.

Roxane daughter of the Sogdianian Oxyartes. All sources record that Alexander married her after falling in love with her on sight, but he probably hoped by the match to establish stability in a region that had given him much difficulty.

Sisygambis mother of **Darius III**. After her capture at Issus, Alexander preserved her royal honours.

Statira wife of **Darius III**; she was captured at the battle of Issus, but died two years later in 331 BC. Ancient sources sometimes mistakenly refer to Darius' elder daughter **Barsine (2)** by this name.

Xenophon general and author (*c.* 431–355 BC) who recounted his march as one of the leaders of the Ten Thousand from Cunaxa to the Black Sea in his *Anabasis*. Arrian consciously imitates Xenophon's style in his own *Anabasis*.

Xerxes king of **Persia** (485–465 BC) whose invasion of Greece in 480 included the Persian victory in the battle of Thermopylae and the capture of Athens. It was in response to this invasion that the **Corinthian League** ostensibly declared the war of revenge that Alexander led against Persia.

Zeus king of the Greek pantheon; father of many heroes and gods, among them **Heracles** and **Dionysus**.